HISTORY AND LEGENDS
of
THE ALAMO
and
OTHER MISSIONS
IN AND AROUND SAN ANTONIO

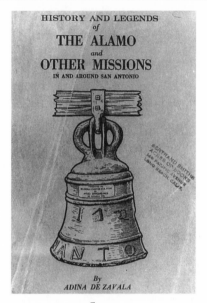

by
Adina De Zavala
Edited and Introduced by
Richard R. Flores

D1502488

Arte Público Press
Houston, Texas
1996

This volume is made possible through grants from the Summerlee Foundation and the Rockefeller Foundation.

Recovering the past, creating the future

Arte Público Press
University of Houston
Houston, Texas 77204-2090

Cover : Mural in G.B. Dealey Library
by Eugene Savage titled *Texas of Yesterday*
Cover design by Mark Piñon

De Zavala, Adina, 1861-1955
    History and Legends of the Alamo and other
    missions in and around San Antonio /
    by De Zavala
        p.   cm.
    ISBN 1-55885-181-X (paper : alk. paper)
        1. Spanish mission buildings—Texas—San
Antonio Region—History. 2. Alamo (San Antonio,
Tex.)—History. 3. Missions—Texas—San Antonio
Region—History. 4. San Antonio Region (Tex.)—
Church history. 5. San Antonio (Tex.)—History.
    I. Title.
F394.S2D196   1996
976.4'351—dc20   96-19969
                                                    CIP

Table of Contents

ADINA DE ZAVALA AND
THE POLITICS OF RESTORATION

Introduction

The life of Adina De Zavala was perhaps as tumultuous, heroic, noble, and contradictory as was her life's passion—the Alamo, and more specifically, Texas history. From resolutions of praise upon her death to notes of reprise from former colleagues and collaborators, Adina De Zavala was, without a doubt, a woman whose resolve and determination were not to be underestimated. A descendent of one of Mexico's and Texas's foremost political families, she had witnessed first-hand a crucial period in American life; as a chronicler, collector, and self-taught historian on all things Texan, she was committed to Texas history's presentation and restoration. Her greatest accomplishment remains the least known: it was her vision and tenacity that led to the preservation of the Alamo, an irony that she, the consummate keeper of records, could not appreciate. For criticizing the misconstrued sense of history by the gatekeepers of the Alamo, she became the most stigmatized of its heroines, but there were other honors, other accomplishments, other battles for which she was remembered.

Adina De Zavala was a woman of predictable passions and complexity of character. In a time long before women's suffrage, she was making and writing history. She was educated when few people, men or women, were. A public and self-made intellectual, she participated in the academic forays of her time. Of partial Mexican heritage, at a time when Mexicans were being socially and economically exploited, she became perhaps the most fervent defender of "Texas" history and culture. And yet, embedded in her work, in her ardor to preserve and recover the material treasures and oral renderings of previous Indian, Spanish and Mexican habitations of Texas, there was an Utopian desire to socially restore and recognize a romantically perceived past.

Adina De Zavala was a patriot of Texas, unabashedly so; however, unlike the Alamo defenders, her life cannot be reduced to a singular act of heroism but must encompass an understanding of the *longue durée*. She lived and toiled for ninety-three years to recover the past so as to set it right, to celebrate Texas history so as to augment it, to restore the achievements of Mexico and Spain and a sense of culture lost.

History and Legends of the Alamo is the distillation of more than twenty years of collating, collecting, writing and research. It was compiled from personally recovered historical documents, previously published sources, folklore and legends concerning the Alamo and missions in other areas of Texas. It was published at the author's expense and lists her personal residence as the place of publication. It is this combination, the historical and legendry, when read in conjunction and against each other that supplies the necessary basis for a critical reading of Texas history on the part of De Zavala. Published after years of working to recover the Alamo from capitalist entrepreneurs and to restore it to its Spanish and Mexican mission past, *History and Legends of the Alamo* is a work at once original, romantic and, embedded in its sedimented layers of factual and fictional texts, critical.

Adina De Zavala was born on November 28, 1861, at Zavala Point, just a short distance from the historic battlefield of San Jacinto near Houston, Texas, where the forces of Sam Houston defeated those of Antonio López de Santa Anna a few weeks after the Battle of the Alamo. She was a granddaughter of Lorenzo de Zavala, a Mexican statesman who also became the first Vice-President of the Republic of Texas. Lorenzo de Zavala was deeply influenced by the emerging spirit of liberalism and played a major role in constructing the Mexican Constitution of 1824, modeling it after its U.S. precursor. He was twice elected governor of the State of Mexico, serving also as Mexico's ambassador to France. He and his first wife, Teresa Correa, had a son Lorenzo, Jr., and in 1831, he married Emily West with whom he had three children: Augustín, Ricardo and Emily.

After serving the Mexican government, de Zavala and his family moved to a plot of land at Zavala Point. It is here that he encountered and collaborated with the founders of the Texas Republic, citing the annulment of the Mexican constitution by President Santa Anna as his reason for joining the Texas forces. Already an established statesman and historian, de Zavala's intellectual and political acumen was recognized by his Texas colleagues, and led to his appointment as the first Vice-President of the Texas Republic under the presidency of James Burnett.

There are various interpretations of the events that preceded the Battle of the Alamo and the move for an independent Texas. In February 1836, General Antonio López de Santa Anna, dictator and president of Mexico, approached the town of San Antonio de Béxar in the province of Coahuila y Tejas for the purpose of enforcing a centralist regime against those who sought to follow the federalist constitution of 1824.

Mexico gained its independence from Spain in 1821, and, like many post-colonial governments, its search for a political and national identity was forged through fractionalized political strife. The main source of discontent was over political ideology: should Mexico develop as a strong centralist state, with power located in the center, or as a cohesively structured federalist nation that allowed more autonomy to its member states? The balance of power teetered in one direction then the other for several years until 1824, when the issue was seemingly settled with the writing of a constitution forming the United States of Mexico as a federalist republic.

It was during the struggle for independence that Moses Austin petitioned the Spanish Crown for permission to settle in Coahuila y Tejas. While he died before achieving his goal, his son, Stephen F. Austin, received colonization rights from the recently established Mexican government. Many of Austin's early frontiersmen, as well as those who soon followed, came seeking opportunity in this new land, but found the presence of Mexicans an unwanted sight. As Arnoldo De León states,

> The immigrants, then, did not arrive in Texas with open minds concerning the native Tejanos: their two-hundred-year experience with "different" peoples had so shaped their psyche that their immediate reaction was negative rather than positive.... They had retained impressions acquired before their arrival in the state then reapplied and transposed those racial attitudes upon the native *casta*.[1]

By 1827, twelve thousand Anglo-Americans had entered Mexico and were living in Texas, outnumbering the Mexicans in the province by 5,000 people. And, by 1835, Mexicans citizens in Texas were 7,800 to 30,000 Anglo-Americans. These numbers alarmed Mexican officials and, in an effort to curb the growing immigration from the United States, they passed an emancipation proclamation in 1829 forbidding slavery. While slavery was not a practice in Mexico, this law was aimed at the growing number of U. S. citizens holding slaves in the Mexican province of Texas.

Another issue was the relative distance between Texas and Mexico City. Texas was appended to the state of Coahuila for governmental purposes. Citizens of Coahuila y Tejas, both Mexican and Anglo-American, were discouraged by the inefficiency of the Mexican government and by the distance to the state capital, Saltillo, where government and appellate court offices for Coahuila y Tejas were housed. Austin, in 1833, traveled to Mexico City to try to persuade President Santa Anna to allow Texas to become an independent Mexican state. Santa Anna refused, but he did agree to allow citizens of the province more latitude in conducting their affairs, including a revision of the tariff laws, repeal of the anti-immigration law and institution of trial by jury.

Tensions between Anglo-Americans in Texas and the Mexican government came to a head when Santa Anna discarded the Constitution of 1824, causing both Mexicans and Anglo-Americans in Texas to call for independence. In an effort to suppress this movement, Santa Anna led his forces north and made his move on San Antonio de Béxar and the Alamo. Less than two hundred men, organized into a small militia, gathered to defend this former Franciscan mission against Santa Anna's forces late in February 1836. On March 6, the Mexicans, greatly outnumbering those in the Alamo, made their final siege, taking the Alamo and leaving no prisoners.

This proved to be a decisive point in rallying support for the cause of Texas independence. Soon afterward, at the battles of Goliad and San Jacinto, as Texas nationalist legend has inscribed in all Texas school children's repertoire of populist history, the battle cry of "Remember the Alamo!" led the Texan forces. And on April 21, Sam Houston's troops engaged

Santa Anna's forces at the "Battle of San Jacinto," capturing the Mexican leader several days later on his retreat south.

Critical to any historical portrait of this era are several factors. First, as noted above, the initial dispute in Texas stemmed from both Mexicans and Anglo-Americans seeking to restore a federalist government in Mexico. Mexicans in the province also tired of Santa Anna's exploits and of the tedious political circumstances affiliated with their distance from the provincial and national capitals in Coahuila and Mexico City. Second, in spite of his unilateral control of Mexican affairs and politics, and his egotistical and personal ambitions, Santa Anna's actions can be viewed as an effort to control an internal uprising in his own country.

Finally, an element that seems quite overlooked is the men who died. The Texas nationalist discourse surrounding the Alamo claims this was a battle between Texans and Mexicans. This is not correct. There were only thirteen native-born Texans in the group, and eleven of them were of Mexican descent; furthermore, native Texans were, by birth, Mexican citizens. Of those remaining, forty-one of them were born in Europe, two were Jews, two were black, and the remainder were Americans from other states in the U. S. (Rosenthal and Groneman 1985). The portrayal of the Battle of the Alamo as a clearly demarcated zone of interests between Texans and Mexicans is clearly unwarranted. Prominent Mexican citizens fought on both sides, dividing their allegiance along lines of political and ideological interests, and not along the ethnically or nationally circumscribed positions that have been fabricated by the custodians of the Alamo and popularized at various levels through collective memory.

During Santa Anna's foray into Texas, de Zavala was meeting with members of the Texas cabinet on Galveston Island. When Sam Houston defeated the Mexican forces and captured Santa Anna not far from where this historic meeting was being held, the Mexican general requested a meeting with his former colleague. De Zavala's son, Lorenzo, Jr., reports the events of this encounter in a letter to Adina years later:

> My Dearest Niece,
>   You cannot imagine the pleasure which I experienced upon receiving your very much wanted letter of the sixth of last month....
>   I have taken cognizance of what Mr. Mitchell said to you with respect to what happened after the battle of San Jacinto in the camp and what he says with respect to my person is true. I was, in effect, the interpreter for General Houston in the first conferences which he had with General Santa Anna after his capture. These took place in the same camp, under the shade of leafy trees where General Houston lay stretched out on his blanket, for he came out slightly wounded on the ankle...
>   ...General Santa Anna who, as can be imagined, was terrified, fearing that because of the cruelties and assassinations which he had committed on Texan prisoners, he would be killed, manifested to me that he was glad to see me and that he knew that I was lending my services in the Texan army as a voluntary aide to General Houston and that he had recommended to his officers that in case I was taken prisoner that they respect my life. Of course, I gave no credence to that assertion. Then he immediately said that he had a very great desire to see and greet Father who was then on the island of Galveston with the rest of the other members of the Texas cabinet. In a few days he arrived at the camp and had very interesting conferences with Santa Anna, which conferences I did not have the pleasure of witnessing ....[2]

Soon after these events, in the Fall of 1836, Lorenzo de Zavala died from a swimming accident near his home.

Adina De Zavala was one of six children born to Augustín de Zavala and Julia Tyrell, whose parents had come to Texas from Ireland.[3] The other children were Florence, Zita, Mary, with whom Adina shared a house for most of her adult life, Thomas, and Augustín P. de Zavala. Adina and her siblings were initially raised at Zavala Point before the family moved to Shavano, Texas, north of San Antonio, when Adina was already in her teens. She attended Ursuline Academy in Galveston, Texas, between 1871 and 1873, graduating from there with distinction. She later took a Teacher's Certificate from Sam Houston Normal College in Huntsville, Texas, in 1879. It wasn't until 1884, however, that Adina began teaching, first in Terrell, Texas, and later in San Antonio until her resignation, stemming from her involvement with the Alamo, in 1907.[4]

Restoring the Past

De Zavala's life-long enthusiasm and commitment to understanding the past was sparked at a young age. She recalls in a short biographical note:

> My father generally took me with him in his visits to his old friends and to the meetings of the Texas veterans.[5] From the conversation of my father and these friends I learned much of their participation in the early struggles and wars and absorbed all the historical facts and legends narrated.[6]

Her interest in history continued to advance and, while in San Antonio, Adina founded the De Zavala Daughters, a group of women dedicated to the preservation of Texas history and historical sites. In 1893 the De Zavala Daughters was admitted into the Daughters of the Republic of Texas, taking as its name the De Zavala Chapter after her well-known grandfather. The DRT, established in 1891, was an organization of women descendants of Texas families from the Republic era who worked to preserve historic sites and the memory of men and women of the Texas Republic. Like the De Zavala

Daughters, the DRT was a growing nineteenth-century effort on the part of women to influence, preserve and define aspects of American history and culture. While little has been written on this subject from the perspective of Texas women, Douglas[7] and McCarthy[8] have documented how women writers and philanthropists, mostly from the Midwest and Northeast, were instrumental in shaping this crucial period in American history. Michael Kammen, in his far-reaching and well-documented history of American culture, includes a brief discussion of such organizations, including the effort to restore the Alamo by De Zavala and others.[9]

De Zavala's Battle for the Alamo

By the time the De Zavala Chapter was admitted into the DRT, Adina De Zavala was already actively engaged in warding off the Alamo's purchase by entrepreneurs from the East coast. The Alamo was originally a Spanish mission named San Antonio de Valero, founded in 1718 under the direction of Fray Antonio de Olivares as part of the Franciscan missions in Texas. The mission complex consisted of a church, friary or *convento*, granary, workshops, storerooms, and housing for the native Indians. The famous facade recognized as the Alamo— not constructed until the mid-nineteenth century—is actually the front of the mission church, completed in 1744. In the 1750's, the roof of the church collapsed due to poor construction materials and workmanship. Still in shambles, Mission San Antonio de Valero was secularized along with all other Texas missions in 1793.

The mission fell into disuse and, left to the perils of abandonment, total disrepair until 1802, when it was occupied by a Spanish cavalry unit, the Segunda Compañía Volante de San Carlos de Parras del Álamo, from which the name "Alamo" stems. This occupation marked the last usage of the Alamo as a church, since it was again abandoned in 1810 and remained so until it was utilized as a fort by the Mexican army from 1821 to 1835.

By the time of the "Battle of the Alamo" in 1836, the mission complex covered two to three acres, and the roofless chapel was 75 feet long and 62 feet wide, with stone walls 22 feet high and 4 feet thick. Attached to the northwest end of the church lay the *convento* or long barracks which was 186 feet long and 18 feet wide and high. The rooms on the upper floor contained an infirmary and those on the first were soldiers' quarters.[10]

In 1841 the Republic of Texas returned the Alamo mission church, along with the other local missions, to the Roman Catholic Church. And in 1848 the Alamo mission was leased to the United States as a U.S. Quartermaster's Depot. The U. S. government renovated the church in 1849, adding the now-famous top center gable and new upper windows. After the Civil War, the Alamo was again used by the Quartermaster's Depot as a grain reception facility. The *convento* or long barracks of the Alamo was sold to Honoré Grenet in 1877, who proceeded to construct wooden porticos above the stone walls. In 1883, Grenet's lease to the mission church was purchased by the state of Texas, placing that portion of the Alamo in the hands of the City of San Antonio. Upon Grenet's death, an advertisement for the sale of the Alamo in 1882 read:

FOR LEASE OR FOR SALE,
to the purchaser of its valuable and constantly kept-up stock of Goods, together with the lease of the ALAMO, and the good will of the business, so long and so profitably enjoyed by its deservedly popular founder.[11]

A buyer for the Grenet business was found in the Hugo-Schmeltzer Company in 1886. From the activities of Grenet and the Hugo-Schmeltzer Co. during the 1880s, it is clear that this portion of the Alamo mission was used primarily for commercial reasons, being described as a "modernized and...mammoth business house," and only secondarily evoking interest as an historical site.[12] Adina De Zavala's pursuits in restoring this portion of the Alamo led to a promise from Gustav Schmeltzer of the Hugo-Schmeltzer Co. "not to sell or offer the property [of the Alamo] to anyone else without...giving the Chapter [of the DRT] the opportunity to acquire it."[13] By this time, De Zavala had been quite active not only in her chapter of the DRT but in establishing herself as a dynamic and bold leader resulting in her 1902 election to the executive committee of the DRT.

De Zavala's initial agreement with Schmeltzer stated that the De Zavala Chapter of the DRT would have the first option on purchasing the appurtenance of the Alamo mission that housed the Hugo-Schmeltzer Co. This would provide the DRT with time to raise the sum of $75,000, the agreed upon price. However, early in 1903, De Zavala received word from her close friend, the Italian sculptor Pompeo Coppini, then living in San Antonio, that a commercial enterprise from the Eastern U.S. was interested in the Hugo-Schmeltzer property. Devising a strategy on how to raise the necessary money, De Zavala heard of a "prominent, rich and very ambitious young woman who may be of some help."[14] This was Clara Driscoll, who initially collaborated with De Zavala and later openly feuded with her over the final historical portrait the Alamo would present.

Driscoll was the daughter of Robert Driscoll, Sr., a wealthy railroad and ranching entrepreneur who lived near Corpus Christi, Texas. Clara Driscoll attended private schools in San Antonio, New York and France, and after her mother's death in May 1899, traveled throughout Europe, to return to Texas in 1903. Before her departure in 1899, however, she wrote a letter to the *San Antonio Express* in which she stated her grave concern over the "hideous" buildings surrounding the Alamo.[15] Once back in Texas, she acted on her concerns and joined the DRT in February, 1903.

De Zavala approached Driscoll about the Alamo, and the two met with Charles Hugo in March 1903, concerning the purchase of the Hugo-Schmeltzer property. After the meeting, Driscoll paid $500 for a thirty-day option on the building, after which an additional sum of forty-five hundred dollars would extend the option to February 10, 1904, giving the DRT enough time to raise the remaining $75,000. It was further agreed upon that the property was "to be purchased for the use and benefit of the Daughters of the Republic of Texas and [was] to be used by them for the purpose of making a park about the Alamo, for no other purposes whatever."[16] By 1904, the DRT had collected a little more than $7,000, at which time Driscoll advanced another $17,812.02 to complete an initial $25,000-down payment that was due in February, 1904. After a year of campaigning, on January 26, 1905, the Twenty-ninth Legislature of the State of Texas appropriated $65,000 to purchase the Alamo.[17]

After acquiring the property, the state, as agreed upon, transferred custodianship of the Alamo to the DRT. On their part, the DRT initially agreed to have the De Zavala Chapter care for the Alamo, based upon De Zavala's initial and continuing efforts in this ordeal; however, this action was blocked by the executive committee of the DRT until the state had officially entrusted them with the property. Then, upon receiving the property, the executive committee gave custodianship of the Alamo to Driscoll and not the De Zavala Chapter, recognizing her financial contributions in this effort. This action led to the first clash between the De Zavala Chapter and the DRT.

Since Clara Driscoll was scheduled to be out of town until December, she appointed her close friend Florence Eager to the position of custodian in her place. But before the mayor of the city presented Eager with the keys, De Zavala claimed them and took possession of the Alamo (for the first time). According to De Zavala, she was ready to deliver the keys to Driscoll "but not to anyone else."[18] Adding to the confusion, turmoil and bitter tension of the moment, the DRT filed suit against De Zavala, demanding that she return all relics to the Alamo and refrain from interfering with future DRT efforts. The legal complaint against De Zavala read as follows:

> Plaintiff (DRT) alleges that on Oct 4, 1905, the State of Texas, acting through S. W. T. Lanhan, Governor, did convey the custody of the Alamo Church property to plaintiff; that defendant (Adina De Zavala) claiming to act for plaintiff took possession of said church, and afterwards about Nov. 1st, 1905, repudiated the right of plaintiff to the possession thereof, and refuses to deliver said property or the relics contained therein to plaintiff....[19]

The DRT eventually withdrew its suit once De Zavala returned the Alamo to their care.

The following April, at its annual convention and with De Zavala's followers in clear control of the meeting, a motion giving custody of the Alamo to the De Zavala Chapter on November 11, 1906, was made. When a motion to substitute Clara Driscoll's name in place of the De Zavala Chapter's failed, Driscoll spitingly offered her resignation, which was refused.[20] With this, De Zavala moved that Driscoll be appointed custodian until November, and when she refused, she continued, "In further compliment to Miss Driscoll, I move that this convention bestow the honor upon the young lady she has expressed the desire should be the actual custodian, her friend, Miss Florence Eager."[21] While Eager accepted this temporary post, De Zavala's courtesy extended no longer than November 11, for on that day she drafted the following telegram to Eager:

The time having arrived at which the Convention of the DRT held at Goliad April 20 and 21, 1906, directed the De Zavala Chapter to assume control of the Alamo, I desire to inform you that De Zavala Chapter is ready to take immediate charge. Are you ready to deliver Custodianship according to said order?[22]

While it seemed that Adina De Zavala and her supporters had succeeded in winning the day, they were on their way to losing the Alamo. At the April convention, Driscoll and her supporters initiated a second San Antonio chapter of the DRT named the Alamo Mission Chapter. It took until 1910 for Driscoll and her colleagues to legally force the De Zavala Chapter from the DRT; before then, however, De Zavala was to garner national attention as the woman who rescued the Alamo—again.

In February 1908, as the Hugo-Schmeltzer building lay vacant, the DRT arranged to temporally lease the building until efforts could be organized to remove the *convento* structure entirely and beautify the area so as to highlight the mission church. Their rational was that the Hugo-Schmeltzer building was not part of the original Alamo mission but constructed at a later date. Outraged by such a desecration and total disregard for historical fact, De Zavala, presenting "authorized" letters from the DRT, received the keys to the building from local authorities and enlisted three men to guard over and forbid entrance to the building. While acting out of moral indignation, the tumultuous politics inside the DRT precipitated this incident. As Ables has adeptly shown, internal conflicts and legal chicanery within the DRT resulted in the election of two different sets of officers: those that supported Clara Driscoll and those siding with De Zavala. When De Zavala claimed the keys to the Hugo-Schmeltzer building, she was charged with a letter, dated February 2, 1908, from Miss Mary Briscoe, the Secretary General, and Mrs. Wharton Bates, the 1st Vice President and Acting President of the

DRT, stating that she, as President of the De Zavala Chapter, was "the Agent for the Daughters of the Republic of Texas, and [had] authority to directly receive the keys."[23] Briscoe and Bates were, as they claimed, officers of the DRT—at least of the faction supporting De Zavala. Local authorities were either unaware of both sets of officers, or if they were, believed they were in no position to determine the legalities of either side's claims.

On February 10, De Zavala was met by the sheriff and other officials carrying an injunction against her for occupying the premises without authorization. In a move that made headlines across the country, De Zavala quickly sealed off the building and barricaded herself within its walls, where she remained for three days, being refused water or food by the local officials. On February 13, De Zavala, under duress but willing to negotiate with state authorities, relinquished the Hugo-Schmeltzer portion of the Alamo to the state superintendent of buildings. Reeling from the negative publicity, the DRT formally denied they were planning to destroy any original structures of the Alamo. However, court papers filed by the DRT revealed their belief that the Hugo-Schmeltzer building was not part of the original Alamo mission complex as well as their plan to "remove this unsightly building and place in lieu thereof a park, museum, or something else."[24]

It appears that De Zavala's effort to preserve the Alamo from destruction, while impassioned, was premeditated and calculated. In a letter to an attorney representing the De Zavala Chapter dated January 10, 1908, she writes the following:

> I have also my original idea in vein & that is to
> take possession bodily of the Alamo building room
> to be vacated by the Hugo & Schmeltzer Co. That is
> by putting an agent in charge & holding the fort. This
> could be done by me in person as president of De
> Zavala C. The H[ugo].S[chmeltzer]. people are afraid

to deliver the keys to us, for fear they may be held
liable or responsible for the rents or for damages, etc.
So we would have to *take* it. Mrs. Bates writes me
just what you told me before—Writes that you say for
us to "act as though there has been no injunction, for
it was really void", & should they try to hold us in
contempt of Court to say you told me to go ahead. So
I really believe I shall be brave enough to go ahead
and take possession—that is—step in when the Hugo
S[chmeltzer] people step out unless you advise me to
the contrary, for though the H[ugo].S[chmeltzer]. people may *not* deliver to us the keys—we can stay
inside & make our own keys. What do you think of it?
...We want the Alamo—nothing *else*—nothing less
will do. We would prefer that it all be under *our* man-
agement Church & Alamo proper but the Church is
not as important-nor in much danger as the Alamo
proper (the building now occupied by the Hugo &
S[chmeltzer]. people).[25]

Adina De Zavala did find the strength to carry out her
plan, and the news of her exploits traveled across the country.
In *Human Life for June*, published in 1908, De Zavala is cen-
trally featured as a defender of the Alamo in the following
story.

The young woman, highly cultured, thoroughly educated, aristocratic—a descendent from the best Spanish blood—is making her fight against business men,
mercenaries, who, she says, "care nothing for historic
association nor for glorious tradition." She maintains
that they would put the old mission to commercial
uses; while they claim that they are but practical
business men, and want to make good use of only
part of the building and enclosure.
    Last February, however, these men, who had
enlisted the aid of a deputy sheriff and others, found
that the American girl of Spanish origin was not to be
bluffed, nor even starved out. Miss De Zavala had
placed guards about the Alamo, but for these the
deputy sheriff and his companions did not seem to

care. It was the young woman herself whom they hesitated to encounter. About eight o'clock one evening, being assured that the "defender of the Alamo" had left for the night, they demanded admission in the name of the law—to which occurrence Miss De Zavala refers with scorn. They broke down one set of doors, but they found the girl on guard duty, and they retreated.

For three days and nights Miss De Zavala remained on post, in the Alamo, alone. Those in intrigue against her, she says, prevented her watchmen and friends from bringing her food. A sister patriot, Miss Lytle, poured coffee through a pipe which she slipped under a window, and in this way the young woman sustained strength to resist the invaders until Governor Campbell took a hand. During the siege all means of communication, telephone wires, etc., were cut off. At night Miss De Zavala was in darkness, for the electric light wires were also cut.

The girl certainly displayed the fighting spirit born in her. De Zavalas fought for the liberty of the people in Spain, Portugal, Ecuador, Bolivia, Mexico, Texas! It is no wonder that she is courageous.

The Alamo tangle bids fair to be soon legally adjusted.[26]

Wasting little time to regain support for the DRT's beautification plans of the Alamo, Driscoll petitioned friends to contribute money for the refurbishment (and destruction) of the Huge-Schmeltzer building.

To All Texans:
As legal custodians of the Alamo, The Daughters of the Republic of Texas request your signature in endorsement of their plan for the beautifying of the Alamo Mission grounds adjoining the Chapel of the Alamo, more generally known as the Hugo-Schmeltzer property.

It is their desire [the DRT] to convert this property into a beautiful park filled with swaying palms and tropical verdure, enclosed by a low way, with arched gateway of Spanish architecture. They also wish to restore the roof of the Chapel of the Alamo, and have a replica of the original doors placed at the entrance to the Church.

The Daughters of the Republic of Texas ask for your support in their honest endeavor to be worthy the obligation imposed upon them by the Twenty-ninth Legislature of the State of Texas.
Clara Driscoll Sevier
Chairman Alamo Auxiliary Committee
Menger Hotel, San Antonio, Texas
or
37 Madison Avenue, New York City[27]

But De Zavala and her associates were adamant in preserving the Hugo-Schmeltzer building, built on the original Alamo mission walls. It took until 1911, at a special meeting convened by Governor Oscar B. Colquitt on December 28 of that year, for the issue to be fully addressed. At this session, held at the St. Anthony Hotel in San Antonio, De Zavala submitted her plats, maps and other evidence showing that the chapel at the time of the battle was in ruins and that "the walls now standing and known as the Hugo-Schmeltzer building, the convent or the monastery, are the original walls of the fortress."[28] The Driscoll faction contended that the convent walls were unimportant, favoring a plan that would remove them entirely from the property in order to provide space for a park and monument. During this debate, Colquitt claimed, "The walls which were then standing, we want to preserve," to which Driscoll replied, "You don't mean to restore it as it was built by the Franciscan fathers before the battle?"[29] The governor concluded that the wooden frame of the Hugo-Schmeltzer building should be removed, but that the two-story stone walls were part of the original Alamo structure and should be preserved and restored. However, to the DRT's delight, funds were extinguished before the work could be completed, and in

1913, while Colquitt was out of the state, his Lt. Governor ordered the demolition of the upper-story walls.

Years later, in her late eighties, De Zavala would reflect back on her effort to influence Colquitt's decision to save the Hugo-Schmeltzer building, recalling the trouble she supposedly had sending Colquitt important documentation.

> Tapped my telephone during "war" to save the Alamo (to get my views and names). Things, documents and pictures, historical matter sent to Gov. Colquitt disappeared after being mailed in P.O. and Gov. Campbell Colquitt *never* received my letters nor *historical* documents nor any material from me. Either they disappeared from P. O. here or by some means at Austin before the Gov. received his mail...a man connected with the one most interested in tearing down the Alamo property was arrested by Federal authorities for taking mail from P.O. (so I was told) and served a prison sentence (so I was told). I always suspected that he may have had something to do with the disappearance of my historical pictures and documents. They were a great loss.[30]

While her official alliance with the DRT ended as a result of this ordeal, De Zavala's interest, passion and vision to protect the Alamo never did. She constantly wrote letters to the Governor, Mayor and the local papers beseeching the DRT to change plans to alter the grounds in any fashion. As of 1935, her greatest dream, she said, was "to see the main building of the Alamo Mission restored. Historically, the church of the Alamo is not of such great importance. It was the building adjoining the long barracks, which witnessed the slaughter of our Texas heroes. But we still have the lower walls of the long barrack and of the arcades facing the patio."[31]

De Zavala's relationship with the DRT never mended. She became their most vocal critic, constantly reminding the public of the DRT's lack of historical detail and myopic vision of the Alamo's historical significance. For their part, the DRT never fully acknowledged De Zavala's contribution, giving Clara Driscoll full credit for saving the Alamo. One example of De Zavala's maligned neglect is found in a pamphlet published by the DRT Library Committee in 1960 and written by Jack C. Butterfield, entitled, "Women of the Alamo." Butterfield rightly credits the DRT and Clara Driscoll for their efforts in preserving the Alamo, but makes no reference to De Zavala—in fact her name fails to appear anywhere in the pamphlet.[32] The irony is that Butterfield was well aware of De Zavala and her vast and voluminous knowledge of the Alamo and Texas history, writing her the following note in 1902:

> I am preparing a little story, the scene of which is laid in San Antonio de Bexar in 1835.... Knowing your interest in all things pertaining to Texas history, I thought perhaps you might be able to assist me.[33]

Perhaps in his own small way, Professor Carlos Castañeda, the eminent University of Texas historian of the Texas revolution, attempted to correct this bias against De Zavala when, upon her death in 1955, he sent to the DRT Library a copy of the State of Texas resolution honoring her. Perhaps, he figured, such a document would not find its way onto the shelves of the DRT library otherwise.[34]

One of De Zavala's most important contributions to the history of the Alamo was finding Don Enrique Esparza, whose father Gregorio had died at the Alamo and who, along with his mother and three siblings, walked out of the Alamo alive after the battle. De Zavala accidentally came upon Don Enrique, although it is unclear how, when he was already a man of seventy-three. She interviewed him and took his story of the battle to the San Antonio newspapers, which published several articles of his account.[35] De Zavala's voluminous knowledge of the Alamo led her to corroborate Esparza's claims and brought her a measure of attention, as well. As the first newspaper story concludes:

> Miss De Zavala thinks that from what she can glean from Esparza, she can add much valuable information to history about the fall of the Alamo, of which very little is now authentically known. No Texas history mentions the escape of anyone from the Alamo but Mrs. Dickinson and child, and the San Antonio lady's discovery is of great value.[36]

In the Battle's Wake

After leaving the DRT, De Zavala continued to work, ceaselessly, for the restoration of historical places. In 1912, she organized the Texas Historical Landmarks Association (THLA), a group that would remain active until soon after her death in 1955. The objectives of the THLA, according to its charter, were:

> 1) to work for the repair, restoration, and preservation of all the missions of Texas; 2) and for the use of the main building of the Alamo—the long two-story Fort (north of the Church of the Alamo [the Hugo-Schmeltzer property]) as a Texas Hall of Fame and a Museum of History, Art, Relics and Literature.

The THLA is credited with identifying a number of historical buildings and sites throughout the State, including its most celebrated, the Spanish Governor's Palace in San Antonio. Like her work with the Alamo, once De Zavala realized the presence and significance of this historical structure, she worked diligently to document and publicize its historical merit. The Spanish Governor's Palace, completed in 1749, was by the 1920s an old, dilapidated home nearly in ruins. Situated on Military Plaza, or Plaza de Armas, in San Antonio, it was De Zavala's tenacious archival work that led to its recognition and purchase by the City of San Antonio. For this effort, the *Texas Pioneer* printed a feature story on De Zavala's work in the August-September 1930 issue, as did the September 19, 1929 issue of the *Christian Science Monitor*.[37]

Even in the early part of the century when De Zavala was most preoccupied with the Alamo, she found time for other civic and academic pursuits. She was appointed to the delegation of the International Congress on Tuberculosis by the Department of Public Health in 1908; [38] she was active in the National Council of Catholic Womens[39] and participated in other religious organizations, such as the St. Anthony's Guild. She was a charter member and fellow of the Texas State Historical Society, an organization that, on numerous occasions, used her as an expert reference for questions on the Alamo. De Zavala was an active member of the Texas Folk-lore Society. She served as a Vice-President from 1926-27, presenting a paper that year at the annual meeting in Austin entitled, "How the Huisache Came to Bloom"; and her paper, "Belief of the Tejas Indians," appeared in Publication no. 1 of the Texas Folk-lore Society, edited by the eminent folklorist, Steth Thompson.[40] And in 1912, John Lomax, another prominent Texas folklorist, wrote her, stating:

> It now appears that you will be the ranking officer present at the meeting of the Folk-lore Society, and we shall expect you, therefore, to preside over the meeting. Please let me have the title of your paper by return mail so that it will be included in the program, which I am now .....[41]

Lomax's respect for De Zavala's vast knowledge of Texas folklore is evident in the following 1911 letter he wrote her in what appears to be a response to a letter she sent correcting him on his folkloric understanding.

Whatever I said about the Mexican Passion Play, I meant the "Pastores". I am just a beginner in the field of folk-lore, and you must pardon frequent and grievous blunders on my part.[42]

De Zavala also served on the Bi-Centennial Commission celebrating the 200th anniversary of the City of San Antonio in 1931, heading the committee charged with designing a Bi-Centennial Medal, chosen, perhaps, as a result of having researched and written an extensive history of the Laetare Medal and its recipients, which is given annually at the University of Notre Dame.[43] Finally, in 1940, at the age of seventy-eight, Adina De Zavala was accepted into the Philosophical Society of Texas.

Like many of her contemporaries, although perhaps more rigorously than most, Adina De Zavala was an habitual letter writer. The most repeated topic of her correspondence was, not surprisingly, Texas history: anyone inquiring about the remotest historical detail was sure to gain a reply from her, especially if they or their descendants might shed historical light on a particular aspect of Texas history. De Zavala's archival files contain letters from Ernest Crockett and Janice C. French, two of the Alamo defender's descendants; from the Mayors of San Antonio and Houston thanking her for reminding them to fly the Texas flag on Texas Independence Day; from Mrs.R. J. Kleberg, Sr., the wife of Robert J. Kleberg of the King Ranch and founder of Kingsville, Texas. She corresponded with contemporary historians and popular writers of Texas history, in addition to her friend Professor Castañeda, already mentioned. She communicated with Eugene Barker, also of the University of Texas-Austin; the Reverend Pierre F. Parisot, whose book, *Reminiscences of a Texas Missionary,* was published in 1899 in San Antonio, and had requested information from her on the Franciscan Friars of Texas and Coahuila, Mexico;[44] Cordelia F. Brodbent, an early writer on *Los Pastores*, the Mexican Shepherd's Play; and numerous others, either commenting on her work or requesting help with their own.

Restoring History through Story

Despite her very public persona, several questions concerning De Zavala's own sense of self remain hidden. It is clear that she was zealous about Texas history and the Alamo, but for what reasons? Why would this woman, a descendent of one of Mexico's political elites, spend her life in pursuit of all things Texan and, knowing today how the Alamo was used to fuel anti-Mexican sentiment, why was she consumed with it? The answers to these questions are not easily distilled from the extensive material she left behind. For one, most of her correspondence consists of letters she received, not those she wrote; second, the few letters of hers that are available are in draft form, and may or may not have been her final thoughts, leaving us with scraps of her formed opinion on a number of issues.

De Zavala's character is further complicated by the realization that several of those with whom she corresponded maintained some very rigid and elitist, if not racist, attitudes towards Mexicans. Pierre Parisot, for instance, in his missionary book refers to Mexicans as a "nomadic" lot coming from the "wilds of the neighboring States of Mexico."[45] Mrs. R. J. Kleberg and her family at the King Ranch were, according to the Mexican folklore of the day, responsible for the social and economic demise of Mexicans in Texas.[46] As one who publicly spoke about Mexican treasures in Texas, both oral and material, could she have been so unwittingly cognizant of their purveyors' demise at the hands of local elites?

The public portrait of De Zavala—one who romanticized, even glorified, a vision of Texas history—is that of a woman of partial Mexican ancestry whose allegiance and politics lie not with her grandfather's "patria," but with the emerging Anglo-American status quo of the day. But this picture, consistent as it may be with her own autobiographical intent, is too facile for comprehending a woman as complicated, committed and socially positioned as De Zavala. Let me clearly iterate that I do not believe we can understand De Zavala, or her remarkable career, from the ethnic politics of today. It would be irresponsible to reductively assume De Zavala's politics from her Mexican name. And yet, the conjuncture of her life's passion, the Alamo, the historical moment, her battles with the DRT and her own writings reveal, upon closer scrutiny, a critical vision of the Alamo and Texas history. I contend that De Zavala's deep desire for restoring material artifacts and historical places stems from a displaced political critique on her part. Furthermore, embedded in her life's work—that desire to preserve and restore the cultures of earlier habitations—is an ecumenical perspicacity of Texas history and society that discerns, through the clouded visibility of the moment, a series of social concerns that remain hidden in her romantic and zealous commitment to the past. This vision, I suggest, comes into sight when her work of material preservation and restoration is brought into relief with her written work.

Tales of the Past

Adina De Zavala wrote profusely, often taking notes or writing initial drafts of letters or historical narratives on envelopes, receipts, or anywhere else she could. Besides *History and Legends of the Alamo*, she wrote short essays, legends, poems, even a brief skit on the six flags that have flown over Texas.[47] Perhaps it was because of her misadventures with the DRT, she saw her work and efforts undermined, receiving little or no recognition, or just her keen sense of history, but De Zavala copyrighted—in her own name—several of her short pamphlets and books, including this volume.

The earliest of her copyrighted materials recorded in the Library of Congress is a print of the Alamo, titled: "Where the Heroes Died," copyrighted April 18, 1908, and which is reproduced in this book. Among the short publications submitted for copyright were: *The Story of the Siege and Fall of the Alamo: A Resumé,* published August 26, 1911; *Margil Vine, the Legend of the first Christmas at the Alamo,* published December 19, 1916; and *History and Legends of the Alamo,* published December 22, 1917. While these materials recount the history and folklore of the Alamo, her 1911 *The Story of the Siege and Fall of the Alamo,* concludes by berating those who would use the Alamo for their own gain. The last two pages of this brief book state:

...The President of the De Zavala Chapter wrote or dictated both memorial and bill presented to the Legislature asking that the property be given into the custody of the Association. The Twenty-ninth Legislature granted the request of the De Zavala Chapter, so unanimously endorsed by the people of Texas, and the property was eventually turned over to the De Zavala Chapter. Here the Hotel Syndicate stepped in and by its machination for the destruction of The Alamo proper caused both the ancient Fortress Building and Church to be snatched from the devoted hands of De Zavala Chapter; and since 1905, the property has been shamefully neglected and put to disgraceful use for these "business interests." A set of men have been trying at each succeeding Legislature to have this main Alamo building torn down in order to put their property to the front and benefit themselves by enhancing the value of their own property....
...Will Texas remember The Alamo and keep faith with the ladies of the De Zavala Chapter, of San Antonio, who saved the Alamo, 1903-1905?
Send in your protests and appeals, at once, to the Governor of Texas, and to your Senator and other

Representatives in the Texas Legislature asking them to save this old Alamo building.

One of De Zavala's lesser known contributions was the editorial work she performed on *The Antiquities of Mexico by Lord Kingsborough*, compiled by Reverend Edmond J. P. Schmitt, a fellow member of the Texas State Historical Society. When Schmitt grew ill and eventually succumbed on May 5, 1901, his project, in the last stages of publication, was completed by De Zavala. Her note on the first page of the book reads:

> The Collator, Rev. Edmond J. P. Schmitt, died May 5, 1901, shortly after the manuscript of this work had been placed in the hands of the printers by me. It was written "between coughs," as he said—and therefore hard to decipher. The proof being in many places meaningless, I had to review the entire work and in some places re-write. He had, toward the last, to depend upon others to look up the materials, and therefore, a few notes which I feel sure he intended to put in, were omitted.

Besides these more formal compositions, De Zavala collected, edited and wrote a number of oral tales and legends. Most list her as the author, although it is clear from her letters that she also received a number of texts from various people she corresponded with; and while several of these are listed as copyrighted, none exist in the Copyright Office of the Library of Congress, except for those already mentioned above.[48]

History and Legends of the Alamo: The History

In 1917, several years after her chapter was voted out of the Daughters of the Republic of Texas, Adina De Zavala privately published *History and Legends of the Alamo and Other Missions in and around San Antonio.* A work consisting of varied narrative forms, it is in many ways the magnum opus of De Zavala's career as a writer of Texas history and folklore. Why it was published privately, I have yet to discover. It may have been because of her intense desire to control its content and details. It is uncertain how many copies were printed, but it was issued in both cloth and paper binding, selling for $1.50 and $1.00 respectively, and was available from De Zavala's Taylor Street address in San Antonio.[49]

Judging from her personal communication, the book sold well. In 1925, the secretary of the Texas Folk-lore Society wrote her petitioning that she send him ten more copies of the book, because the society had exhausted its supply.[50] And, on March 3, 1936, she received a letter from G. B. Dealey of the *Dallas Morning News* claiming that he was unable to find a copy of the book, and when he attempted to receive a copy from the Methodist Publishing House, he was told it was out of print and that a new edition was being considered.[51]

While there is little information on how the book was received, the book jacket of the cloth edition has the following quote from the *San Antonio Express:*

> There is a wealth of romance and history and folklore
> in the neatly-printed, well-bound volume of more
> than 200 pages, making it a real addition to the
> works on the history of the Southwest.[52]

Second, as noted earlier, it was the custom of the Texas State Historical Society to refer questions on the Alamo and Texas missions to her, a recognition accrued, in part, from the quality and accuracy of the book.

History and Legends of the Alamo begins with an extensive and strikingly comprehensive, historical survey of the Alamo. De Zavala reconstructs the history of Mission San Antonio de Valero, or the Alamo, beginning with its founding as a Spanish mission. She includes Spanish documents portraying the allotment of mission lands as well as excerpts from church records from this period. She details how the Secularization Laws of 1793 led to the abandonment of the missions, leading to their occupation by Spanish and Mexican cavalry as frontier outposts.

De Zavala portrays the Battle of the Alamo, the events that precipitated it and its final outcome using diary entries of Fannin's soldiers and letters of Sam Houston, William Travis and others. She incorporates most of the available published work on the Alamo, including Reuben Potter's *The Fall of the Alamo*, H. Yoakum's *History of Texas* and George Garrison's *Texas*. Besides these sources, she also draws from baptismal records from the missions and the cathedral, and includes artistic sketches and plats of the Alamo from Mexican sources. With these early documents, De Zavala provides information on the location of the mission structures, their dimensions, their design and their condition during the Alamo battle.

She concludes her historical chapter with a record of post-battle events and details the mission's structural decline, its use by the U.S. Army and by the Hugo-Schmeltzer Company. She also recounts her efforts to purchase and restore the property. Overall, De Zavala weaves a clear and putatively accurate narrative that chronicles the Indian, Spanish, Mexican, Texan and U.S. presence at the Alamo.

History and Legends of the Alamo: The Legends

Immediately following the historical section, De Zavala switches genres and provides a series of legends related to the Alamo and other San Antonio missions. But unlike the numerous stories that speak of Bowie, Travis or Crockett, these tales have nothing to do with the Alamo "heroes." Instead, they portray a different understanding of turn-of-the-century Texas.

The first legend she recounts tells of ghosts with flaming torches that appear to anyone who attempts to tamper with the walls and physical structure of the Alamo. Following this is a legend about the statue of St. Anthony, the patron of the Mission San Antonio de Valero. Accordingly, all statues were removed from the mission after the Franciscans departed, except for that of St. Anthony, which could not be dislodged. The legend claims that "Saint Anthony held his statue there, because he wished his church to be repaired and placed again at the service of the people he loved, whose mission and town had been given his name, and whom he was still anxious to serve!"[53] The statue was present during the battle in 1836, and years later when St. Joseph's Church was built only a few blocks away, "all ideas of the use of the Alamo church for religious purposes were abandoned, and the statue of St. Anthony gave no more trouble, and was easily moved."[54]

It is the next series of legends that interest me more, because they form a triptych of tales bound with a singular motif. Each narrative under the heading of "The Folk of the Underground Passages" depicts the presence of mysterious characters who emerge from the "enchanted city" to which underground passages of the Alamo are connected.

The first tale, "The Padre's Gift," concerns a man who appears to unsuspecting people and gives them a special gift. According to this legend, the padre is one of the "good people who have power...to pass from the enchanted city of Tejas by way of the underground passages of the Alamo."[55] After providing some brief contextual material, the author, identifying herself as the narrator of the legend, recalls her own encounter with an old man dressed in a religious habit while she was riding outside the city as a young girl. Upon greeting him, she is presented with a thick book written in Spanish. The one condition of receiving the gift is that no one else is to touch the book until she presents it to someone else under the same conditions of privacy. Agreeing, the narrator states, "I have always regretted that I did not ask the old man's name—but I thought, then, only of the precious old treasures and my wonderful good fortune in receiving them."[56]

The second legend concerns the mysterious woman in blue who ascends from the underground passages of the Alamo to seek out a Native Texan woman, "pure and good, well-bred, intelligent, spiritual and patriotic,"[57] upon whom she will bestow a gift. "What is her gift? The gift of seeing to the heart of things! She sees...all that may vitally affect, for good or ill, the people of her city and state whom she ardently loves with a strange devotion."[58] This woman, the legend continues, is ready to help "the rich, the poor, the artist, the artisan, the writer, the children—the whole people of her beloved Texas land."[59]

The third legend describes the events of Ursula, a young girl, missing after playing with friends around the Alamo. Ursula's parents are faced with difficult financial problems due to the father's ill health, and when she fails to come home after playing, a search is organized by people from town. Fearing Ursula has been taken by Indians, the search party is relieved when they find her in a heavy sleep amidst the ruins of the Alamo. Upon her safe arrival home she recounts how, while playing hide 'n seek, she helped a woman who had stumbled and fallen. After aiding the woman, she continued to hide from her friends and she fell into a deep sleep, awakening only after being found by the search party. The woman she helped had given her a small wrapped package and told her to stow it in her pocket. "The mother, realizing her daughter had met the 'good woman' of the underground," examines the package and finds "several very old Spanish gold coins, two diamonds and three pearls...and her first thought was that now, Joseph [her husband], could go to consult and secure the eminent specialists" who could cure his ailing health.[60]

These stories are linked by their motif of gift-giving. However, in place of operating as a form of exchange, this motif serves as an articulation of hope, or more specifically, the nostalgic hope for social restoration. Gift-giving in these legends serves to restore elements of a world displaced by the radical changes instituted by the social and economic reordering of South Texas.

In the first legend, the gift presented is a thick book written in Spanish from a man who comes from the enchanted city of "Tejas." In light of the Anglo-American's "repudiation of the Spanish past" for their own "self-identity,"[61] the use of the referent "Tejas" is instructive. It is derived from a Caddo word adapted by the Spanish as a name for the area, and was later kept by the Mexican government as the name of the province. Its presence indexes a world of Indian, Spanish and Mexican influence, further implied by the gift of the book, a prototypical literary and cultural document, written in the Spanish language. The woman in the legend, whom the author claims is herself, makes an intriguing comment upon receiving the book. "I am sure it is wonderful, but it appears well nigh undecipherable with age, and besides, you see, I do not know the Spanish language well." Upon hearing this the padre responds, "No, use what you can, and pass it on."[62] The woman's comment seemingly contradicts the historical figure of De Zavala who, born into a Mexican family, was accustomed to communicating with her Mexican relatives in Spanish.[63] This legend, therefore, is not autobiographical but a sentimental narrative in which history gives way to hope. By encountering the man from the enchanted and underground city, a place embedded in the unseen reaches of unconscious desire, the young woman in the legend receives a gift that calls attention to and seeks to restore a Spanish and Mexican social and cultural world now lost.

In the "Mysterious Woman in Blue," the recipient of the gift is always a "native Texan woman...eyes of gray...not black" who is intelligent and good-hearted.[64] The description of gray eyes is not a common feature: *Mexicanas* are usually described by their dark, often black or brown, eyes while

Anglo-American women are seen as having blue or light eyes. Gray eyes are an amalgam, neither black or brown nor blue, but a combination of all of them. The woman who receives the gift, I suggest, is identified as neither Mexican nor American, but one who can claim that "All the children are her children—all the people are her friends, and brothers and sisters!"[65]

The issue of social restoration is more clearly found in her gift of seeing. The woman in possession of the gift sees "to the heart of things" with the "clear-eyed vision of Joan of Arc," fighting for "justice" for the "whole people of her beloved Texas land."[66] Seeing to the heart of things is to see beyond the personal and sentimental, beyond the isolated events of every day. The woman's gift of sight restores the unity of experience and vision lost to the reductive processes that render the social world a personal and private affair.

The third legend is that of the lost girl who, after helping an old woman, opens a gift of gold coins, diamonds and pearls. This gift signifies another form of restoration by enabling the father to visit a medical specialist to cure his health. It is consistent with this reading that the gifts offered are forms of wealth and not, strictly speaking, money. That is, the coins and jewels are actually pre-capitalist forms of wealth and exchange and not, as Weber claims, the money-form—the most reified of all forms of exchange.[67]

The gift of wealth serves to restore the father's health, and along with him, the economic and social health of the family since its economic troubles stem from his inability to work. As in the previous legends, the gift bestowed is not meant for personal use, even when given to an individual, but for the good of the "whole people of Texas," as in the gift of seeing—or as in this last text, for the restoration of the family, because the gift of health is really that of economic restoration and stability.

How are we to make sense of De Zavala's two different narratives about the Alamo? What is the relationship between De Zavala's historical text and her collected legendary? Here, I turn to Paul Ricoeur's discussion of historical narrativity, which I find instructive on these points.

Ricoeur states that every narrative "combines two dimensions in various proportions, one chronological and the other nonchronological." By chronological, Ricoeur refers to the "episodic" aspects of narratives which "characterize the story made out of events"; by nonchronological, he means how plots configure "wholes out of scattered events."[68] While Ricoeur refers to the dialectical relationship between chronology and nonchronology in the same text, it is quite clear that he understands texts to be weighted in one direction or another. Finally, as Ricoeur states, an historical event is more than a single occurrence and contributes "to the development of a plot."[69] As such, an historical text is one that not only provides a chronology but situates this chronology within a processual frame. My concern is, first, to see how De Zavala's narratives are weighted in different directions; and second, to demonstrate how the meaning of these two texts can be more fully appreciated through Ricoeur's dialectical relationship: that is, De Zavala's historical narrative is only historical when paired with her collected legends, and these legends make interpretive sense when contrasted with the historical texts.

Equipped with these briefly stated notions of Ricoeur, I now return to De Zavala's writings. I understand her chapter on the history of the Alamo as a chronological narrative that tells an "episodic" story. But this chapter, replete with "data" and "facts" is only a partial history and must be read alongside her nonchronological legendry, since it is there that we find the "plot" to this story. De Zavala's collected legends allow us to understand the "historical" significance of the Alamo, not as a place with a chronology but as an event whose meaning is situated within the larger process of Texas social life.

In order to accomplish this, I turn to the works of Ann Douglas and Fredric Jameson. Building on various literary and critical traditions, including the structuralism of Levi-Strauss, Jameson demonstrates how narratives operate as "symbolic resolution(s) of real political and social contradictions."[70] Placing Jameson's critical perspective alongside Douglas's keen reading of the role of nineteenth-century women in literary and cultural practice makes De Zavala's critical discourse apparent. Following Douglas, the "problem" these legends seek to resolve is the impact of "laissez-faire industrial expansion" and its "inevitable rationalization of the economic order."[71] It is critical to remember that De Zavala's legends were coterminous with capitalist expansion and modernization in South Texas, the effect of which was the dismantling of *Mexicano* traditional society and its subsequent reorganization by capitalist entrepreneurs into a more efficient and pragmatic economic form. Developments in both the railroad and large-scale commercial agriculture were two activities that eroded the traditional, family-based, cattle-ranching society of South Texas and reshaped it to the needs and logic of a market economy.[72] That De Zavala's legends are dialogically responsive to the social and economic displacement experienced by *Mexicanos* at the turn of the century is fairly clear. These Utopian narratives seek to "fix" the problem of socioeconomic displacement by pointing to various forms of restoration and recalling the "enchanted city of Tejas" where social and racial cleavage are unknown.

After these initial legends concerning the Alamo, the book proceeds to document the history of the establishment of the Missions in Texas. With great historical detail and care, including plats of the missions, De Zavala tells of the trials of the early Franciscans in Texas. In conjunction with the chronological formation of the missions, De Zavala continues to weave oral tales concerning these places into her historical account.

Near the end of the book, De Zavala diverges from this subject and provides a brief overview of *Los Pastores,* or the Mexican shepherd's play, in Texas as well as the *Via Crucis* or Way of the Cross, a reenactment of the journey of Christ at the time of his death. Another section is devoted to her grandfather, Lorenzo de Zavala, and the book concludes by celebrating the efforts of the De Zavala Daughters, the historical group she founded.

Restoring the Restorer

How are we to make interpretive sense of the life and work of Adina De Zavala? She was a complex woman, ruled by her passion for all things historical. Of Mexican and Irish ancestry, she was devotedly American. A preserver of Mexican and Spanish material culture, she gave seemingly negligible attention to the contemporary heirs of these artifacts. At one level we must recognize and admire the portrait her deeds and words have painted; on another, we must probe beneath the multitextured surface of this complex image and pose a series of questions, for De Zavala was both an acute chronicler of the past as well as a person shaped by its particular modality.

It is important to recall that during De Zavala's battle to save the Alamo from capitalist entrepreneurs, rural Mexicans in Texas were being economically displaced in the dwindling cattle industry and transformed into wage-laborers in the emerging agricultural industry.[73] Accompanying such a transformation were the various discourses, or "strategies of containment,"[74] that rationalized and supported that social displacement. It is precisely along these lines that the preservation of the Alamo and the concomitant creation of negative images of Mexicans symbolically provided a means to visually subsidize the transformation of Mexicans to a subservient and dependent class.

For one who studied, collected and prided herself in the knowledge of all things Texan and Mexican—to the extent of bringing "grievous blunders" to Lomax's attention—it is difficult to imagine De Zavala being wholly unfamiliar with the social conditions of this period. Could she have missed the growing anti-Mexican sentiment experienced by the émigrés to Texas and San Antonio as they fled the revolutionary turmoil of Mexico? Much of the conflict between Texans and Mexicans was heralded in the local *corridos*, a genre of folklore about which she seemed to have some knowledge—not only did she lecture on a particular text, as noted above, but I found scribbled among her papers a quatrain, written in Spanish, under which she wrote "Corrido is a running rhyme."[75] Contemporary scholarship on the Texas-Mexican *corrido* is quite extensive and demonstrates how the years between 1860 and 1920 were a high-point of *corrido* production, especially of those ballads that sang of the conflict between Mexicans and Texans.[76] Even if De Zavala was unfamiliar with the political elements expressed through these texts, she could hardly escape the events of 1901 concerning the search, chase, arrest and trial of Gregorio Cortez, or the events of 1915 connected with the border skirmishes between the Texas Rangers and a band of Texas-Mexicans known as Los Sediciosos.[77] Why, in the midst of such turmoil, conflict, social and economic upheaval, does Adina De Zavala fixate on the Alamo? It is here, I suggest, that further discussion of De Zavala's sense of Mexicanness is warranted, including some remarks on her own sense of ethnic identity.

De Zavala clearly celebrates all things Texan: historical places, characters and folklore. But she is equally adamant about the Mexican and Spanish roots of Texas. She continues to search the state for evidence and artifacts from these historical periods and construes history as a summation of the past, influenced by social factors from both sides of the border. And yet, as I have shown elsewhere, it is De Zavala's intense effort to understand, interpret and restore the Alamo both as a Spanish mission and place of battle, that distinguishes her understanding of this place from that of Clara Driscoll and the DRT.[78]

But ambiguity remains. While she may have had an inclusive sense of history when it came to Mexican Texas, what were her thoughts about Mexicans as a people, not as places or things? And, likewise, how did she meld her own Mexican ancestry, however partial, with her larger sense of self? These are not easy issues to examine, but De Zavala provides us with a few ideas that lead in interesting directions. In 1949, already in her late eighties, she addresses a letter to Paul Adams regarding a text written for school children about the *San Antonio Story*. Its relevance to this discussion is apparent and I reproduce here in its entirety.

Dear Friends:

It seemed to me that the youth or adult who reads the *San Antonio Story* should be given an overall understanding of how San Antonio came to be, therefore, I sent in the suggestive sketch.

I did not re-read my notes as they were sent in and I am wondering if I have made myself thoroughly understood as to objections to certain terms as "Anglos," "Anglo-Americans," "Latin-Americans," "Yankees," etc.

In a book intended for our schools we should be truthful—accurate in what we say, and try not to offend anyone by our expressions. However, we MUST hold fast to the truth—notwithstanding uninformed and prejudiced opposition. We should set a standard! Other writers should be able, confidently, to take this history as a model—a criterion. We should not copy others' mistakes even if considered popular. It MUST be one! And what a splendid advertisement this would be for our city and schools!

If a German[79] becomes naturalized in the United States, he is a citizen of the United States of America—and entitled to the designation "American"—though born in Europe. And should he be asked in England who he is—he could and should truthfully answer: "I am an American of the United States." This is what our highest authority on Emigration and Naturalization says.

After Mexico won her independence from Spain, and before—there were so many uprisings, revolutions and changes in administrations, and these early settlers were always reaching out and hoping for a stable government. However, they never felt that they really "belonged" until Texas became an independent Republic, March 2, 1836! Then, of course, when Anson Jones, the last President of the Republic of Texas, lowered the Texas flag February 19, 1846, and raised the Stars and Stripes in its stead—they felt that they, too, "belonged" and were citizens of the United States!

Unfortunately, we, in Texas, in the early days of Statehood—and later have often placed in power persons who carelessly or heartlessly permitted neglect and abuse of our early settlers and their descendants—the real owners of the soil before our arrival. They have been for the most part, for years, a confused and "hurt" people. These under-privileged citizens—many descendants of early settlers—know they are NOT Mexicans, for to be one they would have to have been born in Mexico and now hold citizenship there, or have acquired it—yet, when they are questioned as to their citizenship and pressed for an answer they generally say "Mexican," because they have been told continually that they *are* "Mexican." Though puzzled—knowing that they are expected to give that answer—they obligingly do so.

On account of ways and other serious troubles, many of these early settlers and their children were not able to obtain the educational advantages of our citizens elsewhere, though there were many educated people in the early days, and many naturally superior citizens who were looked to for leadership. (See authors of the Memorial to the Mexican Government in 1832. Also Gil Y'Barbo, etc.) These people are "Americans" in every sense of the word—and if we still have descendants of our aborigines—and there were some quite gifted ones here—not so long ago they, too, are preeminently "Americans."

Should we not begin at once to let these under-privileged citizens know that we recognize them as Texans and fellow citizens and fellow Americans? Should we not strive to teach and inculcate a feeling of love, loyalty and pride in our city, state, nation and in all our citizens and young people? And try to instill a sense of responsibility and a desire and determination to work whole heartedly and unselfishly foe the good of all. We, as well as they, are suffering from our short sightedness—from our neglect in meeting our responsibility! Should we not, at once, try to repair our mistakes? It is LATE—but with God's help we may not be TOO LATE![80]

This text is revealing on several counts. First, note that De Zavala speaks of Mexicans in the third person, and includes herself among the list of citizenry, Texans and Americans. But the text is important for a number of other reasons. De Zavala accurately places responsibility for the social demise of Mexicans on "*our* neglect from meeting *our* responsibility" [my emphasis]. Mistakes have been made, she writes, and amends must clearly be made. Furthermore, although these people were not born in Mexico, it is the dominant, Anglo-American class that "continually" reminds these people that they are "Mexicans."

In one of her more telling phrases, De Zavala clearly claims that it is "we, in Texas" who have been abusive and neglectful towards "the real owners of the soil before our arrival." The issue here is land. Like those heroic defenders, not of the Alamo but of the *corridos* of border conflict, ownership of land and the economic resources it provides for those who control it are her concern. Mexicans, due to the abuses inflicted upon them by Texans, have been "confused and 'hurt'" and exist as "under-privileged citizens." De Zavala emphatically pleads that we recognize Mexicans as "Texans and fellow citizens and fellow Americans"; she requests that Mexicans not be treated as second-class members of society but as full participants. While the rhetoric of cultural nationalism is clearly absent from her writing, the goals of shared responsibility and equality, the issues of class displacement and racial abuse, and the subsequent outcome of social and psychological disvaluation are clearly a concern of hers.

Written at the age of eighty-eight, De Zavala's letter displays a keen sense of the inequities of the past that perhaps was not present in her earlier writings. I do not believe these are the musings of an elderly woman who—due to the privileges of old-age—now speaks her mind; De Zavala always spoke her mind. Instead, this text is the product of experience, reflection and knowledge that resulted, perhaps, in a kind of personal and textual reconciliation of her Mexican past and American present.

But what does she make of her Mexican-Irish-Spanish self? To the extent that language serves as an important marker in discussions of ethnic formation and identity, I invoke the following example. In a recent article for the tourist magazine *Texas Highways*, Frank Jennings claims that "Despite her Spanish surname, she [De Zavala] never learned the language."[81] The evidence for Jennings' claim, I suggest, is not so clear; and, judging from De Zavala's papers, there is more cause to believe that she was a dedicated student of the language, if not nearly fluent in the written text.

As a veracious keeper of records, De Zavala left a handwritten and typed record of her personal library holdings.[82] Listed as part of her collection are a number of Mexican history books, written in Spanish, as well as texts for learning Spanish. Furthermore, it is clear that De Zavala traveled through Mexico on more than one occasion and received correspondence in Spanish from a number of people. While some of her Mexican correspondents may not have known English, her Uncle Lorenzo, Jr. did, and on more than one occasion he wrote to her in Spanish.

Another source that suggests she was knowledgeable of Spanish is her copious notes and papers. In more than several places she jotted down phrases, notes and book titles in Spanish. Although it is not clear if she copied this material directly from other sources, Ables quotes De Zavala as stating that, at the time near her resignation as a teacher, she had been studying "Mexican history in Mexico."[83]

While De Zavala's knowledge of Spanish is of interest in and of itself, this issue serves as a marker for her sense of ethnic self. There is no doubt that she considered herself an American, and more importantly, a Texan. But did her clear sense of Texan identity require a rejection of her Mexican heritage? If anything, De Zavala was about remembering, restoring and recollecting the entire past of Texas, including its Spanish and Mexican roots. I cannot imagine she would think otherwise about herself; and yet, based on her letter to Adams, she would not call herself a "Mexican." This is why De Zavala's knowledge of Spanish is significant. I believe Jennings is incorrect in stating that she never learned the language: not only do her personal papers demonstrate a clear effort to do just that, but they further indicate a certain proficiency in reading it. Jennings' discussion of this topic leads one to think that De Zavala was Mexican in name only, alienated from her Mexican heritage. Perhaps her unflinching sense of "Texanness" moves him to claim such a position; I believe another set of factors must be considered on this issue.

It is here, I suggest, that we bring into sharp focus the twin passions that consumed De Zavala's life—places and stories of the past. De Zavala is acutely aware, going back to her letter to Adams, of the treatment Mexicans experienced at the hands of Americans. She claims that any sense of self that is rooted in a "Mexican" identity is the result of its imposition upon people who otherwise seek to be "American." From this statement, we can glean the following possibilities. At one level, De Zavala's identification as an American and Texan appears as a form of ethnic abandonment and reattachment. Instead of accepting her Mexican, lower-status identity, she reattaches herself to her Texan ancestry, one rightly accorded through her Irish lineage. But, even as I suggest this explanation, let me also claim that I do not think this approach answers enough questions. For one, ethnic reattachments are found not only on the part of Mexicans claiming a Texan identity, but are foisted upon "good" Mexicans by local discourses. In an example resulting from De Zavala's own efforts, we have the local San Antonio newspaper referring to Enrique Esparza, De Zavala's eyewitness informant on the Battle of the Alamo, in the following way:

> Esparza tells a straight story. Although he is a Mexican, his gentleness and unassuming frankness are like the typical old Texan.[84]

Reading this description of Esparza alongside De Zavala's celebratory Texan identification serves as a critical reminder of how the hegemonic forces of this period worked their way into local representations of Mexicans, as well as Mexicans' self-references. This leads me to suggest that ethnic reattachments—like that exhibited by De Zavala—while at one level must be considered for their referential content, must also be evaluated in terms of personal repression arising from ethnic hostility and racism. At this level, De Zavala's insistence and fervent declaration of "Texanness" must be seen as a form of personal repression whereby her ethnic self—informed by the same racial sensibilities that turned Esparza into an "old Texan"—has been displaced onto another level of practice. Here I draw on De Zavala's politically unconscious work, both material and discursive, that reveals an embedded political posture that cannot be dismissed. My suggestion, and the crux of my thesis on De Zavala, is that her deep interest in the material and social restoration of a Spanish and Mexican past, expressed through her work of artifactual preservation and historical legendry, results from the displacement of her "Mexican" self onto these other levels of practice.

In an acutely perceptive work, Stallybrass and White argue a similar notion of displacement when they claim that "sentimentality for 'lost' realms can be avoided by mapping the inner articulation of semantic domains/sites of discourse within the historical formation of class subjectivities."[85] Their claim is that displacements, or the discursive shifting of meanings and subjects, are not neutral practices but ones invested with the social meanings of the time. Instrumental for Stallybrass and White, as well as for my own interpretive claims, are the hierarchical relations that emerge from particular historical configurations that lead to the validation of "one set of social practices over against others."[86] De Zavala's passion about Spanish and Mexican places, I contend, emerges, in part, from the anti-Mexican atmosphere of early twentieth-century Texas. In place of validating her own mestizoness—a unique conjuncture of Spanish, Mexican and Irish ancestry—she forges a unified Texan subjectivity and displaces her "cultural otherness" onto historical places. Her life is spent in search of the "lost realms" of Spanish and Mexican Texas precisely because her ethnic sense of self has been displaced by a Texan subjectivity. Displacement, in this case, is linked to the Freudian notion of sublimation, which sheds further light on this discussion.

Ricoeur's ground-breaking work *Freud and Philosophy* allows us to read Freud, not just as an interpreter of the human mind but of the socio-cultural world as well. According to Ricoeur, Freud's notion of sublimation is a "displacement of energy and an innovation of meaning"[87] that is marked by a

profound "unity of disguise and disclosure."[88] De Zavala's celebration of her Texan identity serves as a disguise, I contend,
while her Utopian legends disclose an embedded political critique. But sublimation is itself a mechanism, a response; here
Stallybrass and White offer a particular rationale, since for
them sublimation is inseparable from "cultural domination,"
of which ethnic hostility and racism is, I believe, a particular
form.[89] Sublimation—the displacement of energy that leads to
various shades of disguising and disclosing—is a response to
certain forms of social and cultural hegemonic practices. The
paradox that leads De Zavala to empathize with Mexicans
while celebrating Americanism, to work unceasingly for the
historical preservation of Spain and Mexico's artifactual past
while simultaneously holding little value for her partial Mexican heritage, occurs, I believe, from repressing the depth of
the social, cultural and economic domination experienced by
Mexicans at this time. Personal displacements such as this
are not unheard of for Mexican women of this period. Writing
about De Zavala's colleague and associate in the Texas Folklore Society, José Limón's comments concerning Jovita
González are appropriate for De Zavala as well.[90] She was, he
says, "unsupported by the luxury of a 'growing ethnic-feminist
consciousness,' who perhaps only appears 'to turn a blind eye'
on her role as a historical writing subject with respect to her
native community."[91] But in the case of De Zavala, it was not a
lack of sight but a displaced sense of ethnic self that affected
her. The letter to Adams demonstrates her particular vision
that, like her Woman in Blue, she too saw "to the heart of
things."[92] However, it is only through a critical reading of her
Utopian legends [and the present dissemination of her work]
that the (dialectical) other registers of her sublimated voice
can be heard. The social restoration semantically keyed in De
Zavala's legends serves as the muted and displaced social
voice of De Zavala's subjective speech. Unable to confront
directly the sources that socially and economically displaced

Mexicans, she employed them as the historical rationale of the Alamo; stymied by the racial hierarchies of the period, she displaced her ethnic self onto a Texan identity and a passion for the material past.

Although it is not clear to what extent De Zavala experienced, first-hand, the anti-Mexican climate of this era, she could not escape knowing it, as the following example from her papers demonstrates. On September 13, 1929, she received a letter from the Reverend Charles Taylor, OMI of Sacred Heart Church in Crystal City, Texas, requesting money for his church. His letter begins: "Mexicans, non-Catholics, rural life—are these not the three great problems that confront the Church in America today?... People here need no authority to tell you that their [Mexicans] name is legion...."[93] And yet, even as some members of the Texas Catholic clergy held views like Taylor's, De Zavala's own sense of Catholicism—buried beneath layers of Texas pride—manifests itself in her own religious practice, for also among her papers is a worn holy card, printed in Spanish, of Our Lady of Guadalupe. If not by self-reverentiality, and disguised as it may be, Adina De Zavala was in certain culturally gendered ways, a *mexicana*.[94]

The apparent contradictions surrounding De Zavala are many: a romantic defender of the Alamo, she is forced out of the DRT and her contributions are ignored; a woman of mixed ethnic ancestry, she embraces her own sense of Americanness and Texanness; a romantic chronicler of Texas, she emplots a Utopian vision for a restored "Tejas"; a writer and collector of all matters historical, her accomplishments have been mainly ignored in the present. It is only by historicizing De Zavala herself that these contradictions make interpretive sense. While much of this introduction has in fact historicized De Zavala, let me add the following distinction. As a subject and social actor, De Zavala's ouster from the DRT and her romantic views of Texas are quite understandable: she spoke loudly and vehemently about her own historical knowledge and the makers of the past.[95]

But as a social agent, one who occupies a particular structural position, her life is less clear. To what extent does her ethnic structural slot color the view of the DRT's understanding of her. No doubt they reacted in many ways to De Zavala the actor; brash, confident, outspoken, she was clearly a force to be considered. But as an "ethnic other," in a period when such social positions were more rigid and confining, we see little of her enemy's views. It would be misleading to suggest that De Zavala was treated *only* as an "ethnic other"; she was not, but the level of ethnic prejudice and racism cannot be dismissed. While it is clear that De Zavala's own personal characteristics and historical vision gave the DRT much to wrangle with, the depths of social, ethnic and gender repression of the period were clearly prescriptive forces in her life.

For all her accomplishments, it was the Alamo that remained the singularly most important aspect of her public life. While much that precedes this conclusion has gone to suggest why, let me summarize by stating the following. The Alamo serves as the most salient and ambiguous symbol of Texas. Its semantic imprint dominates the social landscape between Texans and Mexicans, even as its full disclosure reveals deep racial and class fissures between the two. De Zavala lived, paradoxically, in the gulf between the past as a romantic history of "Tejas" and the present as a Utopian longing for its social restoration. She worked diligently and energetically to restore the Alamo as a shrine of Texas liberty—a bastion, in many cases, of anti-Mexican sentiment. And yet, in spite of all her colonial interests—that is, her concern for "things" and "places" of the past with seemingly no concern for their social effect—there remains a critique, a critical discourse, embedded, even repressed, in her work. For we find that the historical frame De Zavala constructs for the Alamo, the plot in which she embeds its story, is the social displacement of Mexicans stemming from the forces of modernity. According to this plot, the fictive restoration of Mexicans is necessary, since their real condition is one of degradation brought forth by the cultural, economic and social reorganization of Texas as an industrialized state. The historical narrative De Zavala provides of the Alamo configures a past for a place, but as a narrative whose plot has itself been displaced, embedded in her collected legends, we find an historical text that prescribes a social place for a people. It is not surprising, following the deep, resistive role that *mexicano* expressive culture has played in Texas, to find De Zavala's critical practice portrayed in such a way.[96] This reading of De Zavala's work serves to counter the monological discourse of the DRT and the growing sentiment surrounding the Alamo in the early 1900s. Her legends that call for a return to "Tejas," precisely *because* of their Utopian impulse, express an allegorical unity that emplots a very different kind of Alamo in a rather unheroic historical narrative. With a fuller discussion of De Zavala's historical and folkloric work still needed, I want, at this point, to allow her embedded critical discourse to remind us that keeping Mexicans in line has been a central plot of the Alamo all along.

[1]Arnoldo de León, *The Tejano Community. 1836-1900* (Albuquerque: University of New Mexico Press, 1982) :11.

[2]This letter is part of the De Zavala (Adina) Papers, Center for American History, University of Texas at Austin, Box 2m127. The original letter is written in Spanish, this English translation is the one contained in the files.

[3]Adina, in contrast to her father and grandfather, inscribed the "de" in her last name with an upper-case "D."

[4]Thesis by Robert Ables, Mexico, DF, Mexico, 1955, a copy of which is in the De Zavala (Adina) Papers, Center for American History, University of Texas at Austin, Box 2m129.

[5]Her father, Augustín de Zavala, served as a captain in the Confederate Navy.

[6]Adina De Zavala Collection, Incarnate Word College, San Antonio, Texas. This collection is still, except for several letter files, in the early stages of being catalogued. As a result, references are to the general collection.

[7]Ann Douglas, *The Feminization of American Culture* (New York: Doubleday, 1977).

[8]Kathleen D. McCarthy, *Women's Culture: American Philanthropy and Art* (Chicago: University of Chicago Press, 1991).

[9]Michael Kammen, *Mystic Chords of Memory: The Transformation of Tradition in American Culture* (New York: Vintage Books/Random House, 1991).

[10]Robert L. Ables, "The Second Battle of the Alamo," *The Southwestern Historical Quarterly*, 3 (January 1967): 376.

[11]Stephen Gould, *The Alamo City Guide* (New York: MacGowan & Slipper Printers, 1882): 16b.

[12]There was, according to Gould (1882), a growing trade in Mexican curiosities and souvenirs of the Alamo, although these items were only loosely tied, if at all, to the physical place of the Alamo.

[13]Quoted in Ables, p. 378.

[14]Ables, p. 381.

[15]Quoted in Ables, p. 379.

[16]Oscar B. Colquitt, *Message of Govenor O. B. Colquitt to the Thirty-third Legislature Relating to the Alamo Property* (Austin: Von Boeckmann-Jones Co., Printers, 1913): 91.

[17]Documents of the Twenty-ninth Legislature—Regular Session for January 23, 1905, contain a resolution thanking the DRT with amendments that specifically recognize De Zavala, Driscoll and others.

[18]Ables, p. 387.

[19]Adina De Zavala Collection, Incarnate Word College, San Antonio, Texas.

[20]Ables, p. 390.

[21]De Zavala (Adina) Papers, Center for American History University of Texas at Austin, Box 2m163. DRT Proceedings, April 21, 1906.

[22]Adina De Zavala File, Daughters of the Republic of Texas Library, The Alamo, San Antonio, Texas.

[23]De Zavala (Adina) Papers, Center for American History, University of Texas at Austin, Box 2m127.

[24]Supplemental petition, "DRT v. ADZ, Docket no. 43344." Quoted in Ables, p. 406.

[25]De Zavala (Adina) Papers, Center for American History, University of Texas at Austin, Box 2m163.

[26]Adina De Zavala File, Daughters of the Republic of Texas Library, The Alamo, San Antonio, Texas.

[27]De Zavala (Adina) Papers, Center for American History, University of Texas at Austin, Box 2m163.

[28]Colquitt, p. 137. It is these same maps and plats that are part of De Zavala's historical chronology in *History and Legends of the Alamo*.

[29]Colquitt, p. 137.

[30]Adina De Zavala Collection, Incarnate Word College, San Antonio, Texas.

[31]*Holland's Magazine*, December, 1935. Adina De Zavala File, Daughters of the Republic of Texas Library, The Alamo, San Antonio, Texas.

[32]Adina De Zavala File, Daughters of the Republic of Texas Library, The Alamo, San Antonio, Texas.

[33]De Zavala (Adina) Papers, Center for American History, University of Texas at Austin. Box 2m128.

[34]Adina De Zavala File, Daughters of the Republic of Texas Library, The Alamo, San Antonio, Texas.

[35]Timothy M. Matovina, *The Alamo Remembered: Tejano Accounts and Perspectives* (Austin: University of Texas Press, 1995).

[36]Matovina, p. 66.

[37]Adina De Zavala Collection, Incarnate Word College, San Antonio, Texas.

[38]De Zavala (Adina) Papers, Center for American History, University of Texas at Austin. Box 2m190.

[39]Adina De Zavala Collection, Incarnate Word College, San Antonio, Texas.

[40]One of the other vice-presidents in the Texas folklore Society was Colonel M. L. Crimmins of Fort Sam Houston in San Antonio, who also served with De Zavala as an officer of the THLA.

[41]De Zavala (Adina) Papers, Center for American History, University of Texas at Austin. Box 2m131.

⁴²De Zavala (Adina) Papers, Center for American History, University of Texas at Austin. Box 2m131.

⁴³Adina De Zavala Collection, Incarnate Word College, San Antonio, Texas. These files contain a hand-drawn sketch of the Bi-Centennial Medal.

⁴⁴For a brief discussion of Parisot, see Richard Flores, *Los Pastores: History and Performance in the Mexican Shepherd's Play of South Texas* (Washington, D.C.: Smithsonian Institution Press, 1995).

⁴⁵See Flores (1995).

⁴⁶For a brief discussion of the King Ranch in the Texas-Mexican folksong, see Richard Flores, "*The Corrido* and the Emergence of Texas-Mexican Social Identity," *The Journal of American Folklore* 105 (1992):166-182.

⁴⁷In an undated note in her own hand, De Zavala states that "there is so much misunderstanding as the national flags which figure in Texas history so this playet was written in response to appeals from classification, for use by societies, schools, clubs, etc." De Zavala (Adina) Papers, Center for American History, University of Texas at Austin. Box 2m165.

⁴⁸Her papers contain the following texts: Legend of the Duck Pond, or the Mysterious Lake; Legend of the Devil's Sink Hole, told to Augustine De Zavala by Mr. Stafford, Standard Oil Company, Also typed as the Punishment of Don Satanus; Signing of the Texas Declaration of Independence; A Texas Removal, in 1773, and the Brave Wanderings of the uprooted Families, dated 1933; An Incident at Mission Nuestra Señora del Refugio, from the manuscript "History of Important Events in Texas, dated 1924; Legend of the Mission Bells of San Augustine at Mission Nuestra Señora de los Delores de las Ais [?], dated 1926; Early Texas Writers, dated 1916; The Capture of San Antonio, 1835; The Voice of the Spirit Guides; Red Feather, or The Origin of the Red Bird; The Enchaned Rock, The Hill of the Original Woman in Blue, dated 1936; The Witch Doctor Cave; Origin, History and Present Status of the Missions of the San Antonio Valley, possibly a prepared talk. These are all found in the De Zavala (Adina) Papers, Center for American History, University of Texas at Austin.

⁴⁹From an advertisement of the book found among her papers in the Adina De Zavala Collection, Incarnate Word College, San Antonio, Texas.

⁵⁰Adina De Zavala Collection, Incarnate Word College, San Antonio, Texas. Letter file, 1925-26.

⁵¹Adina De Zavala Collection, Incarnate Word College, San Antonio, Texas.

⁵²Adina De Zavala Collection, Incarnate Word College, San Antonio, Texas.

⁵³Adina De Zavala, *History and Legends of the Alamo and Other Missions in and Around San Antonio* (San Antonio, 1917): 57.

[54]De Zavala, 1917, p. 57.

[55]De Zavala, 1917, p. 59

[56]De Zavala, 1917, p. 60

[57]De Zavala, 1917, p. 61

[58]De Zavala, 1917, p. 61.

[59]De Zavala, 1917, p. 62.

[60]De Zavala, 1917, p. 65.

[61]David J. Weber, *The Spanish Frontier in North America* (New Haven: Yale University Press, 1992) : 430.

[62]De Zavala, 1917, p. 60.

[63]For example, the letter quoted earlier from her uncle, Lorenzo de Zavala, Jr., was written entirely in Spanish.

[64]De Zavala, 1917, p. 61

[65]De Zavala, 1917, p. 61

[66]De Zavala, 1917. pp. 61-62.

[67]Max Weber, *From Max Weber: Essays in Sociology* (New York: Oxford University Press, 1946): 331.

[68]Paul Ricoeur, "Narrative Time," *Critical Inquiry* 7 (1980): 178.

[69]Ricoeur, 1980, p. 171.

[70]Fredric Jameson, *The Political Unconscious* (Ithaca: Cornell University Press, 1981): 80.

[71]Douglas, p. 12.

[72]David Montejano, *Anglos and Mexicans in the Making of Texas*, 1836-1986 (Austin: University of Texas Press, 1987); Arnoldo de León and Kenneth Stewart, "A Tale of Three Cities: A Comparative Analysis of the Socio-Economic Conditions of Mexican-Americans in Los Angeles, Tucson, and San Antonio," *Journal of the West* 24 (1985): 64-74.

[73]Montejano (1987) ; De León (1985).

[74]Jameson, p. 10.

[75]De Zavala (Adina) Papers, Center for American History, University of Texas at Austin. Box 2m129.

[76]Américo Paredes, *With His Pistol in His Hand: A Border Ballad and its Hero* (Austin: University of Texas Press, 1958); José Limón, "Folklore, Social Conflict and the United States-Mexico Border," *Handbook of American Folklore,* ed. Richard Dorson (Bloomington: Indiana University Press, 1983): 216-226; Flores (1992).

[77]Flores (1992).

[78]Flores (1995).

[79]This is a rather interesting example, especially soon after World War II and the anti-German sentiment it produced.

[80]De Zavala (Adina) Papers, Center for American History, University of Texas at Austin. Box 2m163.

[81]*Texas Highways* 42 (March, 1995): 16.

[82]Adina De Zavala Collection, Incarnate Word College, San Antonio, Texas.

[83]Ables, p. 373.

[84]Matovina, p. 67.

[85]Peter Stallybrass and Allon White, *The Politics and Poetics of Transgression* (Ithaca: Cornell University Press 1986): 196.

[86]Stallybrass and White, p. 197.

[87]Paul Ricoeur, *Freud and Philosophy: An Essay on Interpretation* (New Haven: Yale University Press 1970): 514.

[88]Ricoeur 1970, p. 519.

[89]Stallybrass and White, p. 197.

[90]While it is not clear how close De Zavala and González were, De Zavala refers to her several times in her notes from meetings they attended, specifically referencing a talk she gave on "The social conditions in Southern Texas." De Zavala (Adina) Papers, Center for American History, University of Texas at Austin. Box 2m138.

[91]Jossé Limón, *Dancing With the Devil* (Madison: University of Wisconsin Press, 1994): 74.

[92]The legend of the Woman in Blue seems to have been particularly important for De Zavala. Not only does it play a key role in her embedded political critique, but she collected numerous variants of the legend as well as disseminated it to people she knew. For example, in a letter to James Walsh of New York, she writes, "I am writing other legends and stories. I think you will be interested in the Woman in Blue. You will find a reference to her in the chronicles of the early Tejas Indians—in my little book—also she appears in the histories of the kindred or associate tribes. I am fascinated by her." Adina De Zavala Collection, Incarnate Word College, San Antonio, Texas.

[93]Adina De Zavala Collection, Incarnate Word College, San Antonio, Texas.

[94]See Jeanette Rodríguez, *Our Lady of Guadalupe: Faith and Empowerment among Mexican-American Women* (Austin: University of Texas Press, 1994), for an overview of the meaning and importance of Our Lady of Guadalupe in the lives of Mexican and Mexican-American women.

[95]The distinction between social actors, subjects and agents (developed in the next paragraph) are drawn from Michel-Rolph Trouillot, *Silencing the Past: Power and the Production of History* (Boston: Beacon Press, 1995): 23.

[96]For a fuller discussion and examples of this point, see Flores (1992 and 1994); Limón (1983 and 1995) ; Paredes (1958).

Select Bibliography of De Zavala's Published Sources

Brown, John Henry. 1892. *History of Texas from 1685 to 1892. 2 vols.* Austin: L. E. Daniell.

Brown, John Henry. 1896. *Indian Wars and Pioneers of Texas.* Austin: L. E. Daniell.

Corner, William. 1890. *San Antonio de Bexar: A Guide and History.* San Antonio: Bainbrifge & Corner.

Documentos para la historia eclesiática y civil de la Provincia de Texas o Nueva Philipinas, 1720-1779. Madrid: Ediciones José Porrúa Turanzas, 1966.

Espinosa, Fr. Isidro Félix. 1746. *Chrónica apostólica y seráphica de todos los colegios de propaganda fide de esta Nueva España.* Mexico: Por la viuda de J. B. de Hogal, 1746-92.

Foote, henry Stuart. 1841. *Texas and the Texans; or, Advance of the Anglo-Americans to the Southwest Including a History of Leading Events in Mexico, From the Conquest of Fernando Cortés to the Termination of the Texas Revolution. 2 vols.* Philadelphia: Thomas, Cowperthwait & Co.

Garrison, George P. 1906. *Texas: A Contest of Civilizations.* Boston: Houghton Mifflin Co.

Portillo, Estaban L. 1886. *Apuntes para la historia antiqua de Coahuila y Texas.* Satillo: Biblioteca de la Universidad Autónoma de Coahuila.

Potter, Reuben M. 1878. *The Fall of the Alamo.* reprint, Hillsdale, N.J.: Otterden Press, 1977.

Yoakum, H. 1855. *History of Texas from Its First Settlement in 1685 to Its Annexation to the United States in 1846. 2 vols.* New York: Redfield; facsimile, Austin: Steck-Vaughn Co., 1939.

HISTORY AND LEGENDS
of
THE ALAMO
and
OTHER MISSIONS
in and around
SAN ANTONIO

Church of the Alamo as it is today.

By

Adina De Zavala

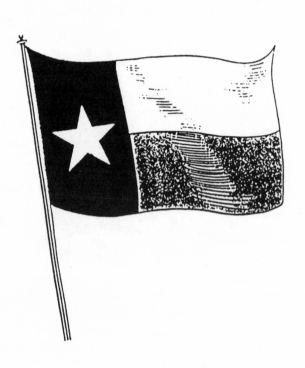

TO THE "DE ZAVALA DAUGHTERS,"

Noble, Loyal, Unselfish, Patriotic Women in Whose
Veins Course the Blood of the Heroes,
Statesmen, Patriots, Pioneers,
and Founders of Texas,

and to

DE ZAVALA CHAPTER,

This Little Book
Is Affectionately Dedicated
By The Writer.

Give Me the Land Where the Ruins are Spread.

"²...Give me the land where the ruins are spread,
And the living tread light on the hearts of the dead;
Yes, give me a land that is blest by the dust
And bright with the deeds of the down-trodden just.
Yes, give me the land where the battle's red blast
Has flashed to the future the fame of the past;
Yes, give me the land that hath legends and lays
That tell of the memories of long vanished days:
Yes, give me a land that hath story and song,
Enshrine the strife of the right with the wrong;
Yes, give me a land with a grave in each spot
And names in the graves that shall not be forgot."

Abraham J. Ryan.

FOREWORD

I wish to express my thanks to Mr. Rolla Taylor, an artist of San Antonio, Texas, for copying faded pictures; to Mesdames Adele B. Looscan and Jessie B. Howe, of Houston, Texas, for kindly assistance; to Mr. Fernando M. Urbina, of Mexico City, for copies from various Mexican archives; and to Mrs. Laura V. Grinnan of Austin, Texas, for help in the Spanish translations.

The history of the Alamo is placed first, as it is of the most general interest. Mission San Francisco is given next, because it is the oldest of all and a review of its history will give a better understanding of the rest. Mission San José is placed last, as it was in reality founded later than the Missions of Concepción and San Juan, although the latter were not brought to the vicinity of San Antonio until ten years later.

A larger and fuller history of the Important Events of Texas and of the Missions of Texas will soon be ready for publication.

(Adina De Zavala.)

San Antonio, Texas,
   141 Taylor Street.
      December 8, 1917.

TEXAS

Empire Majestic, with thy head so proud,
Pillowed on mountain heights of snow and cloud;
And kingly feet laved by the tepid tide
Of Aztec waters, sun-kissed, free and wide!
Realm of eternal spring and blessedness,
Of flower's breath, and mock-bird songs that cease
Not, all the golden months of the year!
Land of cerulean sky, low-dipped, and clear!
Oh, prairies boundless, breeze-tossed, cattle-nipped!
Oh, hidden streams, translucent and deer-sipped!
Oh, sweet hills verdant-footed, purple-hazed!
Oh, fields of cotton-snow and golden maize,
Oh, valleys of low-lying, blue-green wheat,
Up where the mesa and the cold waves meet!
What wonder that men's blood leapt forth, to flow
Chivalric, for thee, at the Alamo?
Land of my birth, and soul's intensest love!
Dear is thy soil, thy calm, blue sky, above;
Dear are thy aims to all my eager heart,
And dear thy people, of myself a part.

(Belle Hunt Shortridge in Lone Star Lights.)

"Dear is thy flag, its red and white and blue,
And dear thy "Lone Star," ever pointing true.
Dear are thy Landmarks—every stone and tree
That tell of love and hearts' blood poured for thee
That Race, and Heir, might ever still aspire —
Their hearts, and souls and minds reach upward! Higher!
Oh, may this sacred heritage of martyrs brave,
Demand response, and shame each knave!
Until thy empire, known the wide world o'er,
A Haven prove till time shall be no more."

(Adina De Zavala.)

THE ALAMO
(Mission San Antonio de Valero)

What the people of the present day speak of as "The Alamo" is known in the ancient records and to the early settlers of Texas as Mission San Antonio de Valero.

The locality of "The Alamo" (Mission San Antonio de Valero) was suggested as a mission site by Father Damian Manzanet, in 1690, but the mission itself was founded later by the perseverance of Father Antonio de San Buenaventura y Olivares who went alone to the Indians who lived in the vicinity of the present City of San Antonio.

Father Olivares wrote to the Viceroy of New Spain, in 1716, telling him of his hopes and plans for Mission San Antonio de Padua, and urged him to send out families, as settlers, for a pueblo; families who should serve as object lessons to the Indians of the life they were expected to lead. In this same letter he stressed the fact that it was necessary that some of these families should be skilled in the useful arts and industries in order to teach the Indians all that should be required to make them useful and capable citizens.

Father Olivares maintained himself alone at San Antonio for some time after he organized his mission, and gathered together the Payaya Indians who spoke the same language as the Xaramas, near the Rio Grande, where he had established the Mission of San Francisco Solano. He won the love and respect of all the Indians in the locality. He was particularly successful with the tribe who formed a village on the east side of the San Antonio River. Unfortunately, his labors were for a time suspended by a serious accident. While crossing a rude bridge made of logs and covered by earth, the foot of the animal he was riding went through a hole, and the priest, thrown suddenly and violently, had his leg broken. A messenger was sent, at once, to the nearest mission on the Rio Grande, for a Father to come to him, and Padre Pedro Muñoz

immediately responded, driving before him on pack animals everything he thought might be needed for the relief of the injured man. He made the journey, without rest, in an incredibly short space of time, administered to his afflicted Brother the consolations of religion and then set his leg.

It was a long time before Father Olivares was able to walk. When he was able to go about again, he changed Mission San Antonio de Valero to the other side of the San Antonio River where what is left of it is seen today, and known as "The Alamo." He lost no time in erecting the mission buildings and perfecting a system of waterworks by which the mission and pueblo were abundantly supplied with water by ditches running from the river. These ditches also served to irrigate the mission lands on which were grown the needed food supplies.

A certified statement still exists to the effect that on May 1, 1718, Don Martín de Alarcón gave to Fray Antonio de San Buenaventura y Olivares possession "of the mission site at the Indian village on the banks of the San Antonio River."

When Alarcón went to establish the Presidio of San Antonio de Bexar, in 1718, he took with him about thirty families, who seem to have been families of members of his company, and settled them in the vicinity of the mission. Father Olivares had some time before this, in obedience to orders, transferred Mission San Francisco Solano to San Antonio de Padua. Mission San Francisco Solano was originally founded by him in the Valley of the Circumcision on January 1, 1700, and was moved several times before its final transfer to San Antonio.

The first baptismal record extant of Mission San Antonio de Valero was entered July 8, 1718. Other interesting records are signed by the Venerable Anthony Margil, founder of most of the Texas missions who visited San Antonio several times and remained at San Antonio de Valero for quite a while after the trouble with the French on the eastern frontier, in 1719.

The Alamo (Mission San Antonio de Valero) was built for a large industrial school to teach, civilize and christianize the Indians of the locality. It was a sort of walled city or fortress, and was composed of several buildings with their courts or patios, and a long rectangular plaza with rows of houses or rooms built along the sides of the walled area, and covering about three acres of ground. All the buildings and the ten-foot wall which surrounded the entire Alamo fortress were of stone. The high wall was needed as a protection against the savage Indians. In this industrial school the Indians were taught to weave coarse cloths, embroidered cotton shawls, blankets, and other needed materials. They were also taught every trade or occupation that was thought useful to them at the period, such as husbandry, stock-raising carpentry, black-smithing, architecture or house construction. They were taught, too, to read and speak Spanish, to write, sing, sew, embroider, draw, carve and paint, each according to his talents. Even their political education was not neglected, they being taught civic government. A governor and alcalde were annually elected by the Indians, and these Indian officials then held authority in the mission pueblo for one year. The full story of the foundation and conduct of this large industrial school under the name of Mission San Antonio de Valero is very interesting. It ceased to be a school and mission somewhere about 1783 or 1785. Contagious diseases, of some kind, wrought great havoc among the Indians at the Alamo in 1763, and greatly depleted their numbers. In fact, it might be said that the establishment declined from the date of the scourge, on account of the loss of so many of its christianized adults. There were no tractable Indians about the vicinity to refill the school and mission, and those brought in from a distance were taken to the mission below, and thus gradually, by reason of the older mission Indians and their children becoming civilized and incorporated with the rest of the population in habits and manners, although still continuing to inhabit the mission and pueblo, this last changed its character and became an ordinary village or pueblo.

The cornerstone of the church of Mission San Antonio de Valero—what is now known as the "Church of the Alamo" or the "Alamo Church"—was laid May 8, 1744, many years after the foundation of the mission and long after the erection of the other buildings of the establishment. The pretty church with its twin towers, arched roof, and graceful dome was entirely finished about 1757—when to the great distress of the inhabitants of the mission it began to crack, and finally "tumbled in" about 1762,—the old records say,—"on account of the stupidity of the builder."

They started to rebuild it, but, owing to a frightful scourge which carried off nearly all the adult Indians of the mission, and other causes, it was never done, and the ancient church came down to comparatively modern history filled with the debris of its two towers, arched roof and dome.*

About the year 1849, Major Babbitt, acting Quartermaster of the Eighth Military Department, took possession of the Alamo Buildings in the name of the United States Government to use them as a Quartermaster's Depot. He found the Church of the Alamo "choked with débris, a conglomeration of stones, mortar and dirt," just as it was left when the twin towers, the dome and the arched roof fell in (about 1762), and, with the disintegration and injury of nearly one hundred years added. He cleared away some of the rubbish, but it was not until 1878, that it was entirely cleared out. On November 15,

*See newspapers of the day and Wm. Corner in San Antonio de Bexar.

Old Font

1878, in removing the débris, nearing the original level of the Church, they uncovered among other objects a beautifully carved baptismal font, belonging to the earliest missionary period of the locality.

Occasionally, officers of the Franciscan order came to Texas on a tour of visitation and inspection and made a report on the mission. We hear of it also through the military channels when writers accompanying the military would be interested enough to describe the missions and country visited.

Father Juan Morfi, who visited Texas with Don Theodore de Croix, the first commandant-general of the "interior provinces," wrote of the "very decadent condition" of Mission San Antonio de Valero in 1778, owing to the "small number of Indians who live in it, scarcely enough to cultivate its small area. The living quarters," he continues, "are beneath an arcade which forms a square with the Church and the residence of the Fathers. The latter has a tower at the principal doorway, where two mortar guns are kept as defense against enemies in case of attack, which is by no means a rare occurrence. In the center of the courtyard there is a well of fine water, although the river is only twenty steps away.* It was constructed with the same caution which was responsible for the tower. The residence is uncomfortable and badly kept, showing its age and careless construction."

*The walls of the Alamo were on the west side of the buildings now fronting east on the west side of Alamo Plaza, opposite the main building of the Fort. The river came in very close, to what is now Losoya Street, and consequently, was but a short distance away.

In the archives of the mission still existing, we find no burials recorded after 1782, no baptisms after 1783. The last marriage was entered in 1785; however, the leaves following this record are missing and there may have been others. It is plain from a note below signed by Father Valdez that there were later baptismal records, at least, although it is possible that they were not of the mission proper, but of the pueblo.

On the 25th day of February 1793, some of the people from the mission and Presidio of Adaes on the eastern frontier, across the Sabine, were settled about Mission San Antonio de Valero, and land, "as much as four pecks of seed corn will cover," was given to each who applied, with fee simple title. They are styled in the records, Adaesenos. They were placed "in possession one by one of their suertes which were allotted to them quietly and peacefully,...using and observing all the ceremonies, formalities and requisites which are necessary and which are required by common use and having also ordered them to pull weeds and throw stones, which they executed to the four winds, in fact of having found themselves royally in possession, etc., and by the same it is given to them that they may take it and profit thereby, they, their heirs and successors..."

———————

Mission San Antonio de Valero was officially secularized in August, 1793, that is, the mission and pueblo were transferred from the government of the missionary Fathers to the ordinary ecclesiastics and officers.

On the last page of the Book of Baptisms is found the following:

"On the 22nd day of August, 1793, I transferred this book of records of the pueblo of San Antonio de Valero to the Archives of the town of San Fernando and presidio of San Antonio de Bexar, by order of the Right Rev. Doctor Don Andrés de Llanos y Valdez, the most worthy Bishop of this

Old Manuscript Showing the Allotment of the Lands.

diocese, dated January 2nd, of the same year by reason of the said pueblo having been aggregated to the curacy of Bexar; and, that it may be known, I sign it.

Fray José Francisco López, Parish Priest."

It seems that this same Father was acting parish priest of San Fernando for some time while in charge of the Mission and Pueblo of Mission San Antonio de Valero.

All the missions in the jurisdiction of Don Pedro de Nava, Commandant-General of the Internal Provinces, were secularized by decree dated April 10, 1794. The Franciscans remained in many instances as pastors of their flocks; but they received their jurisdiction from the Bishops as all other parish-priests, and not from the superior of their order.

Father López transferred the Valero records to his successor as follows:

San Antonio De Bexar, June 14, 1794.

On the day of this date I received from the Rev. Father José Francisco López, who was Minister of the Mission of San Antonio de Valero, until it was delivered into the hands of the ordinary, this book, in which are set down the records of baptisms pertaining to said mission, and performed up to the year 1783—noting that the records which may be searched for from the year 1788 may be found in a new book found in parchment; from leaf 2 to leaf 100, together with these that belong to the following year, and which may be entered hereafter. I make this note that it may serve as an index, and I sign it with the same Rev. Father—date as above.

Bachiller Gavino Valdez.

I delivered this book, on the day of date, to the Parish-Priest, Don Gavino Valdez; and that it may be known I sign.

Fray José Francisco López.

Father Valdez transferred to his successor in charge of San Fernando as follows:

San Antonio de Bexar, July 11, 1804.

"On this day I received from the Señor Cura, the Bachiller Don Gavino Valdez, my predecessor, this book, pertaining to the new pueblo of San Antonio de Valero; and in testimony, we sign it.

"José Clemente Delgado,
"Bachiller Valdez."

A Franciscan Father, while any remained in the province, usually acted as chaplain to the troops stationed about Mission San Antonio de Valero, as well as parish priest of the pueblo of San Antonio de Valero, and often as acting parish priest at San Fernando, hence we find their names signed in such various capacities in the records.

The pueblo of San Antonio de Valero had a separate alcalde up to the year 1809; perhaps later; but under Governor Martínez, it was under the same rule as San Antonio de Bexar.*

On the 2nd day of February, 1814, "baptism is noted as being administered in the Church of Bexar by the chaplain of the company"; (of the Alamo de Parras) but it does not appear that they ceased to use the Chapel of the mission for the administration of the sacraments or religious services "until about the 22nd day of August, 1825, when the curate of San Antonio received the records of baptism, marriages, etc., of the company of the Alamo de Parras from the hands of the chaplain."*

In 1822, the beloved Franciscan, Father José Antonio Díaz de Leon, who was assassinated in 1834, near San Augustine, Texas, baptized at San Antonio de Valero.

Both the civil and ecclesiastical jurisdiction of the pueblo of the Alamo seem to have fluctuated considerably.

"The sacred taper's lights are gone,
Gray moss has clad the altar stone,
The holy image is o'erthrown,
The bell has ceased to toll.

The long ribbed aisles are burst and shrunk,
The holy shrine is ruin sunk,
Departed is the pious monk,
God's blessing on his soul!"

The famous company known as "la compañía volante del Alamo de Parras" came in 1805 and remained at San Antonio de Valero so long that they are referred to in the archives of

*Yoakum, Appendix, page 461.

Bexar as "the ancient company." The troops were first stationed without the walls of the mission, but the depredations of the savages were so frightful and continuous that they were soon compelled to take refuge within the walls. From the long residence of this company in the mission, the mission-fortress finally lost its original and official name and became known, colloquially, to the people about, as "The Alamo." As late as 1831, this same company was in Texas, at Tenoxtitlán, on the Brazos.

During the countless revolutions and uprisings of republicans, royalists, adventurers and Indians, life and property were no longer safe in San Antonio and nearby places. All who could get away did so.

In 1813, when Governor Salcedo surrendered to the Republican Army of the North, the Americans marched into the Alamo Fort and took possession of it, together with all the army stores, the arms, the military chest, etc., liberating seventeen of their countrymen found there and adding them to the ranks. Thus all along the line we find the Alamo in use as a stronghold, first by one party and then the other, during the numerous revolutions which shook this part of New Spain.

After the separation from Spain the troubles incident in the formation of a new government kept the country in a state of unrest for a time.

Then came the settlers from the North American States, and when Santa Anna declared himself dictator, they refused to obey his decrees.

They rose in small bodies all over the province of Texas, captured small forts here and there, and under Stephen F. Austin marched to San Antonio.

A detachment of Texans under Colonels Fannin and Bowie defeated a large body of Mexicans at Mission Concepción, October 28, 1835.[1] After besieging San Antonio for some time, 301 Texans under Colonel Benjamin Milam captured San Antonio

[1]For a full description of this battle see, Alwyn Barr, *Texas in Revolt: The Battle for San Antonio*, 1835 (Austin: University of Texas Press 1900).

under General Cos. Milam was killed and Colonel Francis Johnson, who led the second division succeeded to the command and raised the flag over Bexar. The Headquarters is still in existence, being the old administrative palace on Military Plaza bearing the coat-of-arms over the doorway.

Colonel Johnson was sent to lead an army to the west, and was succeeded in San Antonio by Colonel J. C. Neill. Colonel Neill fully realized the danger of the Texans on the unguarded frontier and sent urgent demands for reinforcements.

The Commander-in-Chief, Sam Houston, sent Colonel Bowie with a small company. Governor Smith sent Colonel William Barrett Travis with the few men the latter could gather. David Crockett and a few others arrived, but all told there were not more than 150 men. In the meantime Colonel Neill had gone home on a leave of absence leaving Travis in command. It was later arranged that both Travis and Bowie should sign all orders until Neill's return. Both Travis and Bowie begged for more men, as did Fannin from Goliad.

Some of the leaders seemed to think that it would be impossible for the Mexicans to reach the settlements before the middle of March, or later. General Houston asked for a furlough and left his command, without notifying or requesting the next officer in rank to take charge. There seemed to be no head at the time of the crisis. The Governor was deposed by the Council of Texas and the Lieutenant-Governor recognized as head by that body. Some continued to address Governor Smith as Governor, others appealed to the Council. The people seemed paralyzed for the time being and failed to realize the urgent need of an immediate rally of men to the front to support Fannin at Goliad and Travis at the Alamo.

When the Texans occupied the Alamo in 1835-1836, the fort was in the same state for defense in which it had been left by General Cos when he surrendered to the Texans in December, 1835. On January 6, Colonel Neill wrote that they had in all about twenty-four pieces of artillery, but that they had "two distinct fortresses to garrison." He later abandoned the fortifications in Bexar (San Antonio) and moved all the guns to the Alamo. Green B. Jameson was placed in charge of the repairs and improvements needed at the Alamo, and was soon at work erecting batteries, planting cannon and planning for better fortification.

The Church in the Alamo was a ruin, and was still filled with débris from its two towers, dome and arched roof, which fell in about 1762. The rooms on the north side of the Church and the west tower rooms retained the arched roof, and were therefore free of débris, and the only part of the Church edifice that was free of débris. The main building of the Alamo fort was the long two-story stone building on the east side of the Plaza and described in the old manuscript as a two-story stone building about "fifty yards square, with arcaded galleries above and below." It had many doors opening out upon the Plaza or main area; and for the defense of the building, these doors, then, had within a semi-circular parapet, for the use of marksmen, composed of a double curtain of hides, upheld by stakes and filled in with rammed earth. Most of the rooms were also loop-holed. This long building was the most securely fortified of any within the fort, and in the upper story, on the south end, was the hospital of the fort.

The Fortified Building

The Main Building of the Alamo where the heroes died, as it looked originally.

(Made from description in old manuscript, plans, pictures, drawings, and descriptions of old settlers and pioneers.)

The Church in The Alamo

Towers, Dome and Arched Roof fell in previous to or about 1762. Never restored or fully rebuilt.

Into this building the men of the Alamo retreated for their last stand. Upstairs, in the hospital in the south end, Bowie was killed. This building divested of its arcaded galleries, roof, and upper story, is still standing on the east side of the upper end of Alamo Plaza in San Antonio, Texas.

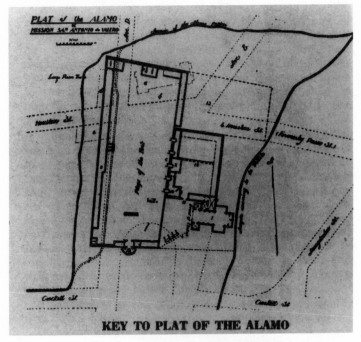

KEY TO PLAT OF THE ALAMO

KEY TO PLAT OF THE ALAMO
(Originally named Mission San Antonio de Valero, and founded as
Industrial School and Mission-Fortress.)

OLD REFERENCES—1836

1   The Church in the Alamo. Cornerstone laid
    May 8, 1744. Towers, dome, and arched roof fell in previ-
    ous to or in 1762, and debris remained untouched until
    about 1850, when much was removed by Major Babbitt,
    U.S.A., in the years he had possession.

2. The fortified main building of the Fort referred to by Pot-
    ter as "the long barrack, a two-story stone building." It
    had, originally, arcaded galleries above and below.*

3. Doors in (2) having within a semi-circular parapet com-
    posed of a double curtain of hides upheld by stakes and
    filled in with rammed earth. Loopholed.

*Documentos para la Historia de la Provincia de Texas, (MS.) Mexican
Archives, Bolton and Barker, With the Makers of Texas.

4. Old Galera or "Prison," also referred to by Potter as the "low barrack."
5. Porte-cochére or entrance to Fort.
6. Stone walls and rooms surrounding Fort.
7. Acequia (ditch) running through Plaza.
8. Rooms used as powder magazines during siege.
9. Cedar post stockade, ditch and earthworks in use during siege.
10. Hospital upstairs in main Alamo building where Bowie was killed and above which, in tower room, a small gun did fine execution. At this corner the flag of the Alamo floated.
11. Entrance to the courtyard and rooms surrounding it. Originally the principal entrance to main building.
12. Courtyard or Patio of the main building where some of the heroes were burned. Originally, this courtyard was surrounded on the four sides by rooms or arcades.
13. A second courtyard existing at an earlier period.
14. Old well that was dug or reopened during siege.
15. Ditch was dug connecting the acequias on the south of the Fort, thus completely surrounding the Alamo by canals. Note cannon and batteries.

NEW REFERENCES—1917.

a. Federal building, Federal courthouse and Post Office.
b. Government lot.
c. Front of the Main building of the old Alamo Fort. The Alamo proper, where the heroes died, which together with the Church (1) is all that is left of the original Alamo.
d. Gibbs Building.
e. Swearingen-McCraw Building.
f. Circular curb of Plaza Garden.

Potter and other historians give fourteen as the number of guns used. Mrs. Dickinson said there were eighteen, and Green B. Jameson and Santa Anna placed the number at twenty-one.

But, as Potter states, "The number has little bearing on the merits of the final defense with which cannon had little to do. These guns were in the hands of men unskilled in their use, and owing to the construction of the works, most of them had little width of range."

*Potter placed the guns as follows: (1) One, a twelve-pounder, was mounted on a high platform of earth formed by the fallen dome and roof of the Church, and pointed west through an embrasure roughly notched in the wall. Another, (2) was aimed north through a similar notch. (3) was fired over the wall to the south, but all on the same platform. The powder magazines, and the women and children, were in the covered rooms of the Church, the rooms on the north and west left intact when the roof fell in. To protect the women and children and magazines and prevent entrance in that quarter, was the mission of these three guns. Marksmen were also stationed around the roofless Church on the heaped-up débris (and on wooden scaffolds where necessary) that they might fire over the roofless walls, using them as parapets. Between the Church and the gate of the Alamo was a battery of four guns (4, 5, 6, 7), all four-pounders, pointing south. The porte-cochére, (the gate of the Alamo) through the low barrack, was covered on the outside by a lunette of stockades and earth, and was mounted with two guns (8, 9). In the southwest angle of the large area was an eighteen-pounder (10), in the center of the west wall was a twelve-pound carronade (11), and in the northwest corner of the same area an eight-pounder (12), and east of this within the north wall, two more guns of the same caliber (13, 14). All the guns of this area were mounted

*Andrade changed the fortifications of the Alamo after its fall. This accounts for some of the difference in the arrangement of the cannon or batteries in the Potter plan.

on high platforms of stockades and earth and fired over the walls.

Of the four additional guns mentioned by Mrs. Dickinson and others, one, a small gun, was placed in the small tower room over the hospital,* in the south end of the main building of the fort, and did fine work in mowing down the enemy as they swarmed into the large area; three cannons were placed in the west wall of the fort near its north corner; Jameson placed two others on a platform near the southern end of the Plaza of the fort. The platforms on which the cannons were, were composed of stakes on end with rocks and dirt between.

The several barriers were covered on the outside by a ditch, except where such a guard was afforded by the irrigating canal, which flowed on the east and west sides of the fort and through it, and served to fill the fosse with water.*

What follows is a copy of a letter sent to General Sam Houston by Engineer Green B. Jameson, with a plan of the Alamo and showing batteries then erected, and those he proposed to erect.

*In Brown's History, Vol. I, page 576, is the following: "When the attack came on, he (Bowie) was confined to his bed in the upper room of the barrack marked (P.). He was there killed on his couch, but not without resistance: for he is said to have shot down with his pistols one or more of the enemy as they entered the chamber." Again, on page 581, is found, "Col. Fulton says: `About the first of August, 1837, I visited the Alamo, in company with Judge Baker, the Chief Justice of Bexar County, who directed my attention to the room I have marked (B.) as the one occupied by Bowie, being on his sick bed, when bayoneted by Santa Anna's minions.' " The room, marked (P.) in the first reference above, and (B.) in the last, is the hospital room in the upper story of the main building of the Alamo and is marked (10) and (J) in plates accompanying this.

*See Potter, Jameson Plat, Plat by Mexican Engineer, Col. Ignacio de Labistida. March, 1836, also Drawing by José Juan Sánchez Estrada, 1829. The originals of Jameson's plats have not been located, with this being one of the few sources available. Copies of Col. Labastida's maps can be found at the Center for American History, The University of Texas at Austin.

Bexar, January 18th, 1836.

Major General Sam Houston,

Sir:

Believing that a letter will meet you at Goliad, and having had more time to make a better plot of the "Fortress Alamo" at this place have embraced this conveyance, to reaquaint you more satisfactorily of the condition and progress of the department, which you have so kindly assigned me.

I send you herewith inclosed a neat plot of the fortress exhibiting its true condition at this time, as also an Index being duplicates of my former addressed to you at Washington, added to which is a recapitulation more explanatory, and showing the improvements already made by me.

I am now fortifying and mounting the cannon. The 18-pounder now on the N.W. *corner of the fortress so as to command the town and the country around.

The officers of every department do more work than the men and also stand guard, and act as patrol every night. I have no doubt but the enemy have spies in town every twenty-four hours, and we are using our utmost endeavors to catch them every night, nor have I any doubt but there are 1500 of the enemy at the town of Rio Grande, and as many more at Laredo, and I believe they know our situation as well as we do ourselves.

We have received 100 bushels of meal and 42 Beeves which will last us for two months yet to come, but no other supplies have come to our relief.

You have heard so much about our situation from our Commander that I shall say nothing further on the subject.

We can rely on aid from the citizens of this town in case of a siege, Saguine* is doing all for the cause he can, as well as many of the most wealthy and influential citizens.[3]

*In his plat it is plainly marked on the southwest corner.

[3] I am certain that De Zavala is referring to Juan Seguín, a captain in the Texas forces.

You can plainly see by the plot that the Alamo never was built by a military people for a fortress, tho' it is strong, there is not a redoubt that will command the whole line of the fort, all is in the plain wall and intended to take advantage with a few pieces of artillery, it is a strong place and better that it should remain as it is after completing the half moon batteries than to rebuild it. The men here will not labour and I cannot ask it of them until they are better clad and fed. We now have 114 men counting officers, the sick and wounded which leaves us about 80 efficient men. 40 in the Alamo and 40 in Town, leaving all of the patrol duty to be done by the officers and which for want of horses has to be performed on foot.

We have had loose discipline until lately. Since we heard of 1000 to 1500 men of the enemy being on their march to this place duty is being done well and punctually in case of an attack we will move all into the Alamo and whip 10 to 1 with our artillery.

If the men here can get a reasonable supply of clothing, provisions and money they will remain the balance of the 4 months, and do duty and fight better than fresh men, they have all been tried and have confidence in themselves.

I can give you full assurance that so far as I am concerned there shall be nothing wanting on my part, neither as an officer or a soldier to promote and sustain the great cause at which we are all aiming, and am at all times respectfully subject to your orders for the verification of which I refer you to my Commander at this place, as will all the officers and men. I have been much flattered for my exertions at this place. I have more than one time received the vote of thanks of the whole Garrison.

I have one other subject which interests me some; to ask of you, if it is not too late, that is to recommend to your notice Capt. G. Navan, who is clerk in my department for the appointment of Suttler at this Post as he is in every way qualified to fill the office. I know of no man who merits it more than he does, as an evidence of his patriotism he has absented himself from his family when he was also receiving a salary of $1800 per annum to aid us in our difficulties.

I am with esteem,

    Very Respectfully,

        Your obt. Servt.,

            G. B. JAMESON.

I will in my next give you a plan of the Town as fortified when we took it. We have too few to garrison both places, and will bring all our forces to the Alamo tomorrow as well as the cannons. In excavating our ditches we can with perfect safety rely on a fall from the two ditches or acqueducts of at least 20 feet, consequently we can make our ditches deep enough with perfect safety, and the earth here is of such a nature that it will not wash, and we can ditch very near the half moon batteries with perfect safety. I will say all that it is necessary in my answer to your official letter on this subject. In regard to the ditch we can have a flood gate at the mouth of it, which will answer for keeping in a supply of water in case of a siege, as also by raising, for cleansing the Fortress. I am too much occupied to copy these papers but I shall be able to show you by demonstration when I have nothing else to attend to that I will not be wanting in my abilities as a topographical Engineer.

        Respectfully, Your Obt. Servt.

            G. B. JAMESON.

This same plat and letters were used by H. Yoakum in the preparation of his *Texas History*, and is referred to in his description of the Alamo as "the plat and letters which lie before me." He sent the sketch on February 12, 1855, to Mr. Francis Giraud asking him to place upon it the measurements—length and thickness of the walls, and to return the sketch to him. He endorsed it: "The enclosed sketch of the Alamo with proposed alterations was drawn by Capt. G. B. Jameson a few days before he was killed at the taking of the Alamo." The plat and key and letters were also copied by Mrs. Mary Jane Briscoe, from papers belonging to Peter W. Gray, in July 1886.

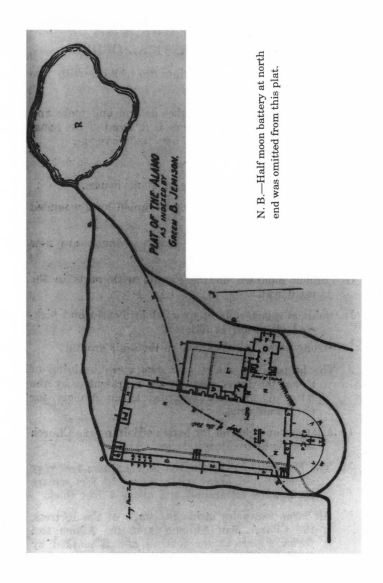

PLAT OF THE ALAMO
AS INDEXED BY
GREEN B. JEMISON.

N. B.—Half moon battery at north end was omitted from this plat.

INDEX TO THE PLAN OF THE ALAMO DESIGNATED
IN ALPHABETICAL ORDER

A. Represents the entrance into the Alamo with two cannon.

B. Temporary redoubts of stakes on end and rocks and dirt between, the long one is in front of the house in which Col. Mendoza now lies wounded.

C. The Guard House.

D. Soldiers quarters built up of stone houses.

E. Headquarters of Alamo now occupied by 2 wounded officers.

F. Batteries and platforms where cannon are now mounted.

G. Cannon mounted on the ground with ports in the main wall.

H. Soldiers quarters built up of doby houses and picketed all round with letter B.

I. Strong stone walls without pickets all around.

J. The hospital upstairs in a two-story building of stone, the lower story being represented by the letter K. and now occupied as an Armory for our small arms.

L. A large stone quartel for horses adjoining the Church San Antonio, Hospitals and Armory.

M. The Magazine in the Church San Antonio, two very efficient and appropriate rooms 10 feet square each, walls all around and above 4 feet thick.

N. All large vacancies inside the walls of the fortress, the Church San Antonio is in the Alamo and forms a part of the fortress and is marked by the letter O.

P. The cannon mounted in the Alamo. Their number corresponding with that of the letters.

Q. The acqueduct as around the fortress by which we are supplied with water, marked with red ink.

R. A lake of water where we contemplate supplying the fortress by ditching from one of the acqueducts laid down.

S. A pass from the present fortress to a contemplated draw-bridge across a contemplated ditch inside a contemplated half moon battery as laid down on the plan.

T. A part of said ditch, as well as a trap door across said ditch, which is contemplated to be raised by a tackle from inside the half moon battery.

U. The hinges on which said bridge is to be raised.

V. The half moon battery at each end of the fortress as contemplated.*

W. A 12-foot ditch around the half moon battery as contemplated.

X. The contemplated ditch where we wish the permanent water to pass thro' the fortress and thence to pass out erecting an arch over each place and also a redoubt for a permanent cannon in case of siege.

Y. A ditch passing under the stone wall to the lake marked R.

*The editor omitted the half moon battery on the north end of the Plaza of the Fort from the plat shown herewith, as it was thought that it was never completed. It corresponded exactly in construction to the one on the south end as shown in the accompanying plat.

You will perceive in this index that I have always marked the parts of notoriety with more letters and characters than one of the same kind.

The letter D represents a large stone building that will answer for a public storehouse. The letter V represents a want of provision, munitions and men.

I would recommend that the doby houses, letter H, be torn down and stone houses erected in their stead. The stone can be obtained out of the old Church San Antonio, which is now a wreck or ruin of a once splendid Church. All we want now is provisions and munitions to stand a siege against an innumerable force tho' we are weak beyond imagination, not being more than 100 strong since Johnson and Grant left, and there could be raised in town 300 men that could besiege us at any time.

———

When on that eventful day in February, 1836, the sentinel posted in the lookout on top of the Church of San Fernando reported that he had seen armed men to the west, it was doubted, and scouts were sent out to reconnoiter. It was found to be true that the Mexican Army was upon them. Upon the hasty retreat of the scout, the Church bells were rung to give the general alarm. Travis ordered all into the Alamo fortress and everything was done that was possible, at the time, in preparation for defense. A large division of Santa Anna's army arrived soon after.

Travis sent out messengers for assistance before the body of the enemy arrived and again before the place was invested.

"Commandancy of Bexar,
"Feb. 23, 3 o'clock, p.m. 1836.

"To Andrew Ponton, Judge, and the Citizens of
Gonzales:

"The enemy in large force is in sight. We want men and provisions. Send them to us. We have 150 men and are determined to defend the Alamo to the last. Give us assistance.

"W. B. Travis, Lieut.-Col. Commanding.

"P.S. Send an express to San Felipe with the news night and day.

"Travis."

He called upon Fannin, at Goliad, feeling confident of his assistance, but with the enemy in the country, and Fannin without food and transportation, the latter was not able to make the march, though he attempted it, desiring to answer the call of a noble and beloved comrade.

The following letter announcing the opening of the siege has been called "the most heroic document among American historical records."*

Commandancy of the Alamo,

Bejar, Feb'y. 24th, 1836.

To the People of Texas and all the Americans in the
world:

Fellow citizens and compatriots—I am besieged, by a thousand or more of the Mexicans under Santa Anna. I have sustained a continual Bombardment and cannonade for 24 hours and have not lost a man. The enemy has demanded a surrender at discretion, otherwise, the garrison are to be put to the sword, if the fort is taken. I have answered the demand with a cannon shot, and our flag still waves proudly from the walls. *I shall never surrender or retreat. Then,* I call on you in the name of Liberty, of patriotism and everything dear to the Mexican character, to come to our aid with all dispatch. The

*George P. Garrison. In "Texas."

enemy is receiving reinforcements daily and will no doubt increase to three or four thousand in four or five days. If this call is neglected, I am determined to sustain myself as long as possible and die like a soldier who never forgets what is due to his own honor and that of his country. VICTORY OR DEATH.

WILLIAM BARRETT TRAVIS,

Lt. Col. Comdt.

P.S. The Lord is on our side. When the enemy appeared in sight we had not three bushels of corn. We have since found in deserted houses 80 or 90 bushels and got into the walls 20 or 30 head of Beeves.

TRAVIS.

Thirty-two heroes from Gonzales and DeWitt's colony, under the command of Captain Albert Martin, answered the call on March 1st, and gave to Texas a sublime example of self-sacrifice.

The noble Bonham, a friend of Travis', determined to stand by his friend and the men of the Alamo, returned March the 3rd, signaled the fort, and dashed in through the Mexican lines on his snow-white steed. "Greater love hath no man than this, that he giveth his life for a friend." James Butler Bonham failed in finding helpers, but he was determined that Travis should not fail for the use of his strong arm and courageous heart, and that he would win or die with him.

And so, through the whole roll call of the Alamo heroes: each did his duty and stood at his post, hungry—because there was no time for eating-and cold, and wearied out with long watching and firing.

At last, Santa Anna determined on the final assault, and called a council of war, and the dawn of the 6th was the time chosen. The night of the 5th was the first respite the weary garrison had had from the continual din of cannon and arms and they sought the needed rest as the Mexican troops ceased firing.

We can imagine the feeling which prompted them as each tried to do that which he thought should be done first.* And then to rest—but this rest was not for long.

At 3 o'clock, at a given signal, three columns of the Mexican Army moved simultaneously on the Alamo, provided with axes, scaling ladders and fascines.

The assault was begun! Again the cannons boomed! Every Texan was at his post, as the enemy showed themselves above the wall, they were mowed down by the shots of the unerring Texans. Three times they wavered and retreated but were driven forward by their own cavalry. At last, one column gained an entrance through a breach on the north,* another then scaled the high wall on the west,* and the third repulsed on the south at the Church, also scaled the western wall. It was impossible for the few men of the Alamo to defend the outer walls long; and most of them soon retreated into the long two-story stone building which was well fortified, "and it was not till then, when they became more concentrated and covered within, that the main struggle began. They were more concentrated as to space, not as to unity of command; for there was no communicating between buildings nor in all cases between rooms. There was little need of command, however, to men who had no choice left but to fall where they stood before the weight of numbers. There was no retreating from point to point, and each group of defenders had to fight and die in the den where it was brought to bay." From the doors, windows, and loopholes of the several rooms of the main building, the crack of the rifle and the hiss of the bullet came fierce and fast; as fast the enemy fell and recoiled in his

*Most of the men gave letters, watches, jewelry, and other keepsakes to Mrs. Dickinson and the other women to be sent to their loved ones. The Mexicans took everything.

*A little east of the center of the north wall of the Federal building would approximate the position of the breach made in the north wall of the Alamo area on that fateful day.

*The high wall on the west stood back beyond the front of the buildings on the west side of the Plaza.

first efforts to charge. The gun beside which Travis fell was now turned against this building, as were also some others, and shot after shot was sent crashing through the galleries and doors and barricades of the several rooms. Each ball was followed by a storm of musketry and a charge; and thus room after room was carried at the point of the bayonet, when all within them died fighting to the last. "The struggle was made up of a number of separate and desperate combats, often hand to hand, between squads of the garrison and bodies of the enemy. *The bloodiest spot about the Fort was the long barrack and the ground in front of it, where the enemy fell in heaps.*"*

A Mexican soldier gave his testimony as follows: "The Texans fought like tigers. The proportion was one to thirty, yet no quarter was asked and each sold his life as dearly as possible. The last moments of the conflict were terrible. The darkness of the rooms, the smoke of the battle and the shrieks of the wounded and dying all added to the terror of the scene. Unable to distinguish friend from foe, the Mexicans actually brained each other in their mad fury. After the battle was over and all were dead, the scene beggared description. The floor of the main building was nearly shoe deep in blood, and weltering there were hundreds of dead men, many still clenched together with one hand while the other hand held the sword, pistol or knife which told how they had died in that last terrible struggle. And thus the curtain went down in darkness and blood on the saddest and sublimest event in the world's history."

Mrs. Dickinson, wife of Lieutenant Dickinson, who was killed in the defense of the Alamo, Mrs. Alsbury, wife of Dr. Alsbury, with their children, and several other women and children, were during the time of the battle in the north rooms of the Church. Mrs. Dickinson and babe were sent on horseback to the Texans at Gonzales, and were soon joined by

*Captain Reuben M. Potter, U.S.A., who was in Matamoros at the time of the seige and fall of the Alamo, and afterwards in San Antonio, Texas.

JAMES BOWIE

WM BARRETT TRAVIS

JAMES BUTLER BONHAM

DAVID CROCKETT

Travis' negro servant who had escaped the guard. The other women were cared for by their relatives in San Antonio and vicinity.

Mrs. Dickinson told how Evans (Master of Ordnance, who had been instructed to fire the magazines when all was over) was followed and killed by the Mexicans as he jumped down from the débris and attempted to enter the room where she was, in the north room of the Church, with torch in hand to carry out his instructions. She also spoke of a gunner named Walker, who was killed in her presence as he was running for the magazine.

None of the women and children were injured during the siege as they were not in the part of the fort where the battle raged. The women and children saw none of the main battle, as there were only the gunners and a few sharpshooters stationed on the roofless walls of the ruined Church to protect the magazines and prevent entrance in that direction, for the main conflict raged in the main building of the fort, the two-story stone building northwest and adjoining the Church and it was impossible for the women to either see or hear anything except the crack of the rifle, the shrieks of the men and the booming of the cannon. The women were only able to tell of the few who were killed in the Church part of the Alamo. "Thermopylae had her messenger to defeat, but the Alamo had none."

The bodies of the dead heroes were ordered by Santa Anna to be piled in heaps and burned, and this order was in part executed in the courtyard or patio of the main Alamo building, north of the Church. Tradition says that the first funeral pyre was lighted in the courtyard but that orders were given later to burn the rest of the bodies elsewhere, and that three pyres were made beyond the walls. The three pyres were to the south, southeast and east by south. When Captain Juan N. Seguín returned to San Antonio after the battle of San Jacinto, he gathered up the charred remains of the bodies of the Alamo heroes and buried them in the Church of San Fernando.*

*So stated over the signature of Seguín.

A. Old Bell "San Antonio," presented to De Zavala Chapter, by Mr. Moses B. Oppenheimer, now of San Antonio, Texas. B. Upper gallery of Alamo Fort as rebuilt by H. Grenet. C. Door leading from gallery of Fort into choir loft of the Church of the Alamo. D. Old Baptismal Font. E. Window of Hospital of Fort in southwest end, showing great thickness of walls. F. Front of Bell "San Antonio," showing date, 1722.

FROM THE DIARY OF DR. J. H. BERNARD, SURGEON OF FANNIN'S COMMAND

"Tuesday, May 17, 1836. Dr. Alsbury in town today from General Felisola, now commander-in-chief, with a pass. He is son-in-law of Angelo Navarro, with whom I live. His wife and sister, together with a negro of Bowie's, were in the Alamo when it was stormed. He has come in order to look after his family and take them off. He gave us all the particulars of the battle of San Jacinto, the capture of Santa Anna, the retreat of the Mexican Army, and the number of volunteers pouring into Texas stimulated thereto by the fate of Fannin and Travis.

Sunday, 22d. General Andrade has received orders to destroy the Alamo and proceed to join the main army at Goliad. The troops have hitherto been extensively engaged in fortifying the Alamo. They are now as busy as bees tearing down.........

Tuesday, May 24, 6 o'clock P.M. As the troops left town this morning (12 A.M.), a large fire streamed up from the Alamo, and, as soon as they had fairly left, Dr. Shackelford and myself, accompanied by Señor Ruiz and some other of the citizens, walked over to see the state in which they left it. We found the fire proceeding from *a church*, where a platform had been built......This was made of wood, and was too far consumed for any attempt to be made to extinguish it. The walls of the church, being built of solid masonry, of course would be but little injured by the fire. The Alamo was completely dismantled, all the *single* walls were levelled, *the fosse filled up,* and the *pickets torn up and burnt.* All the artillery and ammunition that could not be carried off were thrown in the river.

Wednesday, May 25.......After sauntering about the Alamo and calling to mind the startling and interesting scenes that have at different times been acted on this little theater, and the last unparalled in modern history, which forever marks this spot as the Thermopylae of Texas; after looking at the spot where it is said that Travis fell and Crockett closed his immortal career, we went to visit the ashes of those brave defenders of our country, *a hundred rods from the fort or church to where they were burnt*. The bodies had been *reduced to cinders*; occasionally *a bone of a leg or arm* was seen almost entire. Peace to your ashes! Your fame is immortal! The memory of your deeds will remain bright and unsullied in the hearts of your countrymen!"

When Seguín was raised to the rank of colonel and given a considerable force, he was instructed by the general in command to hold memorial services and pay the honors of war to the ashes of the Alamo heroes. This he did February 25, 1837. The account in the Telegraph and Texas Register of March 28, 1837, follows:

"In conformity with an order from the general commanding the army at headquarters, Colonel Seguín, with his command stationed at Bexar, paid the honors of war to the remains of the heroes of the Alamo; the ashes were found in three places, the two smallest heaps were carefully collected, placed in a coffin neatly covered with black, and having the names of Travis, Bowie and Crockett engraved on the inside of the lid, and carried to Bexar, and placed in the parish church, where the Texas flag, a rifle and sword were laid upon it for the purpose of being accompanied by the procession, which formed at three o'clock on the 25th of February: the honors to be paid were announced in the orders of the evening previous and by the tolling knell from daybreak to the hour of interment; at 4 o'clock the procession moved from the church in the following order:

"Field officers, staff officers, civil authorities, clergy, military not attached to the corps and others, pall bearers, coffin, pall bearers, mourners and relatives, music, battalion, citizens.

"The procession then passed through the principal street of the city, crossed the river, passed through the principal avenue on the other side, and halted at the place where the first ashes had been gathered. The coffin was then placed upon the spot and three volleys of musketry were discharged by one of the companies; the procession then moved to the second spot, whence a part of the ashes in the coffin had been taken, where the same honors were paid; the procession then proceeded to the spot and place of interment where the graves had been prepared; the coffin had been placed upon the principal heap of ashes, when Colonel Seguín delivered a short address in Spanish, followed by Major Western in English, and the ashes were buried."

No one knows the exact spot where the ashes of the heroes were buried, though many have pointed out where they think it is; but the old building in which they gave up their lives still stands, and the ancient courtyard in which some were burned and where the blood of heroes is mingled with the soil, still exists sacred to Texans and all patriotic people.

The greatest heritage of the children of Texas and America is the noble example of its great men heroes. Let us not forget their deathless deeds. For the moment we begin to ignore the sublime virtues exemplified by the noble souls of our race, our degeneration has begun.

Let us save our landmarks and sacred battlefields and buildings as reminders and monuments. No monument that could be erected by the hands of man to the memory of the heroes could be as great or as sacred as the Alamo itself, wherein we are brought face to face with the history and scenes from the lives of the men who made the Alamo immortal.

Only two of the buildings of the Alamo still stand, the Alamo proper, where the heroes died and piled the enemy before them in heaps, where the floor was shoe deep in the blood of friend and foe; and the old Church, then a ruin, whose north rooms sheltered the women and children and magazines, and which was defended by a few gunners and sharpshooters.

If you love and appreciate the noble and sublime, do all you can to save these two old buildings and the old courtyard,—all that are left to remind us of the sublime sacrifice of the men of the Alamo.

————

LIST OF HEROES KILLED IN THE ALAMO

In the Texas Almanac for the year 1860 was found a list of the Texan Heroes who defended the Alamo when it was besieged by the Mexican Army commanded by General Santa Anna, and who all perished when that famous fortress was captured, March 6, 1836. This list differs from many that are published, but is believed to be accurate, having been compiled from official and other authentic sources.

W. Barrett Travis, Lt.-Col., Comdr.
James Bowie, Lt.-Col., Comdr.
J. Washington, Colonel, Tenn.
J. B. Bonham, Captain, South Carolina.
— Forsyth, Captain, New York.
— Harrison, Captain, Tenn.
W. Blazeby, Captain, Louisiana.
W. C. M. Baker, Captain, Miss.
W. R. Carey, Captain, Texas.
S. B. Evans, Captain, Miss.
S. C. Blair, Captain, Texas.
— Gilmore, Captain, Tenn.
John Jones, Lieutenant.
Almaron Dickinson, Lieutenant, Louisiana.
I. G. Baugh, Adjutant.
Chas. Despalier, Aide to Travis.
Robert Evans, Master of Ordn'ce, Ireland.
Elial Melton, Lt. Quartermast'r.
— Anderson, Asst. Quartermast'r.
— Burnell, Asst. Qr. Master.
— Williamson, Sergt. Major.
D. Michison, Surgeon.
Amos Pollard, Surgeon.
— Thompson, Surgeon.
Green B. Jameson, Ensign.
David Crockett, Private, Tennessee.
E. Nelson, Private, South Carolina.
— Nelson, Private, Texas.
W. H. Smith, Private, Texas.
Lewis Johnson, Private, Texas.
E. T. Mitchell, Private, Georgia.

F. Desangue, Private, Pennsylvania.
— Thruston, Private, Kentucky.
— Moore, Private.
Christopher, Parker, Private, Mississippi.
C. Huskell, Private.
— Rose, Private, Texas.
John Blair, Private.
—Kiddeson, Private.
Wm. Wells, Private, Tennessee.
Wm. Cumming, Private, Pennsylvania.
— Valentine, Private.
— Cochran, Private.
R. W. Ballantine, Private.
S. Halloway, Private.
Isaac White, Private.
— Day, Private.
Robert Muselman, Private, New Orleans.
Robert Crossman, Private.
Richard Starr, Private, England.
L. G. Garrett, Private, New Orleans.
Robert B. Moore, Private.
Richard Dimkin, Private, England.
Wm. Linn, Private, Mass.
— Hutchinson, Private.
Wm. Johnson, Private, Penn.
E. Nelson, Private.
Geo. Tumlinson, Private.
Wm. Deardoff, Private.
Daniel Bourne, Private, England.
— Ingram, Private, England.
W. T. Lewis, Private, Wales.
Charles Zanco, Private, Denmark.
Jas. L. Ewing, Private.
Robert Cunningham, Private.
S. Burns, Private, Ireland.
George Neggin, Private, South Carolina.
— Robinson, Private, Scotland.
— Harris, Private, Kentucky.
John Flanders, Private.
Isaac Ryan, Private, Opelonsas, La.
David Wilson, Private, Texas.
John M. Hays, Private, Tenn.
— Stuart, Private.
W. K. Simpson, Private.
W. D. Sutherland, Private, Texas.
D. W. Howell, Private, New Orleans.
— Butler, Private, New Orleans.
Chas. Smith, Private.
— McGregor, Private, Scotland.
— Rusk, Private.

— Hawkins, Private, Ireland.
Samuel Holloway, Private.
— Brown, Private.
T. Jackson, Private, Ireland.
— John, Clerk to Deangue.
George C. Kimbell, Lieutenant, Gonzales.
James George, Sergeant, Gonzales.
Dolphin Ward, Private, Gonzales.
Thos. Jackson, Private, Gonzales.
Geo. W. Cottle, Private, Gonzales.
Andrew Kent, Private, Gonzales.
Thos. R. Miller, Private, Gonzales.
Isaac Baker, Private, Gonzales.
Wm. King, Private, Gonzales.
Jesse McKoy, Private, Gonzales.
Claiborne Wright, Private, Gonzales.
W. Fishback, Private, Gonzales.
Isaac Milsaps, Private, Gonzales.
Albert Martin, Private, Gonzales.
Galba Fuqua, Private, Gonzales.
John Davis, Private, Gonzales.
R. A. M. Thomas, Private, Gonzales.
Wm. Fuhbaigh, Private, Gonzales.
John G. King, Private, Gonzales.
Jacob Durst, Private, Gonzales.
M. L. Sewell, Private, Gonzales.
Robert White, Private, Gonzales.
A. Devault, Private, Gonzales.
John Harris, Private, Gonzales.
David Kent, Private, Gonzales.
W. E. Summers, Private, Gonzales.
M. Autry, Private.

———

For many years the Alamo was abandoned as a great tomb, a place of horror to many who recalled the story of the frightful sacrifice of the heroes of 1836.

As the civil jurisdiction of Texas passed from Mexico, the ecclesiastical jurisdiction passed also, and the Rt. Rev. J. M. Odin thought best to have the Spanish title confirmed, and on January 13th and 18th, 1841, the Congress of the Republic of Texas passed an act granting "the Church of the Alamo," and the other mission Churches with their out-lots, to the Catholic

Church, thus settling the title for the benefit of the newcomers to the country, for "the title to the Church was complete without the aid of the act of 1841," as it was theirs, "either by direct grant or by ancient possession."*

About 1847, after the annexation of Texas, the Quartermaster of the United States Army took possession of the Alamo claiming the property as belonging to the United States. It was used for an arsenal several years, for offices, and as a Quartermaster's depot. In April, 1847, the United States acknowledged to hold as tenant of the Bishop of Texas, Rt. Rev. John M. Odin; and Mr. Bryan Callaghan, of San Antonio, acted as agent for the Bishop, part of the time, in receiving the rents. The tenancy of the United States continued until the breaking out of the Civil War, in 1861, and was resumed after the war—the military authorities of the Confederate States during the war occupying the property, in the same manner, as tenants of the Church.

In 1851, the City of San Antonio set up a claim to the Alamo, but lost its suit.

In 1865, the Bishop, wishing to turn the Alamo Church over to the use of the German Catholics of San Antonio, directed his secretary and vice-chancellor to notify the United States to vacate the building. A polite note was addressed to Major General Merritt asking "possession of said Church in order to furnish a suitable and convenient place of worship to the German Catholic Congregation of San Antonio." The note was signed by Thomas J. Johnston and J. T. Fourey, Secretary and Vice-Chancellor to the Bishop. Major General Merritt replied that "the government required this building for the use of the Qr. Mr. Dept. for the present," that it was then "used for receiving grains, and its vacation by the Government would be attended with great inconvenience and serious loss."

*Messrs. Upson and Welder, of San Antonio, Texas, in opinion rendered February 2, 1886

The German Catholics were accommodated elsewhere, nearby, and this incident caused the loss of the Church of the Alamo as a parish Church, and eventually its sale, as it was thought, that, as a Church, it was not needed so close to the new German parish Church.

In 1879, Bishop A. D. Pellicer conveyed to H. Grenet, for the sum of Twenty Thousand Dollars, all the interest of the Catholic Church in the Alamo, exclusive of the Alamo Church.

In 1883, the Rt. Rev. John C. Neraz sold the Church of the Alamo to the State of Texas for Twenty Thousand Dollars. The City of San Antonio applied for the custody and was given charge.

The people of San Antonio had looked upon the old Alamo building as public property for years, as Mr. Honoré Grenet, the owner, had publicly announced his intention of devoting it to the memory of the heroes of Texas, by gift to the people. Part of the old building was long used as a Museum. The sudden death of Mr. Grenet, before title to the property was executed to the public, deprived the people of this benefaction. Mr. Grenet built wooden galleries around the two-story building (which had been comparatively little damaged in 1836) to represent the former arcaded galleries of stone, and erected towers, bristling with wooden cannon, and a battlemented top of wood over the old stone fortress building, and painted the words "The Alamo Building" on the west and south sides. He thus, as he said, restored the outer appearance of the main building of the Alamo (as closely as he could do at the time, and with the material used) in an endeavor to keep fresh in the minds of the people of San Antonio and Texas the memory of the heroic deeds enacted therein.

THE ALAMO AS REPAIRED BY GRENET

In 1886, after the death of Honore Grenet, the Alamo property, which included the main building of the fort proper, was sold at public outcry by his administrator, George M. Kalteyer, to Hugo and Schmeltzer, a firm composed of Charles Hugo, Gustav Schmeltzer, and Wm. Heuermann, for Twenty-Eight Thousand Dollars.

TESTIMONY OF MR. GUSTAV SCHMELTZER

In order to assist in keeping a complete and correct record of the several transactions relative to the purchase of that part of the old Alamo (the main building of the Alamo) occupied by the firm of Hugo, Schmeltzer & Co., I wish to state that Miss Adina De Zavala called to see me about the year 1892, with reference to securing the Alamo property owned by us; explaining the objects of the society of which she was President, and asked me to obtain for her the promise of all the owners, not to sell or offer the property to any one else without notifying her, and giving the Chapter the opportunity to acquire it, to save it to the people of Texas, to be utilized as a Hall of Fame and Museum of History, Art, Literature and Relics.

This object meeting with my full approval, I spoke to the other parties in interest, and on her second visit, informed her that we would do as she had asked, giving her the refusal of the property. Miss De Zavala called again at various times to inquire if we remembered our promise, and we answered that we did, and were in no hurry to sell. In 1900, she called again and stated that the Chapter was about to start an active campaign for the purchase money, and asked us to set the price. On consultation with Mr. Hugo and the other owners, we agreed to contribute $10,000.00 and make the purchase price (to her Chapter) $75,000.00.

Miss De Zavala immediately went to Galveston and Houston in behalf of the cause, and shortly thereafter the frightful disaster of the Galveston storm occurred; Miss De Zavala just missing by a few days being caught in Galveston. On account of the necessity of aiding the storm sufferers, the De Zavala Chapter again postponed its call for money for the purchase of the Alamo, and it was not until 1903, that the Chapter felt justified in bringing the matter before the public again. Miss De Zavala then brought and introduced to me the Chairman selected by herself, and ratified by the vote of the Chapter to take charge of the collections for the purchase, and to prosecute the work outlined by the Chapter. A written option was paid for and signed, and on February 10, 1904, the payment of the $25,000 was completed and the several notes arranging for the balance of the amount due were duly made out and signed.[4]

(Signed.) G. SCHMELTZER.

San Antonio, Texas, September 24, 1908.

Affidavits as to signature of Mr. G. Schmeltzer were sworn to by Mr. Aug. Briam, Jr., who worked for the different companies of the Hugo, Schmeltzer people for 25 years, and who was secretary of the corporation at the time of the agreement and sale of the Alamo property. By Mr. Charles Heuermann, son of one of the members of the firm, who was also employed in the business.

By Mr. A. Sartor, a life-long friend of Mr. G. Schmeltzer.

By Mr. W. A. Wurzbach, who was also employed by the firm and was acquainted with Mr. G. Schmeltzer for 30 years.

By Mr. J. N. Brown, President of the Alamo National Bank, of San Antonio, Texas.

All subscribed and sworn to this 10th day of February, 1914.

I, Wade H. Bliss, a Notary Public in and for Bexar County, Texas, do hereby certify that the foregoing is a true and correct copy of a statement dated September 24, 1908, signed "G. Schmeltzer," and of the affidavits attached thereto.

---

[4]These initial financial transactions were undertaken with the assistance of Clara Driscoll.

Witness my hand and seal of office this 10th day of February, 1914.

(SEAL.)   WADE H. BLISS,
                              Notary Public, Bexar County, Texas.

De Zavala Chapter, descendants of the heroes and founders of Texas, pioneers in the work of conserving the history, relics, manuscripts, books, and historic places of Texas, conceived the idea of saving the main building of the Alamo Fortress and reconsecrating it to the memory of the heroes of the Alamo to be used as a Texas Hall of Fame and a Museum of History, Art, Relics and Literature, to be forever free for the use of Texans and all within the borders of Texas.

An option was obtained on the property by Miss Adina De Zavala, President of the society as shown in the document by Mr. Gustav Schmeltzer, cited above. Later, payments were made, and notes signed, and work seriously undertaken to raise the purchase money.

The raising of the money seemed sure, as all the people of Texas approached appeared enthusiastic and willing to contribute to save the building; but as a certain fixed sum was necessary on certain dates to meet the payments, De Zavala Chapter decided to ask the Legislature to appropriate the money for the balance due and offered on their part to give clear title to the property and the money already paid in (about $20,000.00) and to take charge of the buildings and maintain them in good order and repair without cost to the State, and to repair and restore to its former beauty the old "long barrack" or Fortress building proper where the heroes died, on the condition that the old main building of the Alamo—"the old barrack"—should be used as a Hall of Fame and a Museum of History, Relics, Art and Literature, and forever devoted to the memory of the heroes of Texas, and that the care and custody should remain with the

Association (De Zavala Chapter), and that it should be repaired only under its direction.

The President of De Zavala Chapter, Miss Adina De Zavala, wrote or dictated both memorial and bill presented to the Legislature asking that the property be given into the custody of the Association.

The Twenty-Ninth Legislature accepted the terms and granted the request of De Zavala Chapter, so unanimously endorsed by the people of Texas and her sister chapters, and the property was eventually turned over to that society.

At once, various parties, and a syndicate began their machinations to secure control of the Alamo in order to bring about the destruction of the Alamo proper, the main building of the Fort.* The idea was that if the Alamo Fort proper was out of the way, the park or Plaza would be extended back to property in which these people were interested, thus giving them an Alamo Plaza frontage. Long the battle waged—it was De Zavala Daughters versus Commercialism! New combinations and new syndicates were formed from time to time, as new interests entered the contests to destroy the Alamo proper, purchased by Texas and the De Zavala Daughters in 1906, but, the latter firmly stood their ground. The methods used by the interests are almost unbelievable! They finally created a division among the women of the general society and their friends. The breach has not been thoroughly healed to this day—but, the syndicates concerned are dead, and most of their promoters, and they did not accomplish their purpose! although, some of the same people effected the destruction of the upper story of the ancient Alamo Fort, about 1913, leaving the lower story with its arcades unroofed to the elements as we see it today.

*The two-story stone building, the main building of the fortress referred to by Potter as the "long barrack."

THE MEN OF THE ALAMO.

(By James Jeffrey Roche.)

To Texans at Gonzales town ride, Ranger, for your life,
Nor stop to say good-bye to home, or friend, or child,
      or wife,
But pass the word from ranch to ranch, to every Texan
      sword,
That fifty hundred Mexicans have crossed Nueces ford,
With Castrillon and perjured Cos, Sesma, and Almonte
And Santa Anna ravenous for vengeance and for prey.
They smite the land with fire and sword; the grass
      shall never grow
Where northward sweeps that locust horde on
      San Antonio.
Now who shall bar the foemen's path, to gain a breathing
      space?
'Til Houston and his scattered men shall meet them face to
      face?
Who holds his life as less than naught when home and
      honor call,
And counts the guerdon full and fair for liberty to fall?
Oh, who but Barrett Travis, the bravest of them all!
With seven score of riflemen to play the ranchers' game
And feed a counter fire to hold the sweeping prairie
      flame.
For Bowie of the broken blade is there to cheer them on
With Evans of Concepción, who conquered Castrillon,
And o'er the heads the Texas flag defiant floats on high
And no man thinks of yielding and no man fears to die.

But ere the siege is held a week a cry is heard without,
A clash of arms, a rifle peal, the Rangers' ringing shout.
And two and thirty beardless boys have bravely hewn
      their way
To die with Travis, if they must, to conquer if they may.
Was ever bravery so cheap in glory's mart before
In all the days of chivalry, in all the deeds of war?
But once again the foemen gaze in wonderment and fear

To see a stranger break their lines and hear the Texans
　　　cheer.
Oh, how they cheered to welcome him and those spent
　　　starving men
For Davy Crockett by their side was worth an army then!
The wounded ones forgot their wounds; the dying drew
　　　a breath
To hail the king of border men, then turned to laugh at death.
For all knew Davy Crockett, the generous and bold,
And strong and rugged as the quartz that hides the heart
　　　of gold.
His simple creed for word or deed true as the bullet sped
And hit the target straight: "Be sure you're right,
　　　then go ahead."
And were they right who fought that fight for Texas
　　　by his side?
They questioned not, they faltered not, they only fought
　　　and died.
Who hath an enemy like these, in mercy slay him straight,
A thousand Mexicans lay dead outside the convent gate
And half a thousand more must die before the fortress
　　　falls
And still the tide of war beats high around those
　　　'leaguered walls.
At last the bloody breach was won; the weakened lines
　　　gave way.
The wolves were swarming in the court; the lions stand
　　　at bay.
The leader meets him in the breach and wins the soldier's
　　　prize.
A foreman's bosom sheathes his sword when gallant
　　　Travis dies.
Now let the victor feast at will until his crest be red,
We may not know what rapture fills the vulture with
　　　the dead.
Let Santa Anna's valiant sword right bravely hew and
　　　hack
The senseless corse; its hands are cold; they will not
　　　strike him back.
Let Bowie die, but 'ware the hand that wields his deadly
　　　knife.

Four went to slay and one came back, so dear he sold
      his life.
And last of all did Crockett fall, too proud to sue for
      grace,
So grand in death the butcher dared not look upon his
      dauntless face.

But far on San Jacinto's field the Texan toils are set
And Alamo's dread memory the Texan steel shall whet.
And fame shall tell their deeds—who fell, till all the
      years are run.
Thermopylae left one alive—the Alamo left none.

Showing How Mission Courtyard or Patio looked.

Legends of the Alamo

GHOSTS OF THE ALAMO

There's the tramp of a ghost on the low winds tonight,
    And echo that drifts like a dream on its way;
There's the blur of the specter that leaves for the fight,
    Grave-risen at last from a long vanished day;
There's the shout and the call of grim soul unto soul
As they rise one by one, out of death's shadowed glen
    To follow the bugle—the drum's muffled roll,
    Where the Ghosts of the Alamo gather again.

I hear Crockett's voice as he leaps from the dust
    And waits at the call for an answering hail;
And Bowie caresses a blade red with rust
    As deep in the shadows he turns to the trail;
Still lost in the darkness that covers their sleep
    Their bodies may rest in a sand-mounded den,
But their spirits have come from the red, starry steep
    Where Ghosts of the Alamo gather again.

You think they've forgotten—because they have slept—
    The day Santa Anna charged in with his slaves;
Where five thousand men 'gainst a few hundred swept
And stormed the last rampart that stood for their graves?
You think they've forgotten; but faint, from afar,
    Brave Travis is calling the roll of his men
And a voice answers "Here!" Through the shadows that bar
    Where Ghosts of the Alamo gather again.

There's a flash on a blade—and you thought it a star?
There's a light on the plain—and you thought it the moon?
You thought the wind echoed that anthem of war?

Not knowing the lilt of an old border tune;
Gray shade after shade, stirred again unto breath;
Gray phantom by phantom they charge down the glen,
Where souls hold a hate that is greater than death,
Where Ghosts of the Alamo gather again.
—Grantland Rice, in New York Tribune.

THE GHOSTS OF THE ALAMO.

It is a well-known fact that the papers of San Antonio, years ago, from time to time, chronicled marvelous tales of ghosts appearing at the Alamo. That the Alamo was guarded by ghosts was one of the current folktales of the country. When General Andrade, the Mexican general, sought to destroy the Alamo after the battle of San Jacinto, in 1836, it is said that his men were everywhere met by spirits with flaming swords who barred their progress and soon frightened them off; that almost as fast as new relays of men were sent with orders to destroy the walls, they were overcome by fright; nor could threats or punishment induce them to return. They were permitted by the ghosts for a space to disarm the batteries, but the moment the walls of the buildings were threatened, there was the flaming sword in ghostly hands. It is a matter of history that the Alamo buildings were not destroyed, and not much injured by Andrade.* The Alamo was dismantled of its works, guns, etc., "the fosse filled up, and the pickets torn up and burned," but only the *single* outer walls of the mission-square were injured. The reason it was not destroyed, say the current tales of the day, was because of fear of the threats and prophecy of "the spirits with the flaming swords" whom the Mexican soldiers

*See the comprehensive History of Texas, Dr. Bernard, Kendall, Potter and other historians.

feared more than they feared their officers. These spirits ordered them to desist in hollow tones which struck terror to their hearts, "Depart, touch not these walls! He who desecrates these walls shall meet a horrible Fate! Multiplied afflictions shall seize upon him and a horrible and agonizing and avenging torture shall be his death!"

Was this prophecy fulfilled? Those who know the old folk tale say, "It was, and will ever be." And among other things you will hear if you doubt, is: "Search into the miserable lives and deaths of those responsible for the tearing down of part of the Alamo!" and, "Is it not, at least, a strange coincidence that the man who, more than any other one person, was deliberately responsible for the destruction of the upper story of the old Alamo Fortress met such a horrible, agonizing fate?— entombed alive and consumed by flames—that his worst enemy could not fail to be moved with pity."

<hr/>

LEGEND OF THE STATUE OF SAINT ANTHONY AT THE CHURCH OF THE ALAMO

Saint Anthony of Padua was patron of the Church and Mission of San Antonio de Valero. A statute of Saint Anthony occupied one of the niches in front of the Church which is now known as the CHURCH OF THE ALAMO.

At some time in the past it was decided to dismantle the old ruined Church of Saint Anthony of Padua, which had been a ruin since about 1762, when its two towers, dome and arched roof had tumbled in; for though several attempts had been made to repair and rebuild it, it had never been done. Accordingly, a man was sent with orders to bring away the statuary ornamenting the front niches. The statue of Santo Domingo in the lower left niche was removed and the man attempted to take down the statue of Saint Anthony. He could not move it. He reported his lack of success and another man was sent to help him, but their combined efforts failed. Thinking that the stone of which the statue was carved was unusually solid and heavy, more men were sent until five men—try as they might—still failed to dislodge the statue. At different times during the course of the succeeding years efforts were made to remove the statue by different parties who boasted of their ability, but they all failed.

And the old people chatted; and finally the story grew that "Saint Anthony held his statue there, because he wished his church to be repaired and placed again at the service of the people he loved, whose mission and town had been given his name, and whom he was still anxious to serve! This is perfectly plain," said they, "because there was no difficulty experienced in lifting out the other statues, only with his!"

However that may be, people of a later date saw the statue still filling its niche. It was there in 1837, and almost to modern times. When the German Catholic Congregation of San Antonio desired a Church building, the Bishop of the diocese, in 1865, requested Major-General Merritt to vacate the Church of the Alamo that he might present it to them for their use. The government, having no building which they could substitute for the storage of grains, replied that its vacation would be attended with great inconvenience and serious loss, and declined to do so, and the Catholics, not wishing to make trouble or delay their own work, chose a place elsewhere. When St. Joseph's Catholic Church was built, but a short distance from the Church of the Alamo, all idea of the use of the Alamo Church for religious purposes was abandoned, and the statue of St. Anthony gave no more trouble, and was easily removed.*

The Church of the Alamo was sold to the State of Texas in 1883.

*Every legend related to the writer was told with a smile, a shrug, and a shake of the head, and a "I do not know, that is what they say," as if the narrator was afraid the listener might believe it to be an actual experience within the knowledge of the speaker.

THE FOLK OF THE UNDERGROUND PASSAGES.

In the enchanted city to which the underground passages of the missions have connection are many inhabitants; and now and then, it seems, they may, and do appear in this workaday world of ours—if the folk-tellers are right. Some of the legends clustering around these interesting people follow:

THE PADRE'S GIFT

The old inhabitants of San Antonio de Bexar were very particular to train their children in habits of courtesy to all—to the stranger as well as to their fellow-citizens—but particular stress was laid upon courtesy to the aged. They told tales of "angels' visits unawares," and of "noblemen in disguise," and cautioned them, "Never judge a man by the coat he wears," and such other injunctions, till the children, properly trained by example and precept, were noted for their beautiful and gentle courtesy to strangers and to the aged. One tale which particularly held the attention of all children, aroused their imagination and peculiarly fascinated them, was the tale of the Padre's Gift.

"Now, children, some day you may meet the Padre; he is very old and wears his long mantle. If you meet him and are courteous, you will surely receive a gift. He never goes empty-armed, and all he meets are dowered."

When questioned about the truth of the tale, the old folk-tellers answered: "Yes, they say, the Padre really makes visits, but when he will come, no one knows, although it is said that there have been many children who have received the Gift! They say that Señora G.'s mother received a most wonderful gift—though they never say much about it, we believe it is true." Or, "I am told that little José C.'s father was presented with the deed to property that the family had long lost, when he was a boy." Or, "After the Indians stole all the cattle from the F. family, they say that the little boy, Francisco, one

Some of the Folk-Tellers.

day met the Padre and returned home with a bag of dou-
bloons."

It is needless to say that the children were always on the
lookout for the Padre, and the writer has known some who
have asserted that they had really met the Padre and
received a gift. The Padre is one of the good people who have
power, it seems, to pass from the enchanted city of Tejas by
way of the underground passages of the Alamo. In the light of
the past's strange coincidences, the narrator often wonders if
she, too, has not received the Padre's Gift, though at that time
she had never heard of the Padre.

"Riding out one morning I stopped at the "Little Drunk
Spring,"* and there, with staff in hand, covered by a long
brown cloak, stood a very old man with a wonderfully fine

*The "Little Drunk Spring" is about eleven miles northwest of San Anto-
nio.

face. "Buenos días," said I." "Buenos días," responded the old gentleman with a courteous salute. "Have you come far?" I asked. "No, señorita, just across the Leon." "Oh, from the Coy settlement!" I responded, for I knew the places round about. "Sí, señorita, and below. I have brought something to leave in your care," said he. "Leave in my care! What is it? How do you know me?" I asked. "We all know you," he responded. "The gift is to be left in your care for your use, for life, on one condition; that you name your successor and exact the same promise I shall exact of you; namely, that no other hand shall touch this package while you live." Reaching down into a large olla by his side, which I had not hitherto noticed, he pulled out a packet carefully tied up in oil skins. Unwrapping it he showed me a thick book which appeared to be made of parchment and filled with writing. I looked into it and saw that it was written in the Spanish language. "May I have someone translate it for me?" I asked. "I am sure it is wonderful, but it appears well nigh indecipherable with age, and besides, you see, I do not know the Spanish language well." "No, use what you can, and pass it on. Promise that no hand but yours shall touch this gift until it is bequeathed by you as I now bequeath it to you." I promised, delighted to receive such old and precious treasures, and the good old man, not only gave me the packet, which he carefully rewrapped and replaced in the olla, but, much to my surprise, lifted the olla with all its well-filled contents up to the saddle in front of me, saying, "It is all yours." Bidding me God speed, he cautioned me to be careful not to fall, and delightedly I started home. I have always regretted that I did not ask the old man's name—but I thought, then, only of the precious old treasures and my wonderful good fortune in receiving them. Truth is stranger than fiction." Has she received the Padre's gift? She does not know, but often wonders if she, too, had not really met the Padre.

———

THE MYSTERIOUS WOMAN IN BLUE AND HER
GIFT TO SAN ANTONIO BY THE HANDS OF
ONE WOMAN IN EVERY GENERATION

Out of the underground passages of the Alamo she comes once in a generation, or, when her gift has lapsed—this Mysterious Woman in Blue. Her Gift is not to the first person she happens to meet—but she searches until she finds a worthy recipient. And, strange to tell, tradition says, she always selects a native Texan, of the same type of woman, tall, eyes of gray—changeable with her moods, dark, fine hair—not black. In character the woman is superior, pure and good, well-bred, intelligent, spiritual and patriotic. She may be young or old or middle-aged. Stranger yet, the woman to whom the Gift is given does not always know that she possesses the Gift of the Woman in Blue, though she is always ready to use her talents for the good of others.

What is the Gift? The gift of seeing to the heart of things! She sees with the clear-eyed vision of a Joan of Arc all that may vitally affect, for good or ill, the people of her city and State whom she ardently loves with a strange devotion. All the children are her children—all the people are to her friends, and brothers and sisters! There is no cant, and no pretense—it is real.

She is here now—the Woman with the Gift for San Antonio, and oh, how we need her! She will help you and she will help me, if we find her! Who is she?

Tradition says she is always busy on the side of right, humanity, truth, justice and patriotism—that you cannot keep her hidden or covered, try as you might—not in the whole city full—because she has the Gift. She is a Mascot to those who help on her work, and the "Devil's Own Luck" to those who hinder. Find her if you are wise, search until you do. Who is she? She may be known by her works, perhaps, though the finest of that is in secret. If you are clear-eyed, she will be made manifest. Or another clue may be obtained from those who have tried to frustrate her work. They know who she is from the ill-luck which has followed them! If you need to see straight, and deep, find her. Do you need counsel and guidance. Trust to her. Tradition further says that she is always ready to help the rich, the poor, the artist, the artisan, the writer, the children—the whole people of her beloved Texas land. She has the Gift and therefore cannot choose but use it for San Antonio. Do you know her? If you do not profit by the Gift the fault is yours, not that of the Mysterious Woman in Blue, nor of the Woman who holds the precious Gift as Almoner for San Antonio.

THE COURTEOUS AND KINDLY CHILD AND THE "GOOD PEOPLE" OF THE UNDERGROUND PASSAGEWAY

The Alamo has always been credited with being the abode of ghosts—and some of them marvelous ghosts. Every one knows the story of the ghosts with the flaming swords who are forever stationed to protect the Alamo fortress. This old Fort also boasts of a number of ghosts who have a predeliction for stormy weather and who do not confine their sphere of action to any special apartment, but who manifest themselves in all parts of the Fort. At the time that part of the Fort was used as a prison for detention of city prisoners— many of the inmates—prisoners and officers alike, bore testimony to the strange and unaccountable noises—the rattling of chains, the distinct military tread of ghostly sentinels, the clank of sword and spur being heard, especially on rainy or stormy nights. Other singular and fascinating tales refer to the "good people" who are believed to inhabit the vast underground passageways leading from the old fortress and connecting with all the other missions of the San Antonio Valley and the Ancient Government Palace. One of the more modern of these tales follows:

A beautiful and cultivated gentlewoman lived on the east side of the San Antonio River in a strongly built rock house. Everything in the place betokened refinement and culture. One afternoon she sat alone sewing; looking up from her sewing, she sighed, as gazing toward the town she watched the slow and painful progress of her husband on his return from a trip for the mail. He had been injured in one of the early Indian fights and had been incapacitated ever since. He was up and down continually, but never seemingly making any headway toward health, and this had continued for seven years—soon after the first anniversary of his little girl's birth. There was almost no way for women to make money in those days, and speculation as to the future caused the brave little woman much anxiety. When he came in she said, "O Joseph, I was just praying that some time Ursula might meet the good woman of the underground passage! There might still be hope for you! Ursula is so kind and gentle and loving that she could not fail to win the good will of these good people. I am living in that hope. You know the good fortune that befell Mrs. Ramón's little Mary!" "Dear Ann, I know the good fortune that befell Mary and her mother, but you know I do not believe in any 'underground people' or 'the good woman of the underground passage!' I still think that some friend chose this method—of helping them. I am really surprised that you repeat the oldfolk tales current here about—but I think, dear, that in your case the wish is father to the desire to believe, for your heart is set on my visiting the celebrated Doctor ————
————." The couple then became engrossed in the bundle of mail which had arrived and some business matters were discussed at length. It was quite late before they thought of the time, and the continued absence of little Ursula, who had gone over to the old Alamo Fort to play with some of her little friends and pick wild flowers in the fields. The mother decided to go to

look for the children should have been at home long before. As she neared the Alamo Fort, and all was still, she became nervous, for in those days there was still the possibility of Indian raids. She passed around the Fort and called, but everything was quiet; there were no children to be found anywhere. Much alarmed, she visited the nearest house and the people said that the children had returned to the town long ago. Not wishing needlessly to distress her husband, she went around the place and on into San Antonio to the homes of some of the children, hoping, but not believing that her child had followed one of her friends to her home. But none of them had seen her since they had separated to pluck the wild flowers, or, play hide-and-seek. They thought it strange that she had gone home without telling them; however, they had reconciled it to themselves by saying that she may have gone too far, and become tired.

The mother, now almost frantic, called upon the men to take up the search while she went back home to try if possible to divert her husband who was powerless to render aid.

All thought of Indians, and the men started out to examine the vicinity of the Alamo, where the children had been at play, for signs of them, but no trace of Indians could be found. A number carried lanterns, and it occurred to some to examine the ruins, thinking that it may have been possible for her to have fallen among the rocks from the housetops in such a way as to render her unconscious. They had about abandoned all hope when some of them entered the arched room fronting the baluarte on the south side of the courtyard adjoining the Church. They were about to leave when they caught a gleam of something white in the shadow, and there was little Ursula fast asleep with her lap full of wild flowers. These she carefully gathered up, when the happy women in the party kissed her awake, and she was soon restored to the arms of her distracted parents.

When questioned, Ursula explained that the children were playing "hide-and-seek" and while she was hiding, a dear old lady who had entered the Alamo, caught her dress on a thorn bush and had fallen down. Ursula had helped her up and had given her some of her flowers. After she had rested, Ursula had carried her bundles and assisted her out of the Alamo. Just then, she saw the children dart about, and thinking they were looking for her, she dashed back to her hiding place. She did not know how she came to fall asleep. The old lady gave her something small wrapped up and motioned her to put it in her pocket. And there it was in her pocket. With suppressed excitement, the mother held out her hand for the package. It suddenly flashed upon her that her little girl had really met the "good woman" of the underground way. In the package were several very old Spanish gold coins, two diamonds and three pearls. Without doubt she had met the "good woman of the underground passage," and her first thought was that now, Joseph, her husband, could go to consult and secure the services of the eminent specialist so long looked forward to. She fell on her knees in thanksgiving, and then, pulling the child to her side, covered her with kisses.

LEGEND OF THE FIRST CHRISTMAS AT "THE ALAMO"

THE MARGIL VINE

At the first Christmas season celebrated at Mission San Antonio de Valero (The Alamo), in 1718, the good padres made the Crib of Bethlehem as realistic as possible, and the Indian children and neophytes were taking part in adorning the crib and bringing gifts to the Christ-Child.

Some brought beads and hung them where the lights would make them glisten; others, pretty colored stones or

Little Shavano.

pebbles; others, bits of bright Indian blankets—everything and anything that to the crude Indian mind seemed beautiful. And the padres did not chide them, for their intention was to honor the Christ-Child. One afternoon as the Venerable Anthony Margil was re-entering the Mission from a visit to a sick Indian not far away, he came upon a wee Indian boy sobbing. "What has made you sorrowful, little Shavano, at this happy time of the coming visit of the little Christ-Child?" "That is the very trouble," answered little Shavano, "all the rest have a gift for Him, and I can find nothing." "O, never mind that, little Shavano. The Christ sees into your heart and mind; you wish to love, obey and serve Him, do you not?" "Indeed I do!" replied the boy. "Give Him then your heart and service; tell Him this, and that will be the grandest gift." But little Shavano would not be satisfied; he sought the tangible gift, and the good padre, touched by his grief and sympathizing with his aspirations, said to him: "Bring a wide-mouthed olla, Shavano, and I shall help you find a gift." The wee Indian lad did as he was bid, and not far outside the Mission gate, on the acequia, was found a vine with triform green leaves and dark green berries. "We will take this to the little Christ-Child," said the Venerable Anthony Margil. "It is not very pretty," said little Shavano. "Never mind, it will be pretty to the Christ-Child; He will make it pretty," replied the padre. And so consoled, little Shavano helped to dig the vine and planted it in the olla. They carried it to the crib, and setting the olla on one side, twined and festooned the vine over the front of the crib. Little Shavano decided that it was better than nothing, and asked the Christ-Child to be satisfied with the best he could do, and promised to do all in his power during the coming year to serve Him faithfully. The next morning as he renewed his promises to the Christ-Child, he was gazing on the vine, wishing that his gift had been pretty like some of the others, when lo! the dark leaves began to glisten, and the green berries turned to a beautiful scarlet, and festooned as they were about the front of the crib, delighted the boy beyond measure. He ran for the padre, excitedly exclaiming, "The Christ-Child did make my gift beautiful! Come and see it!"

Indian Boys at School, under arcades of the Alamo Patio.

The Venerable Anthony Margil, who was in one sense only a visitor at this mission, took the happy little Indian boy by the hand, and together they joined the procession just then winding through the arcaded galleries surrounding the patio, leading to the chapel, and which followed acolytes with lighted candles. The joyous paean of the Adeste Fideles was borne upward as they moved forward, and these two, the venerable,

noted and learned man and the wee Indian boy, with grateful
hearts united their voices with the chorus of praise chanting:

"With hearts truly grateful,
Come all ye faithful,
To Jesus, to Jesus, in Bethlehem.
See Christ your Saviour,
Heaven's greatest favor,
Let's hasten to adore Him;
Let's hasten to adore Him;
Let's hasten to adore Him,
Our Lord and King.

The Splendor Immortal,
Son of God Eternal;
Concealed in mortal flesh our eyes shall view.
See there the Infant
The swaddling clothes enfold Him.
Let's hasten, etc.

Angels now praise Him,
Loud their voices raising,
The heavenly mansions with joy now ring.
Praise, honor, glory,
To Him who is most holy.
Let's hasten, etc.

To Jesus, born this day,
Grateful homage repay;
To Him who all heavenly gifts doth bring,
Word uncreated,
To our flesh united.
Let's hasten, etc.

This vine is still of spontaneous growth around San Antonio and is called by those of the old days the "Margil Vine."
From that early time its bright red berries come to do honor to
the season of the Christ-Child.

Mission San Francisco de los Tejas

(De los Neches) and (De la Espada)

Mission San Francisco de los Tejas was founded in east Texas, in May, 1690, by Father Damien Manzanet, many hundreds of miles from any other Spanish settlement, and about six miles west of the Neches River on El Camino Real. It was near a stream referred to in the old diaries as the San Pedro, which joins the Neches not far from the village of Nabedache Indians.

The story of the foundation is of interest to those who appreciate great and wonderful courage and noble motives.

The old settlements of Ysleta and others, did not attract much notice from the authorities as they were not in the direction of the coast where the government's attention was directed by the activities of Peñalosa, nor toward the famed but elusive kingdoms of Quivira and Tagago.

In 1630, Father Benavides had suggested in his Memoria that a direct line to Santa Fé should be opened through the Bay of Espíritu Santo—a landmark which since the expedition of Pineda, in 1519, had been prominent on all the maps of the Gulf coast. The king in a royal cédula, issued December 10, 1678, informed the Viceroy that it had been learned that Peñalosa, the disgruntled ex-governor of New Mexico, was attempting to secure for the French government a patent for the exploration of the provinces of Quivira and Tagago, and that in the efforts made by the Spanish Court to learn about these kingdoms, the report of Father Benavides and his suggestions, in 1630, were recalled. The king ordered the viceroy to investigate and give his opinion as to whether it would be well to open up communication with New Mexico by way of the Bay of Espíritu Santo according to Benavides' suggestion.

Though numerous raids on the Florida coast by French corsairs called attention to the necessity of occupying the country, as late as August 2, 1685, the required report had not yet been received by the king and he issued another cédula, quoting the former one verbatim, and repeating his request for a report on the advisability of converting the kingdoms of Quivira and Tagago and opening communication with them by way of the Bay of Espíritu Santo.

The victory now hastened to carry out the royal orders. Two land expeditions were sent out to find the Bay of Espíritu Santo and were unsuccessful, and a third (unless the one to bring in the Frenchman located by Father Manzanet is counted as the third) left Coahuila March 26, 1689, under Captain Alonso de León, accompanied by Father Manzanet. The latter had become interested in the Indians in the far interior through a letter in his possession treating of facts made known by the Venerable Mary Coronel de Agreda, as to certain tribes, and of her entreaties that missionaries be sent to find and bring them to God. It was the pleading of Mary Coronel de Agreda* that had moved Manzanet to search for the French and try to convince the authorities of their presence in Texas and so induce a third expedition that he might accompany it and the sooner reach the Tejas Indians.

On this expedition the Bay of Espíritu Santo was discovered, the Fort built by the French under La Salle was found, and the Chief of the Tejas Indians was interviewed by Manzanet and promised missionaries. The report made to the viceroy as to the beauty, fertility and desirability of the country was such that it was determined to occupy it and assist the Franciscans in their educational and religious work among the wild tribes.

The viceroy soon decided on a second expedition to the Bay of Espíritu Santo, and that Captain Alonso de León should go as commander, taking one hundred and ten soldiers, one hundred and fifty long guns, twelve hundred weight of powder, and three hundred weight of shot. He likewise pro-

*See Mary Coronel of Agreda, this book.

vided for the founding of a mission among the Tejas Indians and for the escort thither of Damián Manzanet and three other priests and a lay-brother. This expedition left Coahuila for the Tejas "on the third day of the Easter feast, March 28, 1690." They reconnoitered the coast country, saw no trace of French thereabouts, set fire to La Salle's Fort and, after remaining six days in the coast country, set out for the Tejas villages, sending ahead a messenger to the governor of the Tejas.

De León found in the neighboring Indian rancherías two French boys. The Spanish, pushing forward, came quite unexpectedly upon the governor of the Tejas and about fifteen of his people who had come out with the messenger sent to them. As soon as the governor saw Manzanet, he recognized him and, going up, embraced him. They sat down and talked by signs for some time, and the governor produced a small sack of powdered tobacco, of the kind they grew, and another small sack of white pinole* of good quality.

Three days later, Monday, May 22, 1690, they entered the Tejas village. It was raining heavily on their arrival. That year it had rained but little, and the corn was suffering from the drought, but every day of the eleven they spent in the village it rained hard.

On the next day the governor expressed a desire to take the priests home with him and told them that they might live in his house. On visiting the governor they formed a procession with the escort of soldiers through the villages. The four priests went on foot, carrying their staffs which bore a crucifix, "singing the Litany of Our Lady, and accompanied by a lay-brother who bore an improvised banner of the Blessed Virgin." On reaching the governor's house, he invited them to enter and look at it.

It was a round structure built of stakes thatched over with grass and about twenty varas high. It had no windows,

*Pinole is parched corn, ground or crushed. It is also used to prepare drinks.

daylight entering through the door only. In the middle of the house was the fire which was never extinguished by day or by night, and over the door on the inner side was a little super-structure of rafters very prettily arranged. Ranged around one-half of the house, inside, were ten beds; these beds consisted of a rug made of reeds, laid on four forked sticks. Over the rug the Indians spread buffalo skins on which they slept. At the head and foot of the bed was attached another carpet, forming a sort of arch, which, lined with a very brilliantly colored piece of reed matting, made what bore some resemblance to a very pretty alcove. In the other half of the house, where there were no beds, there were some shelves about two varas high, and on them were ranged large round baskets made of reeds in which they kept their corn, nuts, acorns, beans, etc. There was also a row of very large earthen pots like the Mexican water jars, these pots being used only to make the atole* when there was a large crowd on the occasion of some ceremony. With the pots were six wooden mortars for pounding the corn in rainy weather (in fair weather it was ground in the courtyard). After examining the governor's house, they were seated outside in the patio and served with a lunch consisting of tamales with nuts, pinole, very well-prepared, corn cooked with frijoles, and ground nuts. Father Manzanet* says: "Soon I noticed outside the patio, opposite the door of the governor's house, another long building in which no inmates could be seen. I asked who dwelt therein, or what purpose it served, and was told that the captains were lodged in that house when the governor called them to a meeting. On the other side I saw yet another and smaller vacant house, and upon my inquiring about this one they answered that in the smaller house the pages of the captains were lodged, for there is a law

*A kind of gruel, made by cooking pounded maize or rice in water.
*The quotations from Manzanet are taken from a "letter of Fray Damián Manzanet to Don Carlos de Sigüenza," 1690, published by the Texas State Historical Association, in Quarterly, Vol. II, 254-312. The original manuscript is the property of the Agricultural and Mechanical College of Texas.

providing that each captain shall bring his page when the governor assembles the captains, and they observe this custom. As soon as they arrive they are lodged in that house, and for each one is laid a large brightly colored reed mat, on which they sleep, with a bolster made of painted reeds at the head; and when they return home, each page carries with him his mat and pillow. While they attend the meeting, the governor provides them with food, until he sends them home.

"The following are the domestic arrangements in the governor's house: each week ten Indian women undertake the housework; each day at sunrise these women come laden with firewood, sweep out the courtyard and the house, carry water from a brook at some distance—(for this water is very good, and though the river is close by, its water is not as good as that of the brook)—and grind corn for the atole, tamales and pinole. Each one of the women goes home for the night, returning to the governor's house next morning.

"As to whether the priests should live in the governor's house........using the Frenchman as an interpreter, I told the governor, with many kind expressions, that his house was very fine, and that I heartily appreciated his desire to have the priests in his household, but that since we had to build a house for the celebration of mass, it might be well to build likewise a dwelling for the priests, because they must live near the church. Thereupon the governor said that we could build the house I asked for in the most suitable place, that he would show us the village and that I might choose the spot....... Accordingly, next day we went with the governor, who took us to the place the French had selected for their settlement, pleasantly and favorably situated on the river bank. We did not locate the convent there because it was so far out of the way of the Indians....

"The next morning I went out with Capt. Alonso de León a little way, and found a delightful spot close to the brook, fine woods, with plum trees like those in Spain. And soon afterwards, on the same day, they began to fell trees and cart the wood, and within three days we had a roomy dwelling and a church wherein to say mass. Very reverently we set in front of the church a very high cross of carved wood.

"On the feast of Corpus Christi, mass was sung, and before mass we had a procession with the blessed sacrament exposed, a large concourse of Indians being assembled, for we had notified them the day before. The soldiers had been given leave to fire as many salutes as they could during the procession, at the elevation, and at the close of mass, and it was the will of the Divine Majesty that in that solitude we should celebrate a memorable feast, which was rendered a source of great consolation by our being able to carry the blessed sacrament exposed and to walk in procession as Christian Catholics are wont to do. After mass we hoisted in the name of His Majesty the royal standard bearing on one side the picture of Christ crucified, and on the other that of the Virgin of Guadalupe. A royal salute was fired, and we sang the Te Deum Laudamus in thanksgiving.

"These Tejas Indians have always had among them an old Indian who was their minister and who presented their offerings to God. They observed the custom never to taste anything eatable without first taking a portion of it to their minister for sacrifice; they did this with the produce of their lands—corn, beans, watermelons, and squashes—as well as with the buffalo meat they obtained by hunting. Their minister had a house reserved for the sacrifices, and when they entered therein they behaved very reverentially, particularly during a sacrifice. They never sacrificed to idols, but only to Him of whom they said He has all power and that from Him come all things, which is recognizing a first cause.

"The captains, as well as the governor himself, all treat this minister with much consideration, and in order to induce him to visit us, as well as to avoid hurting his feelings, the governor sent out the captains with orders to do honor to the Indian priest and bring him with them. They went, and during three days and nights they entertained him with songs and dances, as is their custom, and when they returned home, he accompanied them. They arrived at noon, just as we were about to have dinner. Since I was eager to see the ceremonies of these people, I suggested that we should wait for that priest of theirs and ask him to eat at our table. He came advancing slowly, and bearing himself with much dignity, and with him was a crowd of Indians: men, women, and children. He appeared extremely serious and reserved, and as soon as he reached the place where we were, the governor bade him kiss our robe. This he did, and when we sat down to dinner I asked the governor to let our visitor sit by my side.

"When this Indian priest took his first mouthful, instead of asking a blessing, he made with the food, as he took it out of the dish, a sign like that of the cross, pointing, as it were, to the four winds, or cardinal points. After dinner we gave him clothing for himself and wife, and he was quite pleased.

"Later we were told by an Indian who was then with the Tejas but came from the country beyond—from Coahuila—and who spoke Mexican, that the above-mentioned priest of the Tejas had told all the captains and other Tejas: "Now you will no longer heed me, for these priests who have come to you are the true priests of Ayimat Caddi"—which last name signifies, in their language, "The Great Captain." This was the name he gave to God, for since the only rank or title they know is that of captain, they call "Great Captain" Him whom they consider as great above all things. Similarly, in order to give the governor a distinguishing name, they call him "dezza," which means "Great Lord and Superior to all."

"When the church and the dwelling intended for the priests had been finished, the soldiers carried into these buildings all that was to be left for the priests, and on the morning of the first of June, a week from the feast of Corpus Christi, we consecrated the church and celebrated mass, after which the Te Deum Laudamus was sung in thanksgiving, the soldiers firing a royal salute. The church and village were dedicated to our Holy Father, St. Francis.

"After dinner on that same day, our company left the place, to return hither, but I remained until the next day, when I went to join the others on the way. The night before I left, I called on the governor, bidding him remember that he must take care of the fathers who remained there and try to cause his people to respect them and to receive the Christian doctrine. I told him the fathers would not take anything from them, nor ask them for anything, but rather help them whenever they were able. And the governor said: "I shall take care of the fathers, so that, when you return, they will have no complaint to bring against me; they are perfectly safe, and may remain." I then told him that I should be gratified if his brother and some other one of his relatives would come with me to visit our possessions and bring back numerous presents for those who remained at home, and that our great Captain, the viceroy, was anxious to see them and entertained very kindly feelings towards them. The governor then replied that his brother with two other relatives and a nephew of his would accompany me, and he thus admonished me: "Do not permit anyone to demand service from these men whom you take with you, nor to make them work." From these words of his it is evident that they have among them the idea of rank, and that they distinguish their nobles from the mass of the people.

Manzanet criticized the military officers as follows: "Evidently some of them thought that they were to be made rulers of the Tejas, and forgot his Excellency's express orders concerning the journey, which orders provided that Capt. Alonso should go as commander of the expedition that was to find out whether there were any Frenchmen in that region, and that León and his men should escort thither the priests who accompanied Fray Damián Manzanet. If the Tejas asked for priests and desired baptism, the priests were to remain there. And if the Tejas proved friendly and no danger was to be expected at their hands, no large garrison was to be left behind; if, on the other hand, they proved troublesome, as many soldiers should remain as seemed needful, according to the advice and with the consent of Father Fray Damián Manzanet. It was not in the least necessary for the safety of the priests to leave soldiers among the Tejas, for from the very first they welcomed us with so much affection and good will, that they could hardly do enough to please us. Yet, in the face of all this, Capt. Alonso de León made arrangements to leave fifty men, under the command of Capt. Nicolás Prieto, an incapable and undeserving old man.

"When the time came, the captain told me of his purpose in a private interview, and I replied: "You are under orders from His Excellency, and if you mean to consult with me, the consultation must not take place in private; call your captains and the priests, and in their presence state what you wish to offer for consideration." This reply deeply wounded León, for his passions had blinded him. He called the captains and I called the priests, and Capt. Alonso de León told us that he had planned to leave for the protection of the priests forty or fifty soldiers under a leader, and that he was holding this consultation because His Excellency had ordered that, if soldiers were to be left, it should be with my consent. To this I replied that it was not necessary to leave a military force in the district, since the people were so peaceable and so friendly. In case the priests should need assistance, I requested that three soldiers whom I thought fit for the position should stay there. If he chose to leave a greater number, well and good; but with no consent of mine, for I did not wish more than three to remain. León was annoyed by my proposition, so was his friend Capt. Nicolás Prieto, who was to remain as leader of the forty or fifty soldiers. However, in the end, it was arranged that the three soldiers recommended by me should remain there. They were willing to do so, and were quite content. They belonged to the Zacatecas company. León left for the soldiers nine of the King's horses, some firelocks, a barrel of powder and some shot, and for the priests he left twenty-six loads of flour, twenty cows, two yoke of oxen, ploughs with ploughshares, axes, spades, and other little things.

"On the 2nd day of June we took departure, and the priests* walked with us a little way out of the village. Then we took leave of one another with many tears of joy and gladness, for these men did not sorrow at being left behind, nay, rather, they gave thanks to God for having merited such a grace as to be called to save the souls of the heathen. We arrived at the Trinity on the 3rd of June and found this river very high. On this account we were kept for a week from crossing. Meanwhile, the governor's brother was taken ill and went home.

"We followed the road by which we had come, until we reached the "rancheria" of the Emat, Toaa, Too, Cavas and other Indians, and in this "rancheria" we heard that the Indians on the coast had captured some young Frenchmen. The captain of the "ranchería" told us that although they themselves were at feud with the Indians on the coast, yet there was among them an Indian who held intercourse with those others, and if some of us desired to go and find them, this Indian would take those who wished to go. Captain León decided to go with twenty men for the purpose of trying to rescue the French boys. They reached the coast of the bay and found the Indians whom they sought. These had just arrived from some other portion of the same coast, armed with lances, and soon our people began to treat with them about delivering up the French boys. The Indians were promised horses and clothing if they would consent to give up the boys, and their reply was that they would do so promptly, without causing any trouble. The soldiers then began to enter the "ranchitos" of the Indians, peering with too much curiosity into their belongings, and committing other acts which

*The President, Father Fontecuberta, Father Francisco de Jesús María Casañas, and Father Antonio Bordoy were the priests who remained with Tejas.

incensed the Indians when they found out who was guilty. Later, after the French boys had been delivered over to our men, the Indians, having grown suspicious, commenced to shoot arrows among the soldiers. Two arrows struck Capt. León in the side, but as he wore mail, they did not penetrate; also, the horses were shot down under two other soldiers. There were four Indians killed and two wounded, and our men took the French boys and returned to the main body of the army, which was waiting by the Guadalupe river."

There were some points on which Manzanet took special note on this journey, as follows:

"First, in the preceding year we had everywhere found Indians, while in the year '90 we saw not a single one, until we inspected the Bay of Espíritu Santo and entered the land of Tejas.

"Secondly, in the year before the soldiers all behaved in a peaceable, orderly manner, performing their duties faithfully, so that there was no disorder on the march, and no loss of horses. But in this year '90 there hardly passed a day without someone fighting, or else some officer stabbing a soldier, so that a lay-brother who had come with me was generally kept busy tending the wounded. He treated them with tepid wine, which is, they say, an excellent cure for stabs in the head.

"Thirdly, I noted that there were so many horses and mules that the laden mules were not missed until some article contained in their pack was needed. As to the number of horses, it was never known to the officers.

"Fourthly, Captain León had a chum along, Capt. ...., so honorable that he never failed to play the tale bearer and excite quarrels; so kind-hearted that only his friend León drank chocolate, and the others lukewarm water; so considerate of others that he got up early in the morning to drink chocolate, and would afterwards drink again with the rest; so vigilant that he would keep awake and go at midnight to steal the chocolate out of the boxes; perhaps his vigilance was the reason why, while, by order of His Excellency, Captain León should have left for the priests twelve hundredweight of chocolate and the same quantity of sugar, he left only six hundredweight of each.

"He is so compassionate towards the Indians that because he saw how poor they were, and that their only clothing was the skins of antelopes and buffaloes, he endeavored to provide them in secret with the articles which His Excellency had sent for them—e.g. blankets, flannel, cloth and knives—but he arranged his alms-giving (by first robbing the Indians of what they had) that his gifts were equal to about one-fourth of his robberies.

"Fifth, when the Indians brought certain complaints against the soldiers for entering their houses, Captain León never attempted to remedy things at all. In one particular case, when the brother of the governor of the Tejas came to us, complaining that a crime had been attempted on his wife, I remonstrated with Captain León about his letting such misdeeds go unpunished. I urged that conduct like this would not be tolerated even among Moors and heretics, and should be the more severely reproved in this case because we had come among these heathen people in order to give an example of right living. But León did not say a word—perhaps because he feared exposure.

"For lack of more time I shall now only add that which is the most noteworthy thing of all, namely this: While we were at the Tejas village, after we had distributed clothing to the Indians and to the governor of the Tejas, the governor asked me one evening for a piece of blue baize to make a shroud in which to bury his mother when she died. I told him that cloth would be more suitable, and he answered that he did not want any color other than blue. I then asked him what mysterious reason he had for preferring the blue color, and in reply he said that they were very fond of that color, particularly for burial clothes, because in times past they had been visited frequently by a very beautiful woman who used to come down

—76—

from the hills dressed in blue garments, and that they wished to do as that woman had done. On my asking whether that had been long since, the governor said it had been before his time, but his mother, who was aged, had seen that woman, as had also the other old people. From this it is easily to be seen that they referred to the Madre María de Jesús de Agreda, who was very frequently in those regions, as she herself acknowledged to the Father Custodian of New Mexico, her last visit having been made in 1631, this last fact being evident from her own statement made to the said Father Custodian of New Mexico."

When the military expedition withdrew, three priests were left alone in the wilds of Texas to tell the Indians of the true God. Father Fontecuberta, Father Francisco de Jesús María Casañas, and Father Antonio Bordoy went to work with a will to master the Indian dialects and instruct the Indians. In a few months Father Casañas established a second mission a few miles north from Mission San Francisco, on the Neches River, and called it El Santísimo Nombre de María. The labors of the Fathers were not entirely without reward, since they induced a number of Indians to receive baptism, among them being the Chenisi, the virtual head of the Tejas (Hasinai) tribes. There were innumerable discouragements however; the conduct of the soldiers, privates, and that of most of the officers who had accompanied the expedition into the Tejas country had gone far to undo the good impression the Fathers made. The story of the outrageous conduct of the military in the other Indian rancherías, on their return trip to Mexico, reported by the Chief's relatives who journeyed with them part way, made the majority of the Indians suspicious of the good intentions of the Spaniards.

No provisions or assistance reached these good Fathers far in the interior of Texas until August 4, 1691, when another expedition, commanded by the Governor of Coahuila and Texas, Don Domingo Terán de los Ríos, entered the Tejas country commissioned to enlarge the missions already estab-

lished and found eight others among the Tejas, the Cadoda-
chos, and those near the Guadalupe. The Spaniards then
learned that the President of the Missions, Father Fontecuberta, had died of some dreadful sickness which had carried
off in a single month three hundred of the tribe immediately
surrounding the Mission of San Francisco; and of the Tejas, or
Hasinai tribes or confederacy, more than three thousand had
died during the year 1690-1691. This expedition did little of
anything it was sent out to do, and failed to accomplish any
lasting good to the missions. In fact, it went far to lessen the
respect of the Indians for the Spanish, and while the former
still professed good will toward the Spanish, to secure the presents brought for them, they were constantly pilfering from
the mission and stealing and killing animals, and this began
before the departure of Teran. At the suggestion of their "medicine men," they attributed the disease and deaths among
them to the influence of the new religion that many of them
had professed, and they began to rebel against it, and use
threats against the Spanish. These difficulties were aggravat-
ed by the harshness and evil conduct of the soldiers in their
dealings with the natives. Father Francisco Casañas wrote of
some of the difficulties encountered during his year and three
months residence at Mission San Francisco, and made various
suggestions to the authorities. He explained the many super-
stitions of the Indians; the adverse influence of the "medicine
men"; the evil conduct of the soldiers who had been sent on
the expeditions, and of those who had been left to guard the
missions; the stupendous task of learning the many languages
or dialects, without a knowledge of which it was almost impossible to make the Indians understand. He advised that a
strong garrison be left with each mission but that the soldiers
who formed the garrison should be exemplary married men
only; that they should have their families with them, and thus
form villages around the missions as examples of what was
meant by a village. "In order to convert the Indians," he said,
"the Spaniards must set them a good example, and so I beg,

your Excellency, to consider and plan how this work, so pleasing to the Lord, may not be lost through the sending of criminals from the prisons, vagabonds and unmarried, who if they were turned loose among Christians would do harm, and here, by their depraved lives and atrocities committed, prevent the ministers of the Lord from gathering in the fruit of these souls." For two successive years after Teran's departure, the harvests were destroyed by drouth; the cattle became afflicted with some disease and most of them died; the others were stolen by the Indians; the soldiers at the mission became unruly and offensive; and the savages grew constantly more threatening.

In 1693, fresh supplies were sent out to the mission, and the missionaries again sent letters back describing conditions and setting forth their needs, asking for a sufficient number of soldiers, of the right kind, to protect the priests from violence; but the government did nothing. There was no longer fear of French encroachment, and the authorities ordered the abandonment of the missions and instructed the priests to retire. On the night of October 25, 1693, the priests buried the bells and such other property as they could not take with them, and left the mission for their return to Coahuila. The Indians missed them, and followed in large numbers, overtaking them, and with prayers and tears besought them to remain with them. Father Hidalgo promised to do so, and later returned and lived among the Hasinai (Tejas) for many years. Captain Urrutia also remained with some others.

Father Hidalgo and the other missionaries who thus wandered among the Indians, here and there, seeking to save souls, were left by the government to brave the wilds of Texas alone, to starve or find food, to remain or leave as necessity demanded. As soon as danger from French aggression was removed, the King's representatives seem to have forgotten the souls of the Indians, and the instructions of His Majesty.

Interest in the Texas missions was, however, suddenly reawakened by renewal of French activities in 1715. When it was seen with what ease Saint-Denis appeared at San Juan Bautista del Río Grande, the Spanish were aroused from their lethargy. Saint-Denis plausibly stated that he had entered Texas to buy stock from the missions, which he believed to be still in existence, and that when the Indians found that he was going on to seek the Spanish, they immediately requested him to petition, in their name, that the missionaries be sent back to them. The petition of the Indians was acted upon promptly and favorably, nine missionaries agreeing to go, and Domingo Ramón was appointed to lead a company of twenty-five soldiers to assist the nine missionaries at the missions. They reached the Tejas, June 26, 1716, and were joyfully received, the Indians chanting the calumet of welcome to them. The first mission, San Francisco de los Tejas, was re-established a little further inland—east of the Neches River near the large mounds. A wooden Church was erected with a thatched roof. The mission had its banner with its name emblazoned on it and all the requisites for divine service in the chapel. In the Hasinai nation, La Purísma Concepción was founded, Father Ysidro Espinosa taking charge on July 7th. The Zacatecan Fathers took possession of Nuestra Señora de Guadalupe, among the Nacogdoches Indians, on the 9th of July. On the 10th of the same month, ten leagues to the north of Mission Concepción, Mission San José was founded.*

Saint-Denis wielded a strong and beneficial influence over the Indians and therefore obtained the highest regard of the missionaries, and since he had married into the family of Ramón, and was in Spanish pay at that time, many esteemed him as a suitable person to be placed in charge of the frontier. The missionaries asked that Saint-Denis be appointed governor, with a view of keeping the Indians in subjection. They also clamored for people to be sent out as settlers, to teach the

*Crónica, Padre Espinosa.

Indians steady habits by example, and to encourage them to adopt a settled mode of living, but nothing was done, and they were again, apparently deserted.

SOME OF THE HARDSHIPS EXPERIENCED BY THE MISSIONARIES IN EAST TEXAS IN 1716-1718.—THE FULL STORY COULD NEVER BE TOLD

In the early days of the missions of Texas there was much similarity in the daily routine, experiences and hardships of the missionaries, so that what is told of one mission or missionary may be taken, in general, as applying to all of that period, in the same section of the country, surrounded by the same conditions.

There were two colleges represented in Texas at this period—laborers for the work of the conversion of the Indians being sent from Queretaro and from Zacatecas. Father Isidro Felix de Espinosa was president in charge of those sent from Queretaro, and the Venerable Anthony Margil was president, and in charge of the priests sent from Zacatecas, at the same time the Venerable Anthony Margil who had founded the colleges of Queretaro and Zacatecas, as well as that of Guatemala, and who had been Guardian or head of them all—was in charge of all the missions of Texas, in general.

Father Espinosa, in 1715, says: "From the time the missionaries arrived in the Province of Texas they endured innumerable hardships, and began to sustain themselves with the bread of tears and tribulations...

"....The first disappointment was the desertion of the soldiers who came as escorts—seven of them fled and took with them the animals that belonged to the religious.

"The site of each mission being settled on, the religious remained alone making their straw dwellings, and as a providence for future maintenance they began an abstinence. Their dinner usually consisted of a small quantity of the vegetable purslane, gathered from the fields of the Indians, the only condiments being a little salt and pepper. The Indians occasionally brought a little meal, frijoles and fruits which served to divert rather than satisfy hunger. They rarely had a mouthful of meat—but once, when a goat broke its leg, we cut him up and lived on the remainder for a week. Chocolate, which is usually the chief part of a dinner with us, was very scarce, and between six religious (those that were from the college of Querétaro) we had only two anobas to divide.....and although all had their trials, some more, some less, they considered that they were living very pleasantly, if they did not have to pass a day without celebrating the Holy Sacrifice of the Mass, asking God for the conversion of these people.

"As the Indians were so scattered, the chief endeavor of the missionaries was to persuade them to live together—and although they gave promises of doing so and planting crops and raising their harvests, it was such a task that no minister was able to have the consolation of having all his people together. The missionaries moved to more spacious dwellings with the desire to congregate the Indians—but the land did not afford the capacity that was necessary for the number of persons—about a thousand—that were in each pueblo....As the Fathers knew much of the language of the country, they tried to point out to the Indians their errors, showing them the darkness in which they lived, and tried to impress upon them the great importance of a belief in the one true God and three Divine Persons, and of the necessity of receiving Baptism... Upon one occasion, a priest speaking to one of their teachers, or medicine men, of his errors, after the former was well acquainted with the language, he convinced him that he had held to wrong beliefs, and not having reasons to evade the Catholic truth, the latter confessed that his religion had no more foundation then that he had inherited it from his parents—that he and the others had good hearts and that they would try to follow the teachings of the missionaries. Among the women they found more docility to be taught the truth of God's law—and so there were many women who called for and received Baptism in danger of death, and the missionaries gathered in handsfull of the desired fruit, since of all who died—rarely one went without holy Baptism. That none should miss the great happiness of Baptism before dying, the missionaries made lists of the houses and ranches of the Indians with the number of adults and of children, and the names of the places, and when any Indian came to visit the Fathers, they asked him if all his family were well—and on finding out that anyone was sick they promised to go to see him and this they did; not only to console the family but principally to catechise the sick person and persuade him that he should receive holy Baptism, and although this was a very difficult thing— because many believed that the holy water shortened their lives—the zealous ministers undeceived them with plain reasons, and the sick ones moved from on High voluntarily received Baptism. It was a usual thing at times to have epidemics among the Indians, and the most common was the flux—a bloody dysentery. In winter, they were accustomed to throw coals of fire under the bed to moderate the great rigor of the cold, having high beds and not enough buffalo robes to keep them warm. The fire supplied what they lacked in cover, but was the occasion of their sad infirmity. When the epidemic was raging—the padres would not wait to be called, but saying Mass, mounted their horses and went to visit all the ranches—and at the cost of much labor—they did not return to their missions without having baptized all of the dying. If they met with resistance they repeated the visit another day, asking Heaven that the eyes and souls of those poor Indians would be opened, and God moved by the faith and piety of the Fathers, and pity for the ignorance of those poor people, and the great price of His Blood caused them to receive Baptism.

"The great and unceasing labor that this diligence occasioned the ministers can be seen when one reflects how far distant the ranches of these Indians were from each other—some being distant six and seven leagues....and it was not possible, although one should run, to visit the greater part in a day, for it was necessary sometimes to stop a long time to teach the dying and to convince the well ones that they should not interfere to prevent the salvation of the sick.

"To encourage his ministers and reward their zeal, God performed many wonderful things....The first year that the missions were founded, the chief of the Tejas Indians was sick in his own house at the same time another chief, a relative, was also sick; both being very old and greatly esteemed by all the people. The people, knowing death was near congregated by multitudes—men and women—some coming, others going, so that there was a crowd day and night. There was always around the house more than five hundred persons. I knew in what grave condition the chief was, and mounting my horse went the distance of five leagues to see him....to find out his sickness and console the people—though my principal object was that he should not die without being baptized. I made him understand, in his idiom, how much I felt for him, because he liked all the religious very much, and I gently proposed the necessity of Baptism for his salvation—pointing out the errors of his forefathers. He listened attentively and asked time to answer me. Five days afterwards I repeated the visit, and at the end of it he commanded water to be brought and a vessel, and before those who assisted him he lowered his head and asked that I baptize him, which I did, increasing with the water from my eyes, that already in the vessel. This captain, who by the circumstances of his baptism, I shall call happy—I named Francisco—because when I commenced to teach him I invoked to my aid the seraphic patriarch... Before he died he gave much advice to his son and charged him to take care of the Fathers—saying that they knew the truth and came from far-off lands to save them, with other reasons which made me understand that the holy Baptism had had its effect upon its soul.

"The chief Captain now being baptized, all my anxiety next was to obtain the same happiness for the other sick man, his relative, since I knew that that living skeleton was ready to lay his bones in the earth. I had already catechized him and he asked time, delaying that he should see more clearly. One day, when the sun was very bright and the morning very serene, his wife put him on a bench to bathe him. It seemed to me to be an opportune occasion—that he should wash his soul while he bathed his body. I went to him and asked him softly in his language if he wished to wash his soul as he washed his body, that nothing more was necessary for his eternal happiness, and I repeated anew the holy lavatory, and he answered that he would do so. His wife, ignorant of what I intended did not wish to give me the vessel with which she was bathing him—but he seriously commanded her to bring it full of water—and bowing his head, he made a sign that I should baptize him, saying that which I taught him, and with the name of Francisco, I baptized him much to my delight.

"In two or three days, with the difference of a few hours, my two Franciscos died, and the people were greatly distressed, and spent eight days in their funeral ceremonies.

"Among the Indians, those who had the greatest authority among the Tejas, and even above the chiefs, are the priests whom they call Chenesi. The chief of these, that is, he who takes care of the house of fire and has his house near, that the flame may never lack nourishment, was the most opposed to the Christian priests and fought with much acrimony the holy Baptism, telling the sick that the water which the priests called holy shortened their lives.... This priest, Sata Taxea by name, became sick unto death, and the danger of that poor soul being lost coming to my notice, I made the determination that he should be baptized. It was an undertaking for the powerful arm of God, and I needed special aid and succor from heaven. It was the day of the conversion of St. Paul, and remembering what the Lord did with this persecutor of Christians, and mistrusting my own efforts, I made use of my humble companion, who was at that time Fray Gabriel, a man old and virtuous; and to encourage him for this work, I commanded him for so much obedience that he should go to the house of the sick man—more than three leagues distant—and that he should try to undeceive him of his many errors, and should persuade him that the only door by which he could enter heaven was holy Baptism. The humble religious obeyed, and with great prudence and forethought he began to destroy the hardness of that hard impenitent heart—he felt hopes of carrying out his intent—and repeated the visit in spite of the battles of the evil spirits. Sata Taxea at last freely and spontaneously asked Baptism, and at the instance of the zealous minister, he received it; the new Paul, for so he was named, called together the Indians and told them clearly that all of their beliefs were lies and it was the truth alone which the Fathers preached. May God be praised forever!"....

"In January, 1717, Father Margil went to visit the Ais, notwithstanding a severe cold spell and ice and snow, and founded with much labor the Mission of Dolores. On this occasion he reduced to a town the numerous nation of Tatasis, but the continued rise of the rivers prevented him from carrying his work to completion. In the month of March the rivers went down and he went to make a treaty with the Adaes Indians fifty leagues distant from the Mission of Dolores, and only ten leagues distant from the French Fort, and there he founded Mission San Miguel, and left in charge Father Augustín Patrón, and a lay-brother as his companion. Father Margil then returned to Mission Dolores where he had left his companion, Brother Francisco de Santiago, of mature age and exemplary virtue. But a short time only did he enjoy the consolation of his companionship, for the good religious soon died, and alone Father Margil gave him burial, and to make his death known to his brethren, he sent the only soldier he had, staying alone at the mission.

At this time he received notice that the French wished to settle in the Cadodacho villages and preoccupy the place, and he decided to go and build a mission there—for which Father Francisco Hidalgo very joyfully offered himself. Having provided everything necessary, he set out with a Father and the Captain of the Presidio, but the journey was frustrated because the Tejas Indians they had to guide them, fooled them and took them the wrong way. I do not know if for fear of the French or from their own malice."

No aid had been received from any source by the missionaries since they had gone to the Tejas country early in 1716, and as they were not well provided with necessaries in the beginning, their sufferings constantly increased. Their sufferings for the common necessities were unimaginable and the neglect of the government for almost two years inexcusable. Owing to droughts, in 1717 and 1718, the Indians had a very scanty crop of corn and frijoles, and this cut off what supplies the missionaries had been accustomed to receive from the natives. The fathers sent letters back to their colleges telling of their extreme need, and the colleges in turn informed the government; the Marquis de Valero named a governor who should go at once with the relief under proper escort, but it was two years before it arrived. In the meantime, in 1717, the President of the Missions on the Rio Grande, learning of their distressful condition and anxious to relieve their immediate needs, caused some supplies to be sent in care of a few religious and an escort of fifteen soldiers; but when they reached the Trinity River it was so high that the overflow extended about two leagues to the west of that river and they could get no nearer to the missionaries they had gone to relieve. The latter were more than forty leagues to the east of the Trinity. They waited until the beginning of December, and when they saw that the rains were increasing, they left all the cargo in a little forest of oaks, and returned very disconsolately to the Rio Grande. The religious conductors were very anxious to go to the help of their brothers, but seeing the impassableness of the rivers, they left a written paper in the hands of some of the Tejas Indians who had remained on that side of the river to sow seed; charging them that as soon as the river went down, they should take the paper and give it to the Fathers.

Of course nothing was said to the Indians of the cargo, as they did not wish them to know anything about it, and they did all that was possible to conceal it without attracting attention.

The poor missionaries whom the cargo was intended to relieve knew nothing of it until the latter part of the next July, when a much crumpled and soiled letter was brought to Father Espinosa, eight months after it was written.

In the meantime they had been without corn with which to make bread, for all the Indian ranches put together had but one bushel. They had no meat, or when they were able to get a little, it did not make a mouthful when divided. In the spring, when a handful of corn given them by Indians was sowed, the crop when gathered helped some to supply the table. Quoting again from Father Espinosa: "We had no salt—and when happily we had some frijoles—for lack of salt they were tasteless, and were able to serve as a purge. No meat was to be had or taken, as already the sign of Aries and Taurus had gone up into the sky. Occasionally, the Indians, pitying us, brought us a quarter of a deer—and this, for lack of salt, we did not enjoy. Many days we had nothing to eat—but as necessity is the mother of industry and invention, it occurred to one of the missionaries that the flesh of the crows might not be unfit. They are as small as jays and abound in the trees in the morning. After this, with the aid of a musket we had fresh meat every day. The blackness and hardness of it destroyed the appetite and was repugnant to the sight, but our necessity was so great that for the greater part of the year it made a good dish. When the other missionaries (those from Zacatecas) learned of this discovery, they also made crows their ordinary food. On fast days the appetite was always greater, but the religious were not allowed to fast altogether under the circumstances, as there was nothing substantial to eat at any time, but whenever possible use was made of the known herbs of the country, and some nuts which they gathered to season them. Sometimes the leaves of the mustard served as a pleasant salad, especially if there was a little salty earth to season it. At times, the torment of hunger was relieved when the Indians, occasionally, came with things to eat which they had found.

The need for wax for candles for Mass was also great, but this was supplied for many days by renewing the wicks until all the wax was consumed. Afterwards we used candles of tallow, but we were able to get so little of the Indians that we found ourselves obliged to celebrate a feast day with only one tallow candle, and the wine was so scarce that we were obliged to mix it with some sour grape juice.

"At this time the Venerable Padre Margil came to our mission. His was distant thirty-two leagues, and although at their missions they (the Fathers from Zacatecas) had lacked everything necessary for the table, they were supplied with things for Mass, and as soon as he learned our need for wine and wax he gave me a little bottle of two cuartillas and one pound of wax, all of which we divided among six priests, and it served us as a great consolation because we were able to say some masses on weekdays. Father Margil told me that he had buried a jar of wine for greater necessity."

THE FINDING OF THE CARGO, IT'S PROTECTION, AND THE MEETING WITH THEIR FRIENDS AND BROTHERS

"About a half or quarter of a league from where the cargo was left hidden were some Tejas Indians, who had gone to hunt and dry the meat of the buffalo, and every day many of them went out to hunt. It is truly marvelous how the cargo should have escaped their eyes, for the little grove of oaks was not thick enough to hide anyone who should enter it, and that these Tejas Indians did not see it was simply because the Lord hid it from their sight." These Indians saw the soldiers come with the cargo, and afterwards some of the same Indians met them when they were returning with the unladen mules, and eight months later when some of the party returned to the place where they had camped for so long, the path to the cargo made by the footprints of the animals was still visible, and was so plain that Father Espinosa, who with the Captain of the Presidio had set out with the few mules they could get together, found the place with no trouble, from the directions given him by the note.

As time went on, and no letter had been received from Texas, the President of the Rio Grande Missions, Father Pedro Muñoz, decided that the cargo must have been taken by the Indians, and with a quantity of wine and wax set out with some soldiers to carry relief to the Texas missions. He took with him the religious who had gone the year before and some of the same soldiers. When he reached the place where they had made their camping place before, Father Muñóz sent on the religious with two soldiers who knew where they had hidden the cargo, with instructions that if they should find anything they should return quickly to tell it, but, as a sign of good success to fire a musket before coming back. They found the cargo just as they had left it and, laughing joyfully, the soldiers fired their two muskets as a sign of great success, but to their amazement, at the same time that they were shooting, they heard other shots answering. Knowing that none of those who remained with the Father had any arms, they did not know what to think. All listened, but were perplexed on hearing the shots without knowing whence they came, and to dissipate their doubts, some mounted horses and went to all parts of the surrounding country for a long distance, but they discovered no human footsteps. "They then piously decided that the guards placed by the invisible God who had so long hidden the succor from the eyes of the Indians, who are like lynx to discover and follow up the least trace that they find on the ground, were those who had made the salvo" (salute).

The party from the Rio Grande camped at this place to rest. Father Espinosa and escort, although the captain entertained no hope that the Indians had left anything, set out on their search for the cargo, on St. Ann's day, just a few days after the receipt of the crumpled and faded note. At last they reached the place, and who can picture their joy at finding both the cargo and their friends! Father Espinosa says: "Our joy was doubled and made us pour many tears of thanksgiving." They found everything of the cargo "intact as it had been left the preceding year, and even the bows and arrows which they had put upon the boxes had suffered no detriment." They read their many new and old letters, they found with pleasure that the viceroy had given many needed orders with reference to the province of Texas. The one which pleased them most and for which they had long pleaded was that the next entrada should bring good families as settlers, soldiers and a sufficient number of people, with flocks and herds, ammunition, provisions, oxen, seeds, agricultural tools and everything necessary to cultivate the lands, to establish towns and missions that would contribute to the propagation and conservation of the faith. Another order was "that the government of Coahuila should be joined to that of Texas." It was also ordered that with the consent of the missionary fathers, one or two missions should be established between the San Antonio and Guadalupe Rivers, and that all things necessary for their support and maintenance should be supplied to enable them to cultivate the land and establish the towns and a settlement of Indians; that with perseverance and diligence they should bring the Indians together, and treat them kindly, without violence; that through the hands of the missionaries they should distribute gifts of cloth and glass beads, and of other things destined for them, in the name of his Majesty; and by agreement with the Father missionaries they should endeavor by all means to reduce the Indians to certain limits, and all the different Indian nations—by offering gifts to their leaders and chiefs—and through promises of good treatment, which shall be given to them as promised, if they live peacefully according to our holy religion and recognize our God and King...... That only the soldiers who have families shall remain among the Tejas...... It was further ordered that all the missions of Texas should be under the conduct of Venerable Padre Margil."

There was great rejoicing among the missionaries over this good news, that they were to have government help for the missions, that their advice had been acted upon, and that all else was to be subordinate to the conversion of the Indians and the saving of souls. But alas, the padres were again doomed to disappointment. And that is the history of the Missions of Texas—promises, hopes, disappointments and trials without end for the poor padres; for in the chapter on the Missions it will be seen how the entradas (military trains) came, but left no substantial benefit as had been ordered and promised, and the poor fathers were left again to struggle alone.

———

The next governor appointed was Don Martín de Alarcón who was ordered to carry fifty married soldiers, three master carpenters, a blacksmith, and a stonemason to put the settlement on a firm basis; each person, like the soldiers, to draw a yearly salary of four hundred pesos. When it was discovered that Alarcón on his entry, in 1718, had not obeyed orders with reference to the missions, the missionaries at once sent in a complaint, in which they recited that he had not brought the master mechanics ordered; nor the fifty soldiers; and the soldiers he had brought were idle and hurtful to the missions, as coming from the most corrupt and worthless classes. The poor missionaries were almost heartbroken over the failure of their countrymen to meet their responsibilities.

War broke out between Spain and France during the regency of the Duke of Orleans. The French on the frontier heard of it and invaded the presidio of Penzacola May 19, 1719, after Alarcón's departure; one of the frontier missions of Texas was also attacked and the inhabitants, impelled by fright, retired inland. "The soldiers, overruling the determination of the missionaries to remain, all retreated toward San Antonio."

The Marquis de San Miguel de Aguayo offered his services and fortune in this time of stress to repel the French, and being accepted, escorted the missionaries back to their old missions. His patronage founded Mission San José y San Miguel de Aguayo before his entrada.

Mission Espíritu Santo de Zúñiga, near the presidio of Nuestra Señora de Loreto or La Bahía del Espíritu Santo, was among the establishments founded at this time, but on the whole he accomplished a very small part of what was hoped and longed for by the missionaries, as he did not leave oxen or other stock in sufficient numbers for the missions, nor provisions, nor tools for cultivating the land, nor the families promised them.

In September, the Brigadier Don Pedro de Riviera began the revistas of the presidios of Texas. He suppressed one of the presidios, reduced the garrisons of all the others and so removed all hope from the missionaries that the government would do anything more for the missions. The missionaries protested against the suppression of the Presidio de los Tejas (Nuestra Señora de los Dolores) and petitioned that its former force and that of Adaes be doubled, or if that be not granted, that the captains of the presidios should place at their disposal competent guards for the missions, and for separating the apostate from the heathen Indians. The petition was denied, and the father President, Miguel Sevillano, appealed to His Majesty, complaining of the measures of the viceroy. A royal cédula asked for the viceroy's report. Don Pedro de Riviera defended his arguments, the viceroy defended his action, and against their combined official testimony the letter of the missionary seemed unimportant and the orders were allowed to stand.

When hope of assistance by the government was lost, the Franciscans of Querétaro, in charge of Missions San Francisco de los Neches (de los Tejas), Nuestra Concepción de los Hasinai, and San José de los Nazones asked to have their missions removed to the vicinity of the presidio of San Antonio de Bejar. This was done at the close of 1730, and Mission San Francisco was located about nine miles below San Antonio, on the right or west bank of the San Antonio River and became known as Mission San Francisco de la Espada. Father Juan Morfi says of this mission: (1778) "Mission San Francisco de la Espada, which is the last one, has forty settlers and a total of 133 souls. It sows nine fanegas of corn, though it could raise much more. It has 4,000 head of cattle, sheep and horses. These have been greatly diminished on account of the great number stolen by the Lipans and Comanches. The living quarters of the priests, although rude and unfinished, are fairly comfortable. The houses of the Indians are the same little huts that are found everywhere. The Church was torn down because it was in a dangerous state of dilapidation. Services are held in a low room, capacious and well supplied with sacred vessels and very decent ornaments. This mission has a great deal of good land, with a copious supply of water from the San Antonio River. It is in charge of the Fathers, Fray Juan Botello and Fray Pedro Noreña."*

Today the boundaries of the mission square are quite distinct except on the side facing the river. The well-preserved baluarte or bastion, with its portholes and its many imprints of cannon balls made in the long ago, is a small round tower presenting quite a feudal appearance, projecting outwardly

*The writer has an old mission book bearing the signature of Padre Noreña.

MISSION SAN FRANCISCO DE LA ESPADA 4TH MISSION

from the southeast corner of the square. It is well worth seeing. The well, the acequias, the chapel, and portions of the
mission buildings with arched doors are still to be seen. There
were other baluartes, or bastions, says tradition, but no traces
of them now remain. One was said to be in the south wall,
west of the present one, another toward the north end of the
west side.

The Reverend Francis Bouchu, who came to Texas in
1845 with Bishop Odin, long made his home at this mission of
San Francisco de la Espada, and served as priest all the settlements for many miles about, and to Father Bouchu is owed
the preservation of the baluarte and other buildings. The
front of the chapel of the mission is all that is left of the original structure. The entrance door, unmistakably Moorish,
reminds one of the Alhambra in shape and line. It is built in
the form of a cross. The elevated front, fitted with arches,
serves as a belfry tower, where the three original bells may
still be seen. It is said that some of the mission bells were cast
at the missions, and it may be true, as the early missionaries
seemed prepared to do most everything. However that may
be, they were proficient in another art or accomplishment, for

there are several pretty specimens of wrought-iron work at Mission San Francisco and the other missions. With his own hands Father Bouchu repaired and rebuilt most of the Chapel, and the main mission building, which was originally erected with arcades running along the front and leading to the Chapel.

BALUARTE OR BULWARK

"Padre Francisco," as the mission people called him, fitted up the buildings on the south and east sides for a school-house and they are still used for that purpose. This good Father, who was wonderfully active and persevering, knew something of many subjects. Joining with his priestly vocation a knowledge of practical handicraft, he was a worthy successor to the original founders. He was among other things something of a musician, scientist, historian, photographer, stone mason, carpenter, lawyer, cook, bricklayer and printer. He obtained a printing press and printed catechisms and other necessary books for the poor Mexicans. He preserved all the history possible of the mission and worked faithfully among his poor parishioners until his last illness. Many old relics of the Indian days may be seen at the mission preserved by Father Bouchu; notably, the statue of the Christ carrying His Cross, and the Madre Dolores or Sorrowful Mother, used in the realistic Via Crucis, or the Passion Play of the old mission days.

The square of this mission was the first camping ground of the Texas Army of Independence in the campaign about Bexar, in 1835.

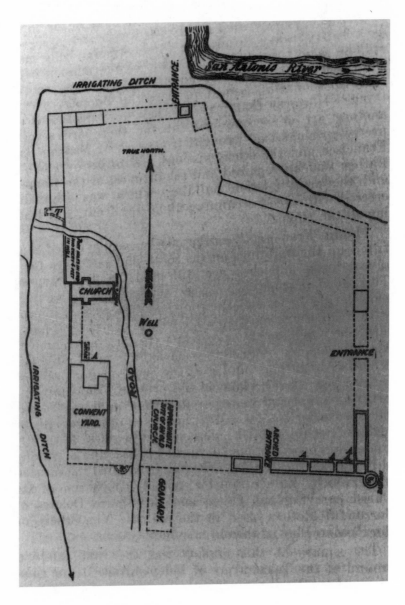

Ground Plan Mission San Francisco de la Espada.

Dotted lines are ruined walls. T stands for bastion or bulwark.
A for arched doorway.

In the city of Agreda, Spain, there lived a beautiful little girl, dainty, graceful and spirituelle, born of noble parentage and surrounded with every comfort. Her parents were persons of education, purposeful and deeply religious. They took a profound interest in public affairs, and entertained all persons of note coming through Agreda; in fact, so general was their hospitality that they may be said to have kept "open house" continually. The great questions and happenings of the day were discussed, tales of travels and hardships were recounted, and the little Mary, who was always present, listened to all with sympathetic heart. The tales of the New World particularly took her fancy, and travelers returning from or going there interested her most of all. The Indians, those strange people of the New World who knew not God, without any means of enlightenment, most excited her sympathy and fired her imagination, and she longed to be like the men—able to go out to them and help them—to help to draw away the dark veil shrouding their intellects and to bring light and salvation to their minds and souls.

As she developed into womanhood, her beautiful character expanded, and she was always to be found where consolation was needed and charity was to be dispensed. Her sympathy was universal, and none were too low or too high for her tender ministrations. Still her thoughts and prayers were chiefly for the benighted Indians of the New World, and she lost no opportunity to point out to all who came her way the great need of the Indians and to urge them to take the perilous voyage across the seas to enlighten those in such unhappiness and darkness of spirit.

She finally determined to devote her time and means to doing all the good possible, and founded a society whose members were to teach all who needed instruction, to succor all who needed aid, and to pray for those whom it was impossible to reach in person. This institution soon became famous throughout the country. The little Mary, now become the learned and distinguished Mary de Agreda, still retained her childlike heart and intense sympathy for the Indians. She prayed for them continually, and for the men who went out to them, and would spend hours on her knees in prayer, begging Providence to succor them. At last it seemed to her that a way was opened to her to visit the New World, and after a long sea voyage and tedious overland route, she found herself among certain tribes of Indians heretofore unheard of in the Old World, who were in every way superior to the vast hordes— who were gentle and well-disposed, whose government was almost civilized, who dwelt together in towns. These towns consisted of a number of round straw houses roofed in conical shape. While they kept a perpetual fire burning, they were not exactly fire-worshippers, though they believed that should the fire die out they would all perish. The fire was built of four logs, one log each pointing north, south, east and west. There was one Great House where they kept the principal fire and from whence the other fires were brought. Great piles of logs for the replenishing of the fire were kept outside the Great House, near at hand. It being impossible for Mary de Agreda to remain long at a time with these Indians, she made them frequent visits, gaining the devoted love of the women and the reverential respect of the men of the tribe, and obtained their promise that they would receive respectfully, as teachers, white men in dark robes whom she would send to them to advance and raise their race and help them in their need.

The picture of the strange and beautiful country and the many in dire need of the land of the Theas or Teas never left her, and she besought all persons going to the New World to endeavor to reach these particular tribes whom she had visited. She wrote pleading letters to the same end to all whom she heard were embarking for that region, and exacted a promise from the Custos (or Guardian) of New Mexico who visited her at her institution in Agreda, that he should see to it that these tribes were reached. Finally her prayers and entreaties were rewarded in this wise. A missionary by name of Damián Manzanet had been sent a copy of the description of the tribes in whom this distinguished woman was interested, with the account of her visits to them, and a request from the Custos of New Mexico that he go to them if possible. He went on to the border of Coahuila to be as near the unknown territory as convenient, and finally was the means of convincing the authorities in New Mexico that there were French in Texas, and he accompanied the next expedition under De León sent into the interior of that country to search for the French. He there found some of the tribes referred to by Mary Coronel de Agreda, and immediately made arrangements to found a mission among them. In May 1689, General Alonso de León refers to her in his report on his expedition to the Tejas. The next year, on his return to the Tejas country, Manzanet and his companions were joyfully and kindly received and shown every consideration. The Governor, or Chief, of the Tejas Indians one day asked Manzanet for some blue baize in which to bury his grandmother when she died.

Manzanet asked him why he desired it blue. The Chief replied that it was because a beautiful woman who had come often to visit their tribe and whom they reverenced wore blue, and they wished to be like her on passing to the other world. The chief said she had not visited them in his time, but that the oldest people remembered her, that she had promised them teachers, and now that Manzanet and his companions had come, the "high priest" or medicine man of the tribe had told them that these were the true teachers who had been expected.

The strange part of the story is that Mary de Agreda had never really been in Texas or the New World in person, but during her state of intense longing and continued prayer, she must have dreamed all or visited them in ecstasy—but so vivid were the dreams—if dreams they were—and so many times were they repeated, and the same country and people held in vision before her mind day after day and month after month, that they became as real to her as those among whom she actually lived. She conversed with these dream people and promised them teachers which she finally caused to be sent as we have seen. Numerous were her writings descriptive of these people, their country, customs and names of tribes, and it was afterwards found to be correct and true.*

Stranger yet is the fact that the people of these tribes saw her, loved and remembered her, and that she seemed real to them. Her appearance and dress were described by the Tejas Indians to the whites coming to the region in 1690, and her memory held in great esteem. The traditions of her visits were handed down in all the tribes akin to the Tejas in various parts of the country.

Mary Coronel of Agreda was born in 1602, died May 24, 1665. Agreda was a small town in Old Castile on the borders of Aragón where one of Mary Coronel's ancestors had built a fine institution and established a society for the promotion of education among the people. In 1619 she joined this society, and became such a valuable member that she was placed at the head in 1626. Her mother also joined the society; and the order with Mary Coronel at its head reached its greatest fame and power for good.

*There are still some of her writings extant and some are preserved in Fordham College, New York.

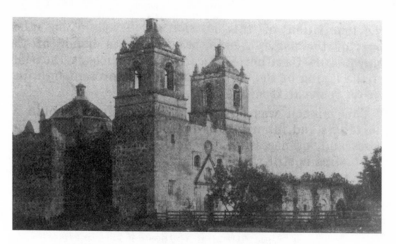

Mission de Nuestra Señora de la Purísima Concepción de Acuña

Mission de Nuestra Señora de la Purísima Concepción de Acuña was originally founded among the Asinais Indians (of the Hasinai or Tejas confederacy) in 1716, and in 1730 was removed to its present site two miles below San Antonio. The early history of this mission, between 1716 to 1731, the dates respectively of its foundation and the laying of its corner stone, is very similar to that of Mission San Francisco de los Tejas, as they were founded near each other and passed through the same general struggles and vicissitudes. In east Texas the mission was called Nuestra Señora de la Purísima Concepción de los Asinais, showing among what Indian tribe it was located.

Its name refers to the doctrine of the Immaculate Conception of the Virgin Mary, which was generally held by Catholics, though not defined as a dogma until December 8, 1854, nearly a century and a half after the foundation of this mission in Texas. The other part of the name, Acuña, was given in honor of the Marquis de Casafuerte, Viceroy of Mexico at the time of the laying of the corner stone of the present building on its removal from East Texas.

This mission was built on the same general plan as the others and intended for religious and scholastic purposes and, of necessity, for defense. The well dug by the padres is still there.

In 1778, Padre Juan Morfi refers to Mission Purísima Concepción, stating that it was founded by the Fathers from the College of the Holy Cross at Querétaro. He further says: "It is controlled today by the College of Zacatecas, to whom the Queretaran Fathers turned over their missions in Texas in order to give all their attention to those of La Pimera (Upper Sonora and Arizona). All of the missions on the San Antonio River are built after the same plan and governed by the same system. The one of which were are speaking is situated upon the road that leads from the Mission of San Antonio (de Valero) to that of San José, on fine land, and is constructed with the same admirable proportions as the other missions. The houses of the Indians form a closed square with those of the ministers and with the Church. The Church is very beautiful and worthy of a large population. It has been constructed with arches of rough sandstone, there being an abundant quarry at the gate of the courtyard. The sacristy is well supplied with ornaments and sacred vessels, and in every respect the Church is properly adorned. The priests' house is low, with arched roofs, and conveniently partitioned. The mission is ministered to by Fathers Fray Francisco López and Fray Mariano Vazconceles."

The Church of this mission is the best preserved of all the mission Churches of Texas. It fronts due west, is built in the form of a cross with the "twin towers" forming two wings at the foot of the cross, and is grand and imposing. The arched stone roof is composed of a series of arches; and over the chancel a beautiful Moorish dome rises graceful in outline, though massive and plain. The choir loft is intact and is entered from the outside, on the south side of the Church. The choir loft of this Church is a duplicate of the Church of the Alamo, except that the latter was entered from the north side by way of the gallery of the main building of the mission, or Alamo Fort. The acoustics of this Church are perfect, and the singing by the little orphan boys from the orphanage nearby, when special services are held there, is wonderfully sweet and effective. The general design of this Church is identical with that of the

A Corner in the Sacristy

Church of the Alamo, except that here the sacristy is on the south side while that of the Church of the Alamo is on the north. The square and barracks have entirely disappeared, but the part of the arcaded residence of the fathers remaining is most interesting. The refectory, or library with its beautifully arched ceilings and its deep recessed shelves, still shows the decoration of the ancient days

In the sacristy now are many objects of interest: the lavatory, the quaint cabinet in the thick walls, the crude and curious old candlesticks, and other articles of the long ago.

The stairway leading to the cellar, back of the sacristy, tradition says, led past underground store rooms, through a subterranean passageway to the river. The old and artistic stone stairs leading to the rooms above the sacristy, the conch shaped doorway and unique windows of those rooms are worth a close inspection, as is also the front door of the Church.

"The upper part of the ornamented facade is not an arch but a simple triangle, and the arch of the doorway is, for want of a better definition, a divided polygon. In the division or center of the arch is a shield with arms and devices, and here and there on the portal facade are cross and scroll, and carved relief pillars at the sides ornamented with carved lozenges."* In angular spaces over the archway is the legend: "ASV PATRONA, Y PRINCESSA ESTA MISSION, Y CON ESTAS ARMAS, ATIENDE EL PVNTO DE SV PVRENZA." This Mission's patroness and princess, with these arms maintain (or uphold) the state (or fact) of her purity. Over this winds, circling in and out, the flagellum or knotted scourge of the order of St. Francis, realistically carved....... These are again surmounted with other designs, and above all on the summit of the facade is a stone bearing the date 1794, and immediately underneath this is a shield with the initials M Ave meaning "Ave María." The only stained glass in all the Missions is the panes of two little windows each side of the upper part of the facade. The front of the Mission Concepción must have been very gorgeous with color, for it was frescoed all over with red and blue quatrefoil crosses of different patterns and with large yellow and orange squares to simulate great dressed stones. This frescoing is rapidly disappearing..... The topmost roofs of the towers are pyramidical and of stone, with smaller corner pyramidal capstones. The upper stories of the towers have each four lookout windows of plain Roman arches. The tops of the side walls of the Church and the circle wall of the central dome have wide stone serrations in the Moorish character, the points of which around the finely proportioned dome stand out like canine teeth. The towers have belfries, and at their bases on either side of the entrance are, on the right, a baptistry

*Wm. Corner, in San Antonio de Bexar, Christmas, 1890.

11x11 feet with massive thick walls, and on the left a similar small chamber... The baptistry walls are frescoed with weird-looking designs, dim and faded, of the Crucifixion and Los Dolores.... A semi-circular font projects from the south wall, its half-bowl carved with what appears to be a symbolical figure with outstretched arms supporting the rim. It is a rude piece of carving, but is artistic. Inside, the stone roof of the chapel

Baptismal Bowl in Baptistry.

with its series of arches and central dome is massive but plain. In each wing of the cross are altars or altar places. In the west is a choir loft."* On October 28, 1835, this mission was the scene of an engagement between the Texans under Colonels Fannin and Bowie and Cos' troops, in which the former, though far outnumbered, were victorious. The fighting took place on the river bank fronting the mission. The Texas troops were quartered here for a while at this period, and in 1849, the United States troops occupied it. It is said that the latter cleared the chapel of an immense amount of accumulated rubbish and bat guano. Bishop Neraz further cleaned it up and re-

*Wm. Corner, in San Antonio de Bexar, Christmas, 1890.

devoted it to Church purposes, dedicating it to Our Lady of Lourdes on May 2, 1887.

It is said that Santa Anna expected to find the Texans at Mission Concepción instead of at the Alamo in 1836, as he considered Mission Concepción far superior as a stronghold. "In the holes in the walls outside are to be found the nesting places of owls, pigeons, doves and other birds. To the south of the Chapel, westerly, are a series of arches which were for-

merly cells, chambers and cloisters for the Mission inmates... To the south, forming a wing easterly, are other buildings, probably the sacristy, superior's vestries and quarters. These have two stories, the upper being approached by a stone staircase. The square of this mission at this date can very hardly be defined, but that the Mission was situated in the southeastern corner of a ramparted square is without doubt.... On April 10, 1794, the lands of Mission Concepción were partitioned in a similar manner to those of the Alamo Mission, among its Indian dependents, setting aside certain portions of the land for the payment of government taxes. This was done by order of the viceroy... The names may be found in our County Records. There were 38 souls at that time in the Mission community, namely 16 men, 12 married women, 1 boy, 6 girls and 3 widows. In 1805 a census showed 41 souls."

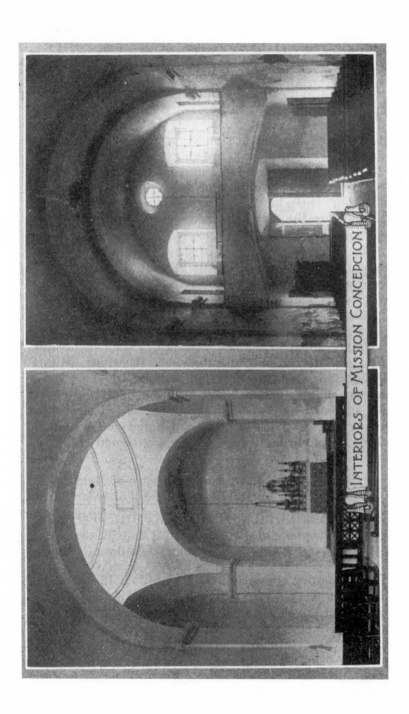

Interiors of Mission Concepcion

A very interesting Spanish document was preserved by Father Bouchu, whose heading when translated reads: "This is the Inventory of the four Mission Churches situated in the neighborhood of the City of San Fernando de Bexar, made by order of the Superiors, and conveying the said Churches to the Ecclesiastical Ordinary of this Diocese of Nuevo Reino de León on the 29th day of February, 1824." This is signed:

"FRANCISCO MAYNES,
Chaplain of the Ancient Company of Bexar
and Parish Priest of this Church.

FRAY JOSÉ ANTONIO DÍAZ DE LEÓN,
Provisional President of these Missions,
commisionado al efecto."

The inventory shows how well supplied these Mission Churches were with precious vestments, sacred vessels and other Church articles. Some of the articles mentioned as belonging to the Mission Concepción are as follows: "Fifteen vestments, nine statues, two silver candlesticks, one silver crucifix, two pairs of silver cruets with plates, one silver bell for the altar (This bell has disappeared; Señor Cura Don Refugio de la Garza is responsible for it.), one silver censer and boat." There were other articles in gold, and 182 more in the inventory than those already specified. The inventory just referred to is very careful to state that "the large bell in the Church of Bexar (San Fernando) belongs to the Church of Mission Concepción." Mission Concepción was completed in twenty-one years, in 1752.

———

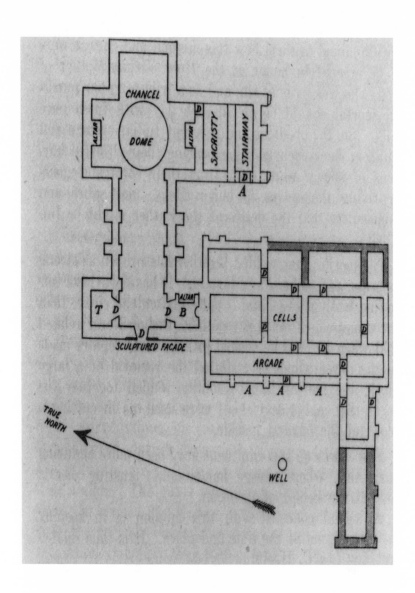

This Mission is built of stone laid in mortar mixed, tradition says, with fresh milk of cows, goats, etc. The stone was quarried "at the gate." A. is arch, B. is baptistry, D. is door, T. is a room under left tower. The shaded part is in ruins. The river is about one-quarter mile towards the west.

In order to guard it, the Monastery had a stone wall with three gateways, as well as two bronze cannons of an eight ounce calibre, with a weight of 3 arrobas 8 libras, (83 lbs. each.) "Apuntes para la Historia Antigua de Coahuila y Texas." Esteban L. Portillo, p. 305.

LEGENDS OF MISSION DE NUESTRA SEÑORA DE LA PURÍSIMA CONCEPCIÓN DE ACUÑA

The true story of the building of this mission runs as follows: When the rock had been quarried, and the foundation of the Church was to be laid, the priest assembled the Indian workers and addressed them. He explained to them how this mission and church were to be erected in honor of the Holy Virgin Mother of God, who was without sin, and as a tribute to her purity the mortar should be mixed each day with fresh pure milk. So, the obedient and reverent Indian women and children came each morning bearing their cheerful burdens of snowy white milk from their cows and goats, depriving themselves to honor Mary, most pure and immaculate that the desire of the Father might be fulfilled.

The mortar thus welded together has proven as strong as brass and as hard as adamant. It has defied the corroding tooth of time, and is more difficult to cleave than the stones which binds it together. Bishop Neraz related that when in 1890 he wished to have some repairs made in the tower which necessitated the removal of a large block, the mortar had so solidly welded together the rocks that mallet and chisel were used, as in cutting a block of the hardest marble.

Few works on this continent have been more enduring than this, where savage hands and trusting hearts obeyed the behest of devotion.

A legend connected with this mission is in keeping with the spirit of the time and place. It is thus related by Mrs. Lee C. Harby:

"The legend runs that one day in the early part of the year when the neophytes were all beyond the mission walls, laboring in the fields preparing for the planting of their crops, a priest went up into the tower to pray without interruption, at the same time to keep watch for the advent of the "wild tribes" which were apt to make a foray upon the peaceful Indians, capture their implements and kill or carry off as many of the workers as possible. For a time he kept his ward but no signs of danger were noticed; gradually his attention became riveted upon his book. Some time elapsed when, upon again looking out, he was horrified to see the Comanches coming down at full ride upon his unsuspecting people. Excitedly, he clanged the bell in notes of warning, and, rushing down the stairs, reported what he had seen afar off. His superior was in a quandry—should he throw the gates wide so that the fleeing throng of Indians could enter and be in safety? If he should do that, then the hordes so close in pursuit and gaining at every step would rush in with them and as there were no soldiers within for their defense nothing would be gained; and all would be slaughtered—priestly teacher as well as Indian convert. How could he leave the poor redmen shut without, at the mercy of the relentless savages? Then he knelt and prayed to the dear Mother in whose honor this mission had been established that she would interpose in their behalf, asking that she would vouchsafe a sign as to what should be done. As he prayed, the pious father glanced up at the statue of the Virgin which surmounting the great gates, looked ever calmly outward at the far, stretching prairies. Lo, as he looked in his agony of supplication, the great statue turned upon its pedestal and, revolving slowly, faced inward, gazing down as with a gracious benediction upon the priest kneeling there. He saw and took it as a sign: The gates were thrown wide and just in time. In rushed the Mission Indians and at their very heels the terrible Comanches followed, even up to the very lintel, but there they paused, held by some unknown power. They did not cross the threshold; the heavy gates closed and those who believed were saved! Then the bell—this very bell*—rang out its jubilee, calling all to a prayer of praise for the miraculous intervention and mercy."

*One of the bells is now in possession of a Texas Historical Society, at Galveston.

Front View of Mission San Juan de Capistrano.

Mission San Juan de Capistrano.

Mission San Juan de Capistrano, six miles below San Antonio, was founded in east Texas among the Nazones, in 1716, under the title of San José de los Nazones. It was transferred to the San Antonio on the left or east bank of the river in 1730, and given the name of San Juan de Capistrano as there was already a San José in the vicinity. The name of San Juan was bestowed in honor of Saint John; and de Capistrano in honor of a noted friar of the Franciscan order born in 1386. The mission was begun March 5, 1731, on the day of the completion of San José.

The pathetic history of Mission Nuestra Señora de Guadalupe, Mission San Francisco de los Neches, and of Mission Concepción between 1716-1730 is in the main the history of the early days of Mission San Juan de Capistrano when under the title of Mission San José de los Nazones.

Mission San Juan de Capistrano is still of interest to visitors with its Chapel, its walled square, its mission well, large gates and some graceful portions of the convent and industrial school with its circular rose window. A Church of pleasing design with a campanile or bell tower on its southwest corner was begun, but it is not certain that the edifice was ever finished or in use, but there was enough of it remaining when viewed by the writer to prove that its destruction was a distinct loss to the architecture of the country, as it differed in style from all the others. The Chapel is small and was wonderfully frescoed in gorgeous colors. It is a narrow rectangle, with a bell tower; the latter is merely an elevation of a portion of the east wall, at the north end, over the main door, with arches in it for the bells. The sacristy is in the south end, and there a number of ancient statues, candlesticks, and

Old Statues, Candlesticks, Missalstand, etc., at Mission San Juan.

altar furnishings can still be seen. It was fast falling into decay when the church authorities decided to repair it, and it is now in good condition. The quaint frescoing, so long exposed to the elements in the roofless Chapel, was so badly ruined that it was impossible to restore it, and it was deemed useless to save what remained.

This mission, while not so grand or imposing as some of the rest, has served, better than the others, to give a general idea of the plan of a complete mission; with its walled square,

Mexican Huts near San Juan Mission.

granary, chapel, Church, well, fields and gardens; living rooms, cells and offices for the missionaries; quarters, workrooms, and school rooms for the Indian neophytes; kitchens and refectories.

The main buildings, unlike the main buildings of the Missions of the Alamo, Concepción, and San José, form part of and are built into the boundary or rampart walls. It is said that in the vicinity of San Juan Mission there are more traces of the Indian in features and characteristics than anywhere else in the interior of Texas.

In relation to the frescoing in the Chapel of this mission, Father Bouchu of Mission Espada, who was an enthusiastic admirer of the missions and a devoted priest who sacrificed his life to the people about the lower missions and in the settlements of that section, gave it as his opinion that the frescoing was of later date than the completion of the Chapel and "was permitted to satisfy the Indian nature's love of color."

Side View of Mission San Juan de Capistrano.

Mr. William Corner gave a full description of the frescoing as he saw it in 1890, and, as the writer does not believe it could be better done, quotes it herewith: "The frescoes are almost obliterated by exposure to the weather and the wonder is that they have not long since been washed entirely off by heavy rains. They are a curious mixture of Old and New World ideas. Detail of Moorish design, a Roman arch, an Indian figure and pigments. A painted rail about four feet high running around the Chapel first attracts the eye, then the elaborately painted Roman Arch in red and orange over the doorway. The design of this decoration is decidedly of a Moorish caste, zigzag strips and blocks of color with corkscrew and tile work, and pillars of red and orange blocks. These pillars are about twelve feet high and support another line or rail of color, and upon this upper line is a series of figures of musicians each playing a different instrument. The figures for some reason are much more indistinct than their instruments, the latter being accurately drawn and easy to distinguish. There is one of these figures over the frescoed arch of the door. It is a mandolin player. The player is indistinct, portions of his chair and instrument plainer; the latter can be made out to be of dark- brown color with the finger board and keys red. To the right of him is a violin player, the best preserved sample of all—the violin and bow are quite distinct, so are the features of the face of the figure; his hair is black, lips red, face and legs orange, feet black; the body of the violin orange; the rest of him and the bow red. To the right of him again is a guitar player dressed in a bluish color, sitting in a red chair, the instrument is quite distinct. Directly opposite this figure, vis-á-vis is a viol player; the instrument being held by the player, fingerboard up, from the left shoulder across the body; head, hands, instrument and bow being distinct, but the body of him is 'played out.' To the right of this ghostly looking viol player is a harp and a chair—but the player is either invisible or vanished. The lower rail, which is the much more elaborate of the two, supports here and there a flower pot and flowers in incongruous colors of bluish green and dull red—carnations and roses being prime favorites, with an occasional cross on a painted pedestal or dado."

There is no record of the partition of the lands about this mission among the Indians, but if Indians remained, they were doubtless given lands. However, at all the missions some were left as caretakers and in many instances the younger and later generations, nothing loath perhaps, were induced to believe by unscrupulous persons that the property was theirs and to dispose of it for various ridiculous sums, from a pair of boots to a few dollars, and the so-called purchasers recorded it as a bona fide sale, when at that date the older and intelligent natives and settlers of the country must have known that the caretakers had no right to so dispose of the property. Some of the caretakers really thought that they were merely trading occupancy—having no idea they were expected to convey a title. Others were likely glad to take advantage of the letter of the law. One of the records shows that María de los Santos López and Bárbara de los Santos López conveyed to the Province of Texas three rooms which they were then occupying in Mission San Juan for the sum of $34.00 on January 28, 1826. This sum was paid to them by the Chief Justice, Antonio Saucedo. What the story back of it is not known. It is a matter of record, however, that the Republic of Texas recognized the title of the Catholic Church to all the missions and their Churches and returned them to that body in 1841.

On the road to the Mission of San Francisco, some distance beyond the Mission of San Juan, is the interesting old fern-covered acqueduct over the Piedra Creek, built to convey water from the San Antonio River to the Mission and lands of San Francisco de la Espada. The building of this acqueduct is considered quite a feat of engineering skill.

OLD ACQUEDUCT
OVER THE PIEDRA CREEK NEAR THE 3rd MISSION.

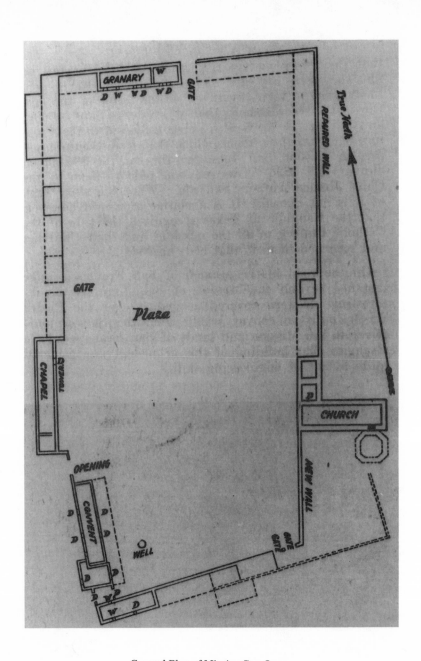

Ground Plan of Mission San Juan.
D. is door, W. is window, dotted lines show old and ruined walls. Granary is partly in ruin. The river is to the west about 100 yards, flowing in a southerly direction.

A LEGEND OF THE MISSIONS

LEE C. HARBY, in New Orleans Times-Democrat.

Here the San Antonio River
Swiftly courses on forever;
Here the mocking birds sweet singing
Sets the mesquite copses ringing;
Here December's sunshine golden
Falls upon the missions olden,
Penetrating dim recesses,
Lighting with its warm caresses
Altars where no priest is praying;
But the lizard brown is straying
In and out of crack and jointing,
While the cross, whose first anointing
Was in tears and bitter sorrow,
From the sunbeams seems to borrow
Something more than earthly glory.
Round the altar reverent gather.
Then it is some ghostly Father,
Gliding to the ruined tower
At this solemn midnight hour,
Sets the rusty bells a swinging—
And the music of its ringing
Sounds into the ears of dead men,
Calling from their graves the red men.

———————————

Thence they come in noiseless trooping,
In the chancel thickly grouping,
Indian warrior, wife and maiden,
Soon the air is heavy laden
With the smoke from censers swinging,
While the priests are slowly bringing
Forth the symbol of their Master.
Peals the bell now louder, faster,
From the ancient mission's tower;
Many voices rise and lower
In an anthem grandly swelling
Faith of priest and convert telling.
Held on high the Host is glowing,
All its golden glory showing

Held on high the Host is glowing,
All its golden glory showing

By the lights which gleam and falter
On the quaint and carven altar,
While the clouds of incense quiver
Stirred by breezes from the river,
Once again the bell's slow pealing
Sounds above the people kneeling
Penitent, their sins confessing,
Bowed beneath the Father's blessing!

———————

Who can tell the thrilling story
Of the missions' slow uprearing?
Of privation, toil and fearing
Borne by these Franciscan friars—
Abnegation of desires,
Sacrifice of every pleasure,
Spending all of life's best treasure
For the glory of their calling?
Now the dust of time is falling
O'er the graves unknown and lowly,
In the missions' confines holy
All the years in silence sleeping;
But when night is slowly creeping
To the birth of Christmas morning,
As the stroke of twelve gives warning
They, from every tomb appearing,
Still their priestly vestments wearing.
Fades the brilliance from the mission,
And a subtle, strange transition
Passes o'er the people praying—
'Tis a change like to the swaying
Of the mist clouds o'er the ocean—
For with neither sound nor motion
Every form fades into spirit,
Back to all they may inherit,
Silent grave and restful sleeping!
And the gray dawn comes a-creeping,
While the ghostly bell is sighing;
Weirdly wail its last notes, dying—
Not an echo even waking—
For the Christmas morn is breaking!

Mission San Joseph y San Miguel de Aguayo

Mission San José de Aguayo, the grandest and most beautiful of the missions of Texas, is situated about four miles below the city of San Antonio, not far from the San Antonio River, or as the old records say, "one league from the presidio of San Antonio de Bexar."

It was named in honor of Saint Joseph, and to compliment a kind friend, the governor and Captain-General of the New Philippines and Nueva Estramadura, San Miguel de Aguayo was added to it.

It was founded by Father Miguel Nuñez de Avo, under the direction of the Venerable Anthony Margil, who, while waiting at Mission San Antonio de Valero to join the expedition of the Marquis de San Miguel de Aguayo to return to East Texas, decided upon a mission for the Pamposas, Suliejames and Pastias Indians thereabouts. Father Margil wrote to Aguayo, who was then preparing for his *entrada* into Texas, telling him of his plans and wishes for the mission. Aguayo approved the foundation and provided that the customary aid be given to it.

Considerable opposition to the foundation of the mission was aroused, as the Indians mentioned above were bitter enemies of the Indians at the Mission San Antonio de Valero and it was thought that the mission as proposed was too close to the villa of Bexar and Mission San Antonio de Valero for such rival tribes. On February 23, 1720, a petition "signed by the *alcalde*, all the *cabildo*, and Father Olivares of Mission San Antonio de Valero, was presented to Juan Valdez, lieutenant general and *alcalde mayor* of the presidio and villa of Bexar," asking him not to give possession of the lands to the missionaries of the College of Zacatecas for the founding of the mission; stating that in the first place all the land in the vicinity had already been given to the College of Querétaro for their Indians, but aside from that fact that the Indians for whom the mission of San José was designed were "ab initio" enemies of the Indians at Mission San Antonio de Valero, and trouble was sure to result and not only ruin the work of the missions but involve the whole community.

It was impossible for Valdez to refuse possession of the lands to the new mission as he had orders from his superior officers to see that the new foundation received its proper quota, so the petition was without results. He arranged for the survey of the property and invited the missionaries of both colleges to be present at the formal giving of possession of the lands to the Fathers of the College of Zacatecas for Mission San José y San Miguel de Aguayo, and detailed Captain Alonso de Cárdenas and his company of eighty men, his sergeant, Nicolás Flores y Valdez, and Captain Lorenzo García to be present as witnesses. The show of arms was likely, not only a part of the formalities, but was also probably intended to overawe the new Indian wards and incline them to docility and peace.

It is a matter for regret that the earliest records of Mission San José have so far not been found. A book entitled:

"Libro de Bautismos, Casamientos, y Entierros, pertenecien-
tas a Misión de Sr. Sn. Josef is still in existence and contains
records beginning in the latter part of 1777.

The baptisms begin September 1777, and extend to
1824. The entries begin with No. 832, and extend to 1211.
The first book, which has disappeared, evidently contained
831 entries. 1067 of the baptisms recorded in the existing
book were entered before the end of 1803. After this date
most of the baptisms were performed for Spaniards, mestizos* and mulattoes.

The marriage entries cover the years 1778 to 1822. The
first entry is No. 335, showing No. 334 to have been contained in the first book. 395 marriages were recorded by the
end of 1796. Very few records after this date were of Indians.

The burial records are for the years 1781 to 1824. The
first entry is No. 847 and the last one No. 1837. After 1804,
there were few burials of Indians, showing as do the other
records the presence of Spaniards, mestizos, and mulattoes
in the pueblo, but almost no Indians.

The day of the completion of Mission San José, March 5,
1731, was celebrated by the laying of the cornerstones of Missions La Purísima Concepción de Acuña, San Juan de Capistrano, and San Francisco de la Espada in the valley of the
San Antonio.

Mission San José, at the height of its activity, was wonderfully prosperous and, in fact, was said to have had "no
equal in all New Spain." It was the residence of the Presi-
dents of the Texas missions, and this famous "pearl of the
missions" was visited by all the prominent people who came
to the Province of Texas in those days.

Captain Don Rafael Martínez Pacheco, a prominent figure in Texas in 1764, refugeed for a time at Mission San
José, and created no little stir, as he had had quite a serious
disagreement with the then governor of the Province. Cap-

*Mestizo seems to denote the offspring of a Spanish father and an Indi-
an mother.

—125—

tain Pike visited San José in 1807, and gives an interesting
description of his visit.

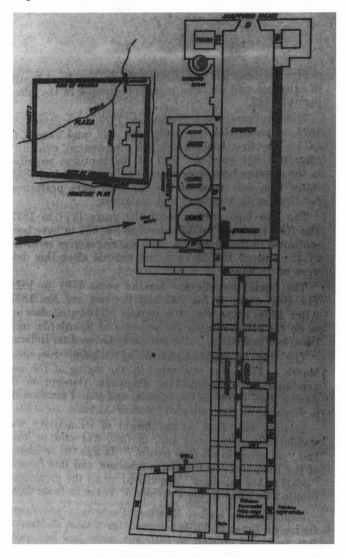

Ground Plan of Mission San José.
Miniature Plan. The dotted lines represent arches or abutments for
arches. The shaded part is the wall that fell in Dec. 1868. D. is door, W. window. The front walls are 5 feet thick, other 3½ and 2½ feet. Material, stone
laid in mortar, quarried at Mission Concepción. The river, running south of
east, is about ¾ of a mile to the north.

—126—

The last President was Padre José Antonio Díaz de León, who was assassinated in east Texas in 1834.

The famous historian, Padre Juan Morfi, who accompanied the first commandant general, Don Theodore de Croix, to Texas, in 1778, gives a very interesting description of Mission San José as follows: "San José de Aguayo, which is situated a little more than half a league from the preceding one (Mission la Purísima Concepción), has from its erection been under the care of the fathers of the College of Zacatecas. It is truly the finest mission in this America and might well be called the queen of all the others; nor has the king in all his line of forts a better constructed or more easily defended stronghold. It forms a very beautiful plaza two hundred and sixteen varas square, with four uniform gates on each of the four sides. A bastion has been erected at each of these gates in order to defend them, and embrasures have been made so that the guns may be fired from shelter in case the gates are stormed. Besides all this, opposite the Church there is fifth gate which may be raised. It is the one most commonly used and opens out on a great plain which was cleared of timber in order to prevent the enemy from surprising the mission. In short, it is so well fortified, that even if the Indians were able to begin a siege, they would gain nothing by it, as the mission has within its granaries enough provisions to last a year and plenty of good water in its wells. The Church, which is almost finished is a large and handsome structure with three arches and a very pretty cupola, although decorated with bold carvings. From its size and beauty it might well be the parish Church of a large city.

"The whole building is well proportioned and constructed of very strong calicanto (mixture of lime and gravel) and a rough, sand granite, very light and porous, which in a few days solidifies with the mixture, and is therefore very suitable for building purposes. It is secured from the quarry of Concepción Mission. The facade is a very costly piece of work on account of the statuary and engraving on it. It is formed of a

Carved Front of the Church of Mission San José.

white stone easily carved. Above the main door a large bal-
cony was built, and it would have a more majestic appearance
if a door had been made to correspond to the window which
gives light for the choir. No one would believe that such deli-
cate workmanship could be found in such a desert. This
proves how much these people can accomplish, and the advantages that would be derived by the State if they were disci-
plined, their talents put to use, and their laziness cured in an
effective manner."

"The residence of the fathers is of two stories, with two
very spacious corridors. The upper one leads to the roof
(azotea), which gives them great pleasure. There they have
erected two vertical quadrants, very well constructed out of a
chalky stone of much consistency, but so soft that when it is
taken from the mine it may be worked with a plane like wood.
When exposed to the air it acquires a polish that is very much
like marble. The railing of the stairs is of the same kind of
stone, as well as a statue of Saint Joseph which has been
placed in a niche at the landing. The railing has been made
very beautiful owing to the ease with which this stone may be
carved.

"From the roof one may hunt without danger, with ease,
and with great success; for I saw in a nearby field so many
ducks, geese and cranes, that they covered the ground and
were so near the house that it would be impossible to miss
them. There are enough rooms for the fathers and for the use
of guests. Besides the general offices of the mission, there are
private ones for the fathers, as well as a capacious and well-
arranged kitchen, a refectory, etc. There is also an armory,
where the guns, bows and lances are kept with which the
Indians of the mission are armed, when in case of an attack or
when a campaign is organized they are utilized as auxiliaries.
There are large, well-built stables, although they are little
used, owing to the cruel custom prevalent throughout all this
country of putting the horses in the fields at all times of the
year. The sacristy of the new Church, where all Divine ser-

vices are held, has an entrance leading from the house of the fathers. It is an arched room, well lighted, very pretty, nicely decorated and well supplied with many rich and decent ornaments, such as duplicates of sacred vessels required for all services. I repeat that there is no mission to equal it in all New Spain. It has reached such a flourishing state through the care of the Rev. Pedro Ramírez, of the College of Zacatecas, chief minister, and President of all the missions of the Province of Texas."

EAST DOOR, BAPTISTRY, SAN JOSÉ.

Mission San José is still worth travelling miles to see although the celebrated carvings on this mission have been ruined and the entire structure more or less destroyed by relic hunters and other vandals. More damage has been done by these vandals than by all the accidents of war or the work of time and the elements. Kendall testifies, in 1842, as to the regard of the Texas troops for this work of art and that though they were quartered there for some time they were so careful of the property that nothing was injured.

Tradition of the oldest settlers gives Huizar as the name of the artist of San José.

Corner truly says, "The hand that chiseled the wonderful facade at the main entrance of the Church, the doorway, the window and pillar capitals of the smaller chapel was one of marvelous cunning. The facade is rich to repletion with the most exquisite carving. Figures of virgins and saints with drapery that looks like drapery, cherubs, heads, sacred hearts, ornate pedestals and recesses with their conch-like canopies, and cornices wonderful..... The window above the archway is a simple wreath of acanthus-like curves and conchoids of surpassing workmanship. The south window of the baptistry is considered by good judges to be the finest gem of architectural ornamentation existing in America today. Its curves and proportions are a perpetual delight to the eye, and often, as the writer has seen and examined it, it is of that kind of art which does not satiate, but ever reveals some fresh beauty in line or curve." Its "reja" or wrought-iron grating should be particularly noted.

The walled square of this mission has entirely disappeared. The roof and one side of the great Church has fallen, but the beautiful front, the graceful arcades of the residence of the fathers, the towers, the baptistry chapel, or sacristy with its serrated enclosing walls and triple-domed roof, and the large granary with flying buttresses and stone-arched roof, still remains. These with the well, storerooms, refectory, kitchen, almoner's room with its "window of the voices," the kitchen, cells, and corridors are a delight to antiquarian and student.

SOUTH WINDOW OF BAPTISTRY, MISSION SAN JOSÉ.

Some of the walls were frescoed in red, blue and yellow, in pretty designs, but little of this is now visible.

The belfry tower is about sixty feet high. It has four lookout windows and a pyramidical stone roof. The unique circular tower built for the winding stairway, of solid hewn steps of heart oak, leading to the second story of the tower was placed in the angle made by the belfry tower and the south wall of the Church. From the second story leading to the upper lookout of the tower are peculiar stairways or ladders, curiously notched, made of solid cedar trunks or branches and dressed and hewn with an axe.

1. Side View Mission San José. 2. Lavatory in Baptistry.
3. and 4. Pillar Capitals. 5. Panel of Baptistry Door.

One stormy night in December, 1868, a large part of the north wall of the Church with the beautiful dome and cupola fell in with a great crash, a result of the work of treasure hunters who had a few days before undermined the wall. A number of persons imagined that there were valuables buried about the mission, and for many decades after Texas became a State of the Union, with the influx of new people there were naturally many undesirables. Some of these made excavations in and out and about Mission San José seeking these imaginary treasures. No valuables were ever found, but great damage was done to the buildings and walls by these idle and usually worthless fellows who dreamed of getting rich quick. The baptistry chapel, or sacristy, is entered now only by the east door through a wing of the cloisters. There is also a door entering from the Church on the north side, but this is now nailed up. This door has been entirely wrecked and carried off piecemeal. The arch and side stones of the east door are beautifully sculptured, and of the wonderfully carved cedar double doors enough still remains to give an idea of the beauty of the Church and mission in its palmy days.

Services are still held in the little chapel occasionally. The wall behind the altar is decked with a hanging of patchwork of Mexican design; and other attempts at beautifying by the simple folk thereabouts are in evidence. There are three very old pictures that were brought from Spain, and were once valuable, they are now mildewed, torn and ruined. One, a picture of the Infant Saviour, has been pronounced by good judges to be unmistakably a Corregio. The others, "The Flight into Egypt" and "The Visit to Saint Elizabeth," when first seen by the writer were still beautiful. The fan-like fluted canopies of the south window and recesses are very effective. The cloisters and cells of two stories are quite extensive with a double series of arches. The outside arches are plain, wide, semi-circular arches. There are pointed Gothic arches inside and on the second floor. Part of the residence near the Church was once of three stories. The mission well is close to the kitchen,

1. Looking toward the Front Door in the Roofless Church. 2. Granary. 3. First View of San José from the Road, near the Granary. 4. Cloisters of Mission San José. 5. Looking toward the Church from the Almoner's Window —the "Window of the Voices."

within the mission walls. The remains of irrigating ditches may still be seen throughout the valley and plain surrounding the mission. One ditch originally flowed close to the walls of the north and east sides. The north end of the granary is of two stories and was used as a dwelling, the upper story being entered by way of one of those peculiarly hewn upright stairs, or ladders, above described.

Granary of San José Mission.

Before the Civil War, in 1859, the Benedictines from St. Vincent's Abbey, Pennsylvania, hoped to establish at Mission San José a college and seminary. They made some few repairs, but the unsettled conditions of the country and the mutterings of war caused them to hurry back to their home college and the project was abandoned.

De Zavala Chapter, descendants of the heroes of Texas, have expended several hundred dollars in repairs on this mission. They have propped up the beautiful front doorway to keep the arch from falling, repaired the roof of the sacristy, and tried to retain all stones and woodwork in place. The De Zavala Daughters and the Texas Historic Landmarks Associa-

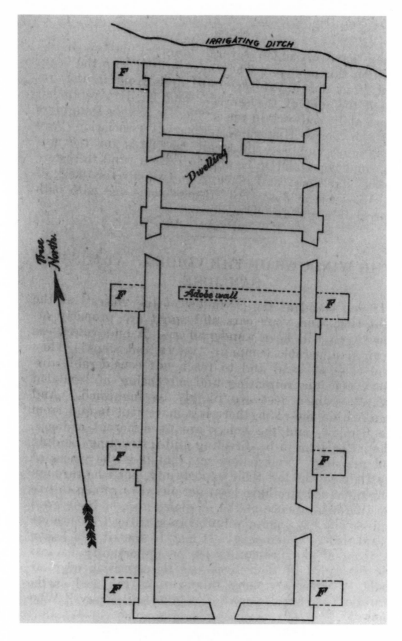

Ground Plan of Granary of Mission San José
F. Flying buttresses, material, rough stone laid in mortar, quarried at
Mission Concepción. The adobe wall is not part of the original. The river
is toward the north.

tion have given much publicity to a call for funds for the missions and hope later to be able to raise a fund to restore the circular tower and place in full repair this work of art, Mission San José, or to inspire some one with both appreciation and funds to do so.*

———

"THE WINDOWS OF THE VOICES," AT MISSION SAN JOSÉ

If you stand at the "window of the voices" at the right time, and your ears and spirit are properly attuned, you will hear wonderful sounds and voices—as of an innumerable company—voices and steps! They seem close at hand and to reach out considerable distance, and the retreating and advancing of sandaled and moccasined feet are plainly distinguished. And then, within the room, there is a movement to and from the window, and the voices are of different cadence. The latter seem to be directing and instructing, chiding and praising! Folktellers say that it is the voices of the Indians who lost their opportunity, but who through longing and desire have been permitted to return to live the life of obedience at the mission—and of their good padres who have again voluntarily sacrificed themselves to aid them. ¡Quién sabe! It may be that it is a lesson to those of the present to let no opportunity be lost for the uplift of their lives and the salvation of their souls. "There are more things in heaven and earth, Horatio, than are dreamed of in your philosophy." Who knows!

*Since this was written, the Right Rev. John W. Shaw, Bishop of the diocese of San Antonio, and Rev. W. W. Hume have been enabled to begin the repair of this mission through a donation for the purpose.

A LEGEND OF THE BELLS OF MISSION SAN JOSÉ

Mission bells have many voices. When one of the Fathers sailed from Spain destined for the early Texas Missions, a near kinsman of his, young and nobly born and full of ardent zeal, wished to accompany him and devote some service to God and King in the New World, and was accepted. Short service it must need be, since Don Ángel de León had plighted his faith to a beautiful and high-born maiden of old Castile, and she had promised to become his wife on his return. Her memory gladdened his days of loneliness and hardship on the frontier. Time passed and the days were fast of loneliness and hardship on the frontier. Time passed and the days were fast rolling on when he should leave the land of Tejas to return to Spain. With the next expedition he was to return, but alas! it was not to be! A sudden raid by the Apaches, and Don Ángel, the young and brave lieutenant, flying to the assistance of the mission soldiers, was laid low by a treacherous arrow. He was buried in consecrated ground close to the walls of mission San José. Tears fell from all eyes at his loss, for he was a universal favorite. Poor Theresa, the maiden in Castile, watched the days until a galleón should return from the New World—for well she knew it would contain a message for her from the dear absent one. The good ship came, and, too, the letter came. She seized it joyfully and eagerly tore it open. Alas! it seemed as if the arrow which had laid Don Ángel low had pierced her heart. She swooned, and lay 'twixt life and death for weeks. The letter from the good padre told the sorrowful tale of Don Ángel's death. As the weeks passed she grew paler and feebler. Her friends tried to rouse her, but their efforts were unavailing. She prayed for tears, but she could not weep. She seemed as but a spirit ready to depart. At last news came that the Mission San José was completed, and but waited a chime of bells for the tower. The next day the bells were to be cast and sent to the New World. This news roused her, and she begged her friends to go with her to see the casting of the bells. A great throng had gathered to do honor to the bells of San José, and all waited for the moment when the molten mass should fill the molds and give birth to the bells. As Theresa reached the place, a sudden inspiration seized her. From her finger she took the ring Don Ángel had given her as a pledge of truth and devotion, and from her neck the golden cross he had hung there, and pausing before the molten mass, with eyes of one looking into the far distance, murmured sadly, "Oh, bells, you go to look upon the grave where my dear one lies. I would go, but cannot, since my days on earth are all too few. Take with you these treasured relics of the one I love. It may be that when you softly ring the Angelus for the first time above his far-off grave, he will hear and know that I was faithful and loved him to the end. Take this message." Then she dropped the golden cross and ring into the furnace and passed out, not noting the throng and the bowed heads and weeping eyes of all the men and women present. She could not weep.

A pious wave swept all present when she had passed,

"And they flung their ornaments,
Silver and gold of rare device, gifts prized,
And kept as heirlooms through long generations,
While Ave Marias trembled on their lips,
Into the matrix of the Mission Bells.
What wonder that their voices are so sweet,
Since they are sanctified by love and faith?"

Theresa was seen no more, save at church and where the poor and lowly needed aid and sympathy—but all who saw her thought of angel spirits. One evening as she sat gazing on the last rays of the setting sun, thinking that those rays shone too upon her loved one's grave, she started, her pale face became wreathed with smiles of angelic sweetness. And her lips murmured: "The Bells, it is the Angelus! and Don Ángel hears!"

"And then her stainless spirit took its flight,
And those who watched caught a dying strain,
Of ravishing melody from golden harps,
And song seraphic and divinely sweet,
And then another letter came to Spain,
From yon mission whose white walls we seen
It told how on the day Theresa died
The bells were baptized, and their silver tongue
For the first time pealed out the Angelus.*

*A similar legend is told of San Gabriel Mission, California, and an extract of the beautiful poem by A. T. Hawley, in The Old Grape Vine and Mission History, by Kate C. Bagly McCormick, is quoted herewith.

The Venerable Anthony Margil.

The Venerable Anthony Margil

One of the most illustrious Franciscans around whose name cluster legends and romance is claimed by Texas with much pride, although Mexico City possesses his tomb.

The Venerable Anthony Margil, one of the earliest pioneers of Texas, founder of the early missions of San Antonio and Texas, devoted his life to the uplifting of his fellow men. He was author, philanthropist, teacher and founder of the first public schools of San Antonio and Texas, industrial, agricultural and literary.

The pupils were taught all useful industries. They were also taught to read, write, spell, sing, draw, carve and everything of use in that day, for which they showed aptitude. They were likewise taught to labor and to have respect for labor, whether of hand or brain.

"Honor and shame from no condition rise,

Act well your part, there all the honor lies."

Anthony Margil was born in Valencia, Spain, August 18, 1657. He joined the Franciscans at an early age, and soon became noted for his eloquence and charity, but caring not for renown, he asked permission of his Superior to go to Spain.* This permission he obtained and, setting sail, arrived at Vera Cruz June 6th, 1683.

His admirers protested that a man of his talents would be wasted in the New World, but men were needed who "should brave the savagery of the Indians, dare their treachery, love them even in their unlovableness, and thus lead them into the fold of the Church." Margil heard the call and answered, "Here am I!" He was athirst for great deeds, full of bravery and heroism, and love of humanity, with a great capacity for sacrifice. He would not stand by to listen for the applause of the civilized world and let some untried, untrained young priest go out to the degraded savages! The greater the need and danger, the greater the necessity for speed, power, earnestness and inspiration in the one who should go to them. So leaving the world to its vain applause, society and its pettiness, civilization and its comforts, casting all these things behind him, Margil joyfully and yet seriously started out to serve the savages of the New World.

He had scarcely reached his destination at Querétaro when he began his apostolic labors, choosing for his work the poorest sections. He walked barefooted over the roughest and

*This should read, New Spain.

most dangerous parts of Yucatán, Tabasco, Chiapas, Suconus-co, and going even as far as Guatemala, reaching the latter place Sept. 21, 1685.

The people of California stress the wonderful labors and long journeys on foot of Padre Junípero Serra, but Texas could perhaps, prove far more wonderful deeds and labors accomplished by Padre Margil if they were more familiar with his life.

One old writer says: "In examining the forgotten pages of our chronicles, we experience a feeling of admiration for the self-sacrificing deeds and great acts of all the early religious who, like Anthony Margil, sought to save the souls of the Indians, and we are often profoundly moved by the zeal and earnestness which caused them to regard as of no consideration the anguish, loneliness and suffering which they endured in this wild country. Anthony Margil passed through the desert carrying for his sustenance a little cooked corn, and this scant nourishment often failing, he was obliged to try palmitos, which was the only edible thing in that barren region. Usually, in this part of the country, the appearance of a missionary, in the view of the savage hordes, was the signal for a discharge of stones and arrows. But these good Fathers did not hesitate, for their fervent love for souls and their unselfish, self-sacrificing spirit made them the more anxious to persevere in order to bring the light of God's love to those benighted untutored hearts, and they were consoled if in return for sacrifices, weariness, hunger and suffering of all sorts, they saved one soul.

Father Margil was made President of the College of Santa Cruz de Querétaro March 11th, 1687. On July 25th, 1706, he was called to found the College of Guadalupe de Zacatecas, of which he was also made President.

In his College and at all times where possible, Father Margil walked barefooted, without sandals, fasted every day in the year, never used meat or fish, and applied the discipline as well as other instruments of penance to himself unmercifully. He slept little, passed the greater part of the night in prayer, as well as also the time allotted for the siesta.

After years of experience with the Indians, upon being questioned by the Royal Audiencia as to what methods he thought most efficacious in civilizing the wild tribes, he replied, "That which seems to me most proper for the introduction of Christ's sweet evangelical Gospel and to carry out the plans that His Majesty has established by law to convert and reduce the wild tribes, is to teach them the Gospel truths and right living, always by the sweetness of persuasion and good example. I intend to set forth with only one companion, without escort or arms, provided I be conceded by the authorities ample faculty to pardon any Indians I may find, who have been prosecuted for any crime, and to assure any fleeing slaves that they shall not receive from my hands any punishment that does not comport with my mission of peace and pity." This power being conceded to him, he began his journey for the sierra, some Indian guides preceding him. He arrived at an Indian ranchería May 21, 1711. "When the Indians saw him, they made threats and a terrible clamor trying to turn him back. When this failed, a party of thirty or more Indians all painted with carbon, carmine and other tints, all armed with bows, arrows, machetes and other weapons, came down from the mountain near them, and made continual gestures that they were going to shoot. Standing under a tree, the brave Father Anthony began to preach to them, with animated voice and gesture. Then he and his companion extended their arms to them waiting, as he said, "whether our weapons had touched their hearts, or their arrows should be buried in our breasts," all that company of savage idolaters remained transfixed, and the servant of God going forward to the Captain of the band gave him a tender embrace, telling him the good that would accrue to them if they would yield themselves to the soft yoke of Christ. After this gain in attention, he further persuaded them with loving words, and founded the first mission sent out from the College of Zacatecas. Reconnoitering the regions of Nuevo León, Coahuila and Texas, he formed the first establishment of Mission Guadalupe on the banks of the Guadalupe, May 1714.

"In 1716, with three fathers and two lay-brothers, he founded the mission of Nuestra Señora de Guadalupe among the Nacogdoches Indians, Los Dolores among the Ays; and San Miguel among the Adaes, on the frontier near the French settlement. When the French destroyed these mission in 1719, Father Margil remained among the Tejas tribes for some time, and then lived on the San Antonio River for more than a year. He then returned to the scene of his missions in East Texas, restored them, and even gave his attention to the French settlers in Louisiana. He remained in this unsettled region for some years, making during this period a dictionary of many of the dialects and idioms of the frontier tribes. Named anew guardian (president) of the College of Guadalupe de Zacatecas, he was compelled to leave his beloved Indians, going back to Mexico in 1723 to arrange for the foundation of new missions. In 1725, he was named for the second time president of the missions that were on the entire northern frontier. At the end of 1725 and beginning of 1726, he traveled over the departments of Guadalajara, Valladolid and Querétaro, in the direction of the Capital of Mexico. Upon this journey during the last days of July, he contracted pneumonia. With great suffering he arrived at the City of Mexico August 2, 1726, and expired on August 4th at the Convent of San Francisco. There was universal weeping and all the demonstration of respect that his virtues deserved.

A pretty legend is told in Texas, to this day, that at the moment of his death all the mission bells rang of their own accord, without hands, and now on this anniversary one may still hear the ringing if with spirit attuned one is near one of his missions. His body was interred in the Church of San Francisco in a sepulchre constructed in the presbyterio on the ceded for this object by the possessor of the entail. On the stone that covered him was very suitably engraved commands of Christ to his Apostles, whom Father Margil came to this country to imitate. "Go to preach; Do not possess gold nor silver nor money in your purse, nor scrip for your journey, nor two coats nor shoes, not "staff," "nor arms for defense." Take my yoke upon you, and you shall find rest to your souls." His remains are now in the Cathedral of Mexico City.

"The remains of the Venerable Padre Margil remained in the church of San Francisco until 1861. On the second of April of that year, Fr. (Bro.) Amor de Montes, being the guardian at the convent, the remains were brought to the Cathedral to be placed on an altar at the foot of the Crucifix in the chapel de la Virgen de la Soledad. They were afterwards placed in the chapel of the Virgen de las Augustias, beneath St. Peter's altar, and remained here for a long time. They were moved from there by the order of Bishop Labistada, (and it would appear this was done in his presence) to the sacristy, to remove them from the large red leather case in which they had been, and to place them in a smaller one, so that they would fit in one of the three sepulchres that Bishop Labistada had ordered. The remains are now in the middle sepulchre next to the remains of the illustrious archbishop Señor Garza in the chapel of the Immaculate Concepción. The inscription on the marble slab marking the place of sepulchre is as follows:

V. Dei Servi F.
A. Jesu Margil.
Cisneros
Obit Die August. Ann. Dom.
1726

In the cell* where Father Margil died, his portrait was placed on the wall at the spot occupied by his bed. It was inscribed: "A true portrait of the Venerable Fray Priest A. M. de Jesús, Apostolic Missionary, who died at this place and Convent of our Patron San Francisco of Mexico, on the sixth of August, 1726, seventy years of age." In the archives of the office of the archepiscopal palace are two boxes lined with brin, with the following inscriptions: "Testimony taken by the Ordinary of Mexico for the beatification of the Rev. F. Fr. A. M. de Jesús." "Testimony taken by the Ordinary of Guadalajara for the beatification of the Rev. F. Fr. A. M. de Jesús."

He accomplished so much that he seemed superhuman to the simple Indians and frontiersman and it is no wonder that in the folklore that has come down to us from that period his name is a first favorite.

*The writer visited this cell in the Convent of San Francisco, Mexico City. This building was torn down, in 1908, much to the regret of all who love history and cherish the memory of great men.

Two Miracle and Mystery Plays of the Missions of Texas

Miracle Plays and Mysteries are two names used to designate the religious drama which developed among Christian nations at the end of the Middle Ages. The origin of the medieval drama was in religion. The Catholic Church forbade the Christians during the early centuries to attend the licentious representations of decadent paganism; but once this immoral theatre had disappeared, the Church contributed to the gradual development of the drama which was not only moral, but also edifying and pious. On certain solemn feasts, such as Easter and Christmas, the Office was interrupted, and the priests represented, in the presence of those assisting, the religious event which was being celebrated. At first the text of the liturgical drama was very brief and in Latin prose, and was taken solely from the Gospel or Office of the day. Gradually, versification and the vernacular crept in. When the vernacular completely supplanted the Latin, and individual inventiveness asserted itself, the drama ceased to be liturgical and left the precincts of the Church without losing its religious character. This evolution seems to have been accomplished in the 12th century. These dramatic pieces were called "plays" or "miracles," the word miracle taken from the word miraculum, from mirari, to wonder—in general—meaning a wonderful thing. The plays or dramas during the great dramatic effort in the fifteenth century were known as "mysteries." The word was doubtless derived from the Latin ministerium and means "act." These sacred dramas were also called by other names of similar significance in the Middle Ages, in Italy, funzione, in Spain, autos, and even our own word drama is of analogous signification. But the dramatic and dogmatic mysteries were soon confused and it was thought that the former derived their name from the latter because the plays so frequently had for subject the mysteries of Christian belief.

We find in the lists of these old dramas "The Mystery of the Siege of Orleans" and "The Mystery of the Destruction of Troy," clearly showing the meaning of the term. After the plays ceased to be liturgical and passed into the hands of the people, the authors, as time wore on, often mingled truth and legend without distinction, though still picturing Biblical personages. Later these plays were given by dramatic societies whose members considered it a great honor to belong to such an association. One of them secured the monopoly of all such plays in Paris. Finally, so many individual inventions, as the comedy features, and fabulous traditions, became mixed with the Biblical stories that it was deemed wisest to forbid these representations in Paris. The provinces soon followed the example of Paris, and the Biblical Dramas gradually became extinct in France. In Spain they were retained long after they had been abandoned in other parts of Europe. When the Spanish Missionaries came to the New World, it is easy to see that it was quite natural for them to institute for the Indians (who were fond of solemn rites, glittering shows and mysterious ceremonies) religious plays and scenes from the Life of Christ, in order to convey to the crude minds of the Indians important Biblical truths, such as the Divine origin of Christ and the stories of His Birth, Passion and Death on the Cross. The Indians became the actors under the guidance of the Fathers, but so far as I have been able to learn, the part of Christ was never taken by the Indians, in Texas, but shown by lifelike limb-hinged figures. The character of Christ was held too sacred—or impossible of worthy interpretation, or perhaps, the missionaries had in mind the corruption of the sacred drama in Europe and wished to leave no room for false interpretation of the Christ. Another character represented by figure was Judas. It may have been deemed too dangerous to be a Judas as he had to hang himself (and they likely knew that someone in playing the part in Europe in the 15th century had remained hanging for so long that his heart failed him and he fainted and had to be cut down and borne away). But the real reason seems to be that no one was willing to take the part of so hated and despised a character. There grew up a hatred and detestation of Judas for the betrayal of Jesus as symbolical of the hatred we should bear to sin (which really betrayed the Savior) that after the influence of the missionaries was withdrawn, it was not many decades before the story of Judas was altered to the extent that the populace in some parts of Mexico, at least, hung Judas in effigy, instead of Judas hanging himself. During the Missionary Period, the Biblical characters were depicted as truly and carefully as the circumstances and actors would permit, and from a religious point of view, were most helpful in conveying the idea and story intended. These scenes became very popular with the Indians and early Mexican settlers, and when the Missions were abandoned, though no longer under the auspices of the Church, they were kept alive by the descendants of these people and have come down to us in several forms; the Pastores and the Via Crucis (or Via Sacra) being the best known.

LOS PASTORES

Los Pastores (The Shepherds) still obtains in most Spanish-speaking communities in Texas, and may be seen during the Christmas season in San Antonio, Texas, along the Rio Grande, on both sides, and in many parts of Mexico. A Franciscan missionary is credited as the author of this particular Nativity play (or exposition) and it would seem that this is correct, as nowhere has this play been found, except in communities which have been at some time under the ecclesiastical jurisdiction of the Franciscan fathers. The play varies slightly in the different communities, no originals have ever been found; the play has been handed down from father to son since the mission days, and from the method of its preservation it is easy to excuse errors and interpolations. Sometime before Christmas, lanterns are hung out to represent the Star of Bethlehem and the coming of Christ, the Light of the World.

These lights are sometimes placed along the roofs of the houses, on trees or on high poles in front of the doors where the celebration is to be held. The play, supposed to be given during advent, is usually given during the period of about three weeks in San Antonio, beginning now about a week before Christmas. Los Pastores, or the story of Christ's Nativity, opens with the singing or chanting of a choir or chorus dressed as shepherds. These shepherds seem to take the part of neighbors or onlookers, in some scenes, and that of simple interpreters in others in which they can fittingly have no part after the fashion of the chorus of the Greek drama. The second scene, but the first scene proper of the story, is the meeting at the temple of the patriarchs who have assembled to select a husband for the Virgin Mary. Many aspired to the honor, but the Divine Will was made manifest and while all are engaged in prayer, blossoms burst forth from the rod borne by Joseph, and a beautiful dove is seen at the same instant to descend and alight on his head. Joseph is accepted and he and the Virgin Mary are espoused.

In the next scene Lucifer holds converse with his imps Satan, Sin, and Leviathan. He announces to his imps that the prophecies of Ezekiel are accomplished and that a Redeemer of mankind is to be given to the world, that he had read the signs, that the maiden selected as the mother of the Redeemer is a Virgin. Where she is now, he knows not, but the birthplace of the Savior is to be in or near Bethlehem, in an humble spot. He tells them by what signs they shall know the maiden, and he commands them to depart and to search the whole world over for her and bring her to him that he may kill her. They all disappear, and Lucifer departs.

The next scene is the Annunciation. The angel Gabriel appears and announces to the illustrious Virgin that she is to become the Mother of God, using the well-known Biblical salutation beginning, "Hail full of grace, the Lord is with thee; Blessed art thou among women, Fear not, Mary, for thou hast found grace with God." Lucifer, followed by his imps, again comes upon the scene. The imps tell him of their inability to locate or find the maiden, but that the whole world is expecting the Messiah. They beg him to give them her name and to aid them in the search. At the pronunciation of her name the angel Michael appears, reminds Lucifer of his downfall, and warns him to desist from his evil intention. However, Lucifer continues his search, locates Joseph and the holy maiden, and through fear of Michael he dare not injure the person of Mary, he poisons Joseph's mind against her, and Joseph becomes suspicious of his spouse. Mary appears sorrowful at Joseph's misunderstanding, but passes her time in prayer and devotion.

Next scene, Joseph is asleep, and an angel of the Lord appears, revealing to him the adorable mystery of the Incarnation, using the Biblical language. "And thou shalt call His name Jesus; for He shall save his people from their sins." Joseph, repentant, hastens to Mary's presence, falls upon his knees before her and implores her pardon.

In the next scene, Mary and Joseph journey to Bethlehem, and on their arrival go from door to door begging for shelter for the night, but they invariably receive the reply that there is no room for them. At last they find shelter in a stable and are glad to rest their weary bodies.

The chorus of shepherds all this while are chanting verses, telling the stories, and interpreting the meaning of the various scenes.

The scene now changes to that of shepherds around a campfire, keeping the nightwatches over their flock. One shepherd goes off to look after his sheep and when he returns tells those around the fire that if each will give him a present, he will relate some wonderful news. Each promise, and he tells them that while he was away he saw an angel who spoke to him, saying, "Glory to God in the Highest and on earth peace to men of good will. Christ is come." Some tell him he has been dreaming, others that he is deceiving them, and that they will not believe him, etc., but just at this juncture an angel appears, saying, "Fear not; for behold, I bring you good tidings of great joy, that shall be to all the people; for this day is born to you a Savior, who is Christ, the Lord, in the city of David. And this shall be a sign unto you; you shall find the infant wrapped in swaddling clothes and laid in the manger." He further warns them of Lucifer, saying, that he will attempt to confuse them, but not to fear or obey him.

The shepherds start on their journey to Bethlehem, Lucifer comes and advises them not to go to Bethlehem, as the roads are infested by beasts of prey, covered with ice and snow. Besides that, they have been deceived that the Messiah has not yet come. They pay no heed but continue on their way, which so enrages Lucifer that he is about to destroy them when the angel Michael and his hosts appear, and Lucifer is vanquished.

The shepherds at last arrive at the manger and adore the Christ Child, each presenting a simple gift, then they sing a lullaby, and with many blessings, depart, singing as they go.

Being arranged and performed by the simpler classes, the costumes and accessories are unique, and the play, very naturally, is a crude survival of the original Pastores, with many comedy features interspersed. For instance, a hermit, who comes out of a cave and joins the shepherds on the journey to Bethlehem, is the clown of the company and with his jokes and jests keep the shepherds in good spirits on their tedious journey.

The hermit is old, with long white hair and beard, and is dressed in a monk's tunic, with girdle of cord, and wears a funny rosary of spools with cross attached.

Satan, in some of the portrayals, has a very long tail composed of firecrackers, and this tail is set on fire when Lucifer and his imps are finally banished by the angel, being a ludicrous imitation of thunder, smoke and sulphur. Satan is made to perform many antics before his banishment with Lucifer, which causes uproarious amusement.

In some places, the evil spirits are thrown into the pit, and you can see them vanish into the flames. Realistic flames are produced by the use of sawdust and powdered resin thrown loosely into the blaze of hidden torches, concealed by an assistant, in the pit. The pit opens by a trap door.

A shepherd, Bartholomew, is a ridiculously sleepy, comical fellow, who cannot shake off his drowsiness and will not even arouse himself to go and adore the Christ Child. Each shepherd goes in turn and pleads with him, after endeavoring to arouse him, but to each he makes some funny excuse, till patience ceases to be a virtue and two shepherds take him up bodily and deposit him in front of the crib. The Divine Presence has the desired effect; he arouses himself, falls upon his knees in contrition, and joins in the adoration.

The scene of the shepherd chorus is very pretty and unique. They come in twos and line up on opposite sides of the stage, facing each other. They each carry a shepherd's crook, this is about five feet long and is entirely covered with paper of every hue. On the top, instead of one hook, there are four which come together and form a sort of crown-like top. This top is also covered with colored paper, and bright ribbon streamers float out from below it, giving the crooks a very gay appearance. Inside the crown of the crooks are suspended many tiny bells or other jingling instruments. As they sing, the shepherds lift and drop the crooks, a musical jingle is thus produced, which adds to the melody and keeps time to the simple tune to which they recite the history of the birth of Christ in rhyme. The lunch baskets which they carry suspended from their shoulders by bright hued streamers are small and trimmed to correspond with the crooks. Sometimes they are made of beautiful beaded work, composed of beads of all colors.

Though the missionaries might not recognize the play at first sight as now performed, it is likely they would recognize the poetry or versicles sung, as they are of a high order and are undoubtedly from the original source.

EL VIA CRUCIS—THE PASSION PLAY

That Los Pastores has survived in more places than the El Via Crucis—Passion Play—is due to many reasons, the chief of which may be that human nature turns to the joyous and from the dolorous.

In the Passion Play the costumes of the principal actors were true to life, and to the period, everything being made as realistic as possible.

Each place made memorable by the moving events in Christ's journey along the road to Golgotha was carefully marked and described. The Franciscans, having had charge of the holy places in Jerusalem for many centuries, well knew the traditional and historical significance of each. The early Christians who dwelt in Jerusalem were wont to visit and pray at the sacred spots sanctified by the sufferings of the Divine Redeemer, and there recall to mind the scenes enacted at each, endeavoring thus to place more vividly before their minds the sufferings of Christ, that they might more nearly unite themselves to Him in spirit. It naturally became the custom for Christians, living elsewhere, to make a pilgrimage to the holy land of Palestine, where the Blessed Lord had lived and died, and there to visit every spot of ground made sacred by His Presence, just as we, of the present day, visit the homes of great men and noted historical places. The Franciscan missionaries, long imbued with a love of these holy places, felt that they could the better teach of the life and sufferings of Christ by a realistic following of Him and arranged "Stations" to correspond to the holy spots in Jerusalem—and taking the people with them from Station to Station began the drama or realistic following of Christ on His way to Calvary. In order to understand this enactment of Christ's journey to Calvary you must place yourself in the attitude of the humble and devoted follower of Christ in Jerusalem, who accompanied Him every step of the way and witnessed the crucifixion. Come with me along the road to Calvary. The scenes are interpreted by the chants and by an interpreting "Voice." The Indians of Texas in the early days of Texas are the congregation—all are the followers of Christ and accompany Him on the sorrowful journey. Assembling before the High Altar, in the Church before starting, they implore pardon of the Most High for the sin of every thought, word, deed and omission, expressing sincere love for God, sorrow for having offended so good a Father, and promising never to sin again.

The people of Jerusalem have heard of this wonderful Savior, of His apprehension at the Garden of Gethsemani, of His having healed the ear of Malchus, the servant of the high-priest, which was cut off by Peter, and they are going to the governor's palace to find Him and hear what the sentence will be. As they move along, the chorus chants:

Forth let the long procession stream,
And through the streets in order wend;
Let the bright waving torches gleam,
The solemn chant ascend.

They have now reached the governor's palace.

SCENE I

In an endeavor to satisfy the Jews, Pilate had Jesus scourged. In this frightful condition he is shown to the people by Pilate. "Behold the Man! Behold I bring Him forth to you that you may know that I find no cause in Him." But they cry out, "Crucify Him, Crucify Him, or you are no friend of Caesar's." Pilate answers, "Take Him you and crucify Him for I find no cause in Him." And Pilate washes his hands before the people, saying, "I am innocent of the blood of this just man. Look you to it." They answer, "Let His Blood be upon us, and upon our children!"

Behold the man! He has been scourged, spat upon, mocked, and derided. An old purple garment has been placed upon Him in mockery of His royalty, a crown of thorns is pressed upon his head for a diadem, and where the thorns pierce the brow the blood trickles down; his hands are tied with cords and a reed placed in them as a mock scepter. The robe falling from His shoulders shows the mangled and lacerated flesh from which the blood oozes. His face is full of anguish.

(A voice is heard: It is not the Jews, but your secret sins of thought, your sins of pride, of criminal pleasures and sensual gratifications which press down those cruel thorns and scourge and mock the patient Jesus.)

They strip off the purple robe, clothe Him with His own garment, and lead Him off to be crucified. The crowd moves off after the Savior, chanting:

Dear Jesus, Thou dost go to die

For very love of me:

Ah! let me bear Thee Company;

I wish to die with Thee.

SCENE II

They have now arrived at the place where the huge cross is. The thorns of the crown still pierce the sacred head of Christ, and to add to His torture He is made to bear the cross upon His lacerated shoulders.

(The voice again interprets: How patiently He suffers for your sins of impatience, selfishness, and rebellion against present duties and God's will.)

With ropes and chains about His body, carrying His cross, He is led on down the road to Calvary. The people follow chanting:

Our sins are manifold and sore;
But pardon them that sin deplore;
And for Thy name's sake make each soul,
That feels and owns its languor, whole.

SCENE III

Jesus falls under the Cross.

See, He is passing over a rough and steep way. He has lost a great quantity of blood and is so weakened He can scarcely walk, yet He struggles on under the great weight of the cross. He stumbles, He Falls. He is rudely struck by the soldiers and dragged to His feet.

(*The voice*: It is not the weight of the cross, or the cruel soldiers, but it is your sins which have made Him suffer so much pain and insult.)

As on He goes the people chant:

Much have we sinned, O Lord! and still
We sin each day we live;
Yet look in pity from on high,
And of Thy grace forgive.

SCENE IV

On Jesus totters under the heavy load, but stops from sheer weariness. He looks up and beholds His afflicted Mother almost fainting with grief at the sight of the sufferings of her Beloved Son. As they gaze at each other, their looks become so many arrows in those tender hearts.

(*The voice* interprets: Weep for your sins of faithlessness and ingratitude which have so afflicted the heart of the loving Savior.)

As the suffering Christ moves on, the crowd follows,
singing:
O how sad, and sore distressed,
Now was she, that Mother Blessed
Of the Sole-begotten One;
Woe begone, with heart's prostration,
Mother meek, the bitter Passion
Sees she of her glorious Son.
For His people's sins rejected,
Sees her Jesus unprotected,
Sees with thorns, with scourges rent;
Sees her Son from judgment taken,
Her beloved in death forsaken,
Till His spirit forth He sent.

SCENE V

The Savior is faint and weak, but is dragged on by His
merciless captors, until on the point of expiring from fatigue
and suffering He again stops by the way. Fearing that He can
stand no more, and wishing Him to bear the disgrace of an
ignominious death on the cross, they constrain Simon, the
Cyrenian, to help carry the cross.

(The voice speaks: You are the Cyrenian who refuses to
patiently carry the Cross of daily trials. Help, for the future,
to carry the Cross by accepting all trials with Christian resignation, even the Death to which you are destined, with all the
pains which may accompany it.)

As on the Savior moves with help from the Cyrenian, the
chant is heard:
Ah, let us not refuse to share
Thy Cross, and pains, and death,
But patiently our sorrows bear,
Trust all to Thy dear care.

SCENE VI

Jesus stops again from weariness, His beautiful face disfigured with wounds and blood and anguish. A compassionate woman, seeing His Face bathed in sweat and Blood, presents him with a towel with which He wipes His Holy Face. And see! He has left upon the towel the imprint of His countenance!

(The voice: You have indeed, a heart of flint if the sufferings of your Meek Savior become not indelibly impressed therein and renew not in you a new and clean heart.)

On the Savior passes, and we hear:
Print in our souls, we pray Thee, deep
The memory of Thy bitter pains,
That we in life may ever keep
Free from disfigurement by Sins.

SCENE VII

Another long stretch, and Jesus is visibly growing weaker and weaker. He stumbles, again He falls, and the heavy cross strikes against His head and shoulders, pressing deeper the cruel thorns, and renewing again with added torture all His wounds.

(The voice: How often you have been pardoned, and how often you have fallen again into sin. Pray that the merits of this second fall of the suffering Savior may enable you to rise again from Sin and persevere in His grace until Death.)

Jesus is dragged up and on, the chorus sings:

Oh let us shun whatever things
Distract the careless heart;
And let us shut our souls against
The tyrant tempter's art;
And weep before the Judge, and strive
His vengeance to appease;
For ah, alas! our sins have wrought
Such sufferings as these.

SCENE VIII

He stumbles forward on His agonizing way, the blood streaming at every step. A crowd of women of Jerusalem have assembled by the side of the road, and are weeping with compassion at His pitiable state. He stops and speaks to them. "Daughters of Jerusalem, weep not for me, but for yourselves and for your children."

(The voice is heard: Bewail your God who goes forth to die: but weep for your sins which lead Him thereunto. You are cruel to yourself if you do not know how to obliterate your faults with tears. Precious blood of the Savior, soften the heart that does not weep for its sins; enlighten the intellect that does not understand the enormity of sin; humble the will that resists God's precious graces.

The Savior can scarcely put one foot before the other, but forces Himself onward. The chanters say:

May we weep for our offences,
For the pains they have deserved,
For the anguish they have caused Thee,
And the love that we have spurned.

SCENE IX

Another long stretch of road and His weakness is extreme. See how His cruel executioners try to hasten His steps when He has scarcely strength to move. He falls for the third time, and lies there under the cross until dragged up by the soldiers who, with harsh words, brutally kick and cuff Him.

(The voice: Weep for those repeated relapses into sin which caused this fall. Weep for your ingratitude which gives this cross such frightful weight. By the merits of the weakness the outraged Jesus suffered, ask for strength to conquer all human respect, and all wicked passions.)

At last the Savior is again able to totter onward, while a hymn is heard:

Quench Thou in us the flames of strife,
From passion's heat preserve our life,
Our bodies keep from perils free,
And give our souls true peace in Thee.

SCENE X

He is now climbing the hill of Calvary. He has arrived, being dragged upward. They are stripping off His garments with violence. His inner garments adhere to the torn flesh, but the cruel executioners strip them off without mercy.

(The voice: Sin will leave your soul naked and defenseless in the hour of your death. While Time is yours, repent and put on the robe of virtue and self-sacrifice.)

Chant:

Strip me of all affection for evil,
Make me loathe all that savors of Sin,
For sin renews all Thy sorrows and woes—
Let me not add to Thy tortures again.

SCENE XI

They drag the Divine Redeemer with ropes, visiting upon Him kicks and blows, until He is finally forced upon the cross. His arms and legs are roughly and cruelly pulled into place. Hear the heart-rending blows! The huge, rough nails pierce His hands and feet! See they have fastened Him to this infamous gibbet and are now straining at the ropes to elevate it! It is done. What torture and anguish He endures. Consumed with the thirst, they give Him gall and vinegar to drink.

(The voice: Behold your sins have brought Him to death. Seek refuge in those wounds and cleanse your soul in that holy blood.)

Chant:

Thirty years among us dwelling,
His appointed time fulfilled,
Born for this, He meets His Passion,
For that this He freely willed;
On the Cross the Lamb is lifted,
Where His life-blood shall be spilled.
He endured the nails, the spitting,
Vinegar, and spear, and reed;
From that holy body broken
Blood and water forth proceed:
Earth, and stars, and sky, and ocean
By that flood from stain are freed.

SCENE XII

After three hours of agony, hanging on the cross between two malefactors, Jesus dies.

(The voice: Behold there on the mountain hangs the Son of God nailed to the Cross. Those eyes streaming with blood; those death-pale lips, those thorns, those nails, those wounds, that pierced side, that blood—all are fountains of mercy. But, alas! see also justice beside this cross with sword in hand! Oh, unhappy being should you persist in sin, and so frustrate the work of your redemption.)

Chant:

At the cross her station keeping,
Stood the mournful Mother weeping,
Close to Jesus to the last:
Who could mark, from tears refraining,
Who, unmoved, behold her languish,
Underneath His cross of anguish
'Mid the fierce, unpitying crowd?
Those five wounds, on Jesus smitten,
May they in my heart be written,
May His wounds transfix me wholly,
may His Cross and Life Blood holy
Ebriate my heart and mind;
Make on me impression deep:
Thus Christ's dying may I carry,
With Him in His Passion tarry,
And His wounds in memory keep.

SCENE XIII

Two of Christ's disciples now take Him down from the Cross and place Him in the arms of His afflicted Mother.

(The voice: What a horrible evil Sin is! Abominable Sin! Murderer of the Son of God, tormentor of the motherly heart! It caused the bodily sacrifice on the part of the Son, a sacrifice in spirit and heart of the Mother.)

Chant:

In her arms her Jesus holding,
Torn but newly from the Cross!
What a sea of tears and sorrows
Did the soul of Mary toss.
Oft and oft His arms and bosom;
Fondly straining to her own;
Oft her pallid lips imprinting
On each wound of her dear Son,
Till at last in wounds of anguish,
Sense and consciousness are gone.

SCENE XIV

The disciples carry the body of Jesus to bury it, and His holy Mother, who is with them, arranges the body in the sepulchre with her own hands. They close the tomb and all withdraw.

(The voice: Let your heart be the grave of Jesus, that He may cleanse and sanctify it, and thus absolved, may you rise with Him at the Last Day.)

Chant:

The Royal Banners forward go;
The Cross shines forth in mystic glow;
Where He in flesh, our flesh who made,
Our sentence bore, our ransom paid:
O Cross, our one reliance, hail!
This holy Passiontide avail
To give fresh merit to the saint,
And pardon to the penitent.

Francis of Assisi,
FOUNDER OF THE FRANCISCANS*

Francis Bernadone of Assisi had been the gayest of a gay set of young noblemen but was turned to the service of God and man and from evil ways by remorseful contemplation during a severe illness.

On Feb. 24, 1208, hearing the Gospel of the day read, he accepted it as if spoken to himself. He understood that the disciples of Christ were to possess neither gold nor silver nor scrip for their journey, nor two coats, nor shoes, nor a staff, and that they were to exhort sinners to repentance and announce the kingdom of God. He left the church after the service and determined to act as became a real disciple. He threw away his shoes, cloak, staff and empty wallet, obtaining a coarse woolen tunic, of "beast color," then worn by the poorest Umbrian peasants, tied it around him with a knotted rope, and went forth at once, exhorting the people of the countryside to penance, brotherly love and peace.

Francis' simple childlike nature fastened on the thought, that if all are from one Father, then all are real kin. Hence his custom of claiming brotherhood with all manner of animate and inanimate things. He was the loving friend of all of God's creatures, the joyous singer of nature. Few lives have been more wholly imbued with the supernatural. Nowhere can there be found a keener insight into the innermost world of spirit; yet so closely were the supernatural and the natural blended in Francis, that his very asceticism was often clothed in the disguise of romance, as witness his wooing of the "Lady of Poverty." He found in all created thing some reflection of the divine perfection and loved to admire in them the beauty, power, wisdom, and goodness of their Creator.

*Compiled mainly from sketch of St. Francis in *Catholic Encyclopedia.*

His personification of the elements in the "Canticle of the Sun" is not therefore merely to be regarded or esteemed as a rhetorical rhapsody. He saw sermons in the stones and good in everything.

Money and wealth alone excepted, Francis most detested all discords and divisions. Peace was his watchword. His exhortations were short, affectionate or pathetic, touching even the hardest and most frivolous, so that Francis soon became, in sooth, a very conqueror of souls. He strove to correct abuses by holding up an ideal. He stretched out his arms in yearning towards those who longed for the "better gifts." The others he left alone. Francis' foremost aim was a religious one. To enkindle the love of God in the world and reanimate the life of the spirit in the hearts of men was his mission. And because Francis ever sought first the kingdom of God and His justice, many other things were added unto him, so that his exquisite Franciscan spirit, as it is called, passing out into the world became an abiding source of inspiration.

For Christmas 1223, Francis conceived the idea of celebrating the Nativity by a realistic reproduction of the Crib of Bethlehem. He endeavored to persuade the Emperor to make a special law for the Christmas season that would compel men to provide food for birds and beasts, as well as for the poor, that all creatures might have occasion to rejoice in the Lord.

Francis gathered his followers, the Franciscans, into an association and made for them a Rule. This Rule was based on Matthew XIX, 21, Matthew XVI, 24, Matthew X, 3, Mark VI, 8, Luke IX, 3, and on the three vows of poverty, chastity and obedience, special stress being laid on poverty which Francis sought to make the special characteristic of his order. It likewise enjoined an Apostolic life with all its renouncements and privations. His followers were forbidden to wear shoes, if not compelled through necessity. They were expected to fast, when able, from the feast of All Saints until the Nativity, during Lent, and every Friday. They were forbidden to ride on horseback unless compelled by manifest necessity or infirmity. "In no wise shall they receive coins or money, either themselves or through an interposed person." He insisted on the duty of labor for "those brothers (members) to whom the Lord has given the grace of working. But they must work in such a way that "they do not extinguish the spirit of prayer and devotion to which all temporal things must be subservient." As reward for their labor, they may receive things needed, with the exception of coins or money. "The brothers (members) shall appropriate nothing for themselves, neither a house, nor place, nor anything, and as pilgrims and strangers in the world, let them go confidently in quest of alms." He appeared to the order to "observe fraternal love and mutual confidence, and beware lest they be angry or troubled on account of the sins of others." The duty of a servant of God, Francis declared, was to lift up the hearts of men and women to spiritual gladness. The Franciscans, his followers, therefore "went among the people, dwelt among them and grappled with the evils of the system under which the people groaned." They worked for their fare doing for the lowest the most menial labor, and to the poorest speaking words of hope such as the world had not heard for many a day, a doctrine of love and cheerfulness.

"Let the Friars," Francis wrote, "take care not to appear gloomy, or sad, like hypocrites, but let them be jovial and merry, showing that they rejoice in the Lord, and becomingly courteous." They wandered from place to place singing in their joy. The wide world was their cloister; hence it mattered not whither they wandered if thus they could save souls. They accommodated themselves to any manner of life, sleeping in haylofts, grottoes, church porches or fields, if nothing better was offered. They toiled with the laborers in the fields, and when none gave them to eat they would beg. In a short while Francis and his companions gained an immense influence and men of different grades of life flocked to the order.

It has been said that Francis is the one Saint whom all people have agreed in canonizing. "Certain it is that those who care little about the order he founded and who have but scant sympathy with the church to which he gave his devout allegiance, even those who believe not Christianity to be Divine, find themselves instinctively, as it were, looking across the ages for guidance to the wonderful Umbrian Poverello. This unique position Francis doubtless owes in no small measure to his singularly lovable and winsome personality. There was about Francis a chivalry and a poetry which gave to his worldliness a singularly romantic charm and beauty. Other saints have seemed entirely dead to the world around them, but Francis was ever thoroughly in touch with the spirit of the age. He delighted in the songs of Provence, rejoiced in the newborn freedom of his native city, and cherished what Dante calls the pleasant sound of his dear land. This exquisite human element in Francis' character was the key to that far-reaching, all-embracing sympathy, which was his characteristic gift. In his heart the whole world found refuge; the poor, the sick and fallen, being the object of his solicitude in an especial manner. Heedless as Francis ever was of the world's judgments in his own regard, it was his constant care to respect the opinions of all and to wound the feelings of none. Wherefore he admonishes the friars to use only low and mean tables, so that if a beggar were to come and sit down near them, he might believe that he was with his equals, and need not blush on account of his poverty. One night the Priory was aroused by the cry: "I am dying!" "Who are you," exclaimed Francis, arising, "and why are you dying?" "I am dying of hunger," answered the voice of one who had been too prone to fasting. Whereupon Francis had a table laid out and sat down beside the famished friar, and lest the latter might be shamed to eat alone, ordered all the other brethren to join in the repast.

Francis, writing to a certain member of the Order, said: "Should there be a brother anywhere in the world who has sinned, no matter how great so ever his fault may be, let him not go away after he has once seen thy face, without showing pity toward him: and if he seek not mercy, ask him if he does not desire it. And by this I will know that you love God and me."

According to medieval conception of justice, the evil-doer being beyond the law, there was no need to keep faith with him, but according to Francis, not only was justice due even to the evil-doers, but justice must be preceded by courtesy, as by a herald. "Courtesy," indeed, in the Saint's quaint concept, "was the younger sister of charity," and one of the qualities of God Himself, "Who of His courtesy," he declares, "gives His sun and His rain to the just and the unjust." This habit of courtesy he ever sought to enjoin on his disciples. "Whoever may come to us," he writes, "whether friend or foe, a thief or a robber, let him be kindly received," and the feast which he spread for the starving brigands sufficed to show that "as he taught so he wrought."

The very animals found in Francis a tender friend and protector, thus we find him pleading with the people to feed the fierce wolf that had ravished their flocks, because, through hunger, "Brother Wolf" had done this wrong. Early legends have left us many an idyllic picture of how beasts and birds alike, susceptible to the charm of Francis' gentle ways, entered into loving companionship with him, how the hunted leveret sought to attract his notice, how the half-frozen bees crawled towards him to be fed, how the wild falcon fluttered around him; how the nightingale sang with him in sweetest content in the ilex grove at the Carceri, and how his "little brethren," the birds, listened so devoutly to his sermon by the roadside that Francis chided himself for not having thought of preaching to them before. Francis' love of nature also stands out in bold relief in the world he moved in. He delighted to commune with wild flowers, crystal springs, and a friendly fire, and to greet the sun as it rose upon the fair Umbrian vale.

Hardly less engaging than his boundless sense of fellow feeling was Francis' downright sincerity and artless simplicity. "Dearly Beloved," he once began a sermon following upon a severe illness, "I have to confess to God and you that during this Lent I have eaten cakes made with lard." And when the guardian insisted, for the sake of warmth, upon Francis having a fox skin sewn under his worn out tunic, the Saint consented only upon condition that a skin of the same size be sewn outside. For it was his unfailing desire and practice never to hide from men that which was known to God. "What a man is in the sight of God," he was wont to repeat, "so much he is and no more." A saying which passed into the "Imitation" and often quoted. Another winning trait of Francis which inspires the deepest affection was his unswerving directness of purpose and unfaltering following after an ideal. "His dearest desire so long as he lived was ever to seek among wise and simple, perfect and imperfect, the means to walk in the ways of truth." To Francis, love was the truest of all truths: hence his deep sense of personal responsibility towards his fellows.

The love of Christ and Him crucified permeated the whole life and character of Francis, and he placed the chief hope of redemption and redress for a suffering humanity in a literal imitation of his Divine Master. The saint imitated the example of Christ as literally as it was in him to do so: barefoot, and in absolute poverty, he proclaimed the reign of love. This heroic imitation of Christ's poverty was perhaps the distinctive mark of Francis' vocation, and he was undoubtedly, as Bossuet expresses it, "the most ardent, enthusiastic, and desperate lover of poverty the world has yet seen."

Francis was a profound mystic in the truest sense of the word. The whole world to him was one luminous ladder, mounting the rungs of which he approached and beheld God.

In August 1224, when Francis had retired with three companions to "that rugged rock 'twixt Tiber and Arno," there to keep a forty days fast and retreat in preparation for Michaelmas, the sufferings of Christ became more than ever the burden of his meditations. Into few souls has the full meaning of the Passion ever so deeply entered. On the feast of the exaltation of the Cross, Sept. 14th, while praying on the mountain side, he beheld the marvelous vision of the seraph, and, as a sequel, there appeared on his body the visible marks of the five wounds of the Crucified which had so long been impressed on his heart. His right side was described as bearing an open wound, which looked as if made by a lance, while through his hands and feet were black nails of flesh, the points of which were bent backwards. This marking was called "the Stigmata."

After the reception of the Stigmata, Francis suffered increasing pains throughout his frail body, already broken by continual mortification. Sensitive as he always was of the weaknesses of others, he was ever so unsparing of himself that at last he felt constrained to ask pardon of his body for having treated it so harshly. Francis' strength and eyesight now failed him. He was almost totally blind. About September, 1225, it was that he composed the "Canticle of the Sun" in which his poetic genius expands itself gloriously.

Some months after this he dictated his last testament, which he describes as "a reminder, a warning and an exhortation." In this touching document, Francis, writing from the fullness of his heart, urges anew with simple eloquence the few but closely defined principles that were to guide his followers: implicit obedience to superiors as holding the place of God, literal observance of the Rule "without gloss," especially as regards poverty, and the duty of manual labor, being solemnly enjoined on all the friars. Francis, in a dying condition, set out for Assisi, but feeling the hand of death upon him, had himself carried to his beloved Portiuncula, that he might breathe his last sigh where his vocation had been revealed to him, and whence his order had struggled into sight. On the way thither he asked to be set down and with painful effort he invoked a beautiful blessing on Assisi. On the eve of his death he blessed all of his companions, saying: "I have done my part: may Christ teach you to do yours." Then wishing to manifest a last token of detachment, and to show he had no longer anything in common with the world, Francis removed his poor habit and lay down on the bare ground, covered simply with a borrowed cloth, rejoicing that he was able to keep faith with his Lady of Poverty to the end. He asked to have the Passion according to St. John read to him and then in faltering tones he himself intoned Psalm CXII. At the concluding verse, "bring my soul out of prison," Francis was led away from earth by "Sister Death" in whose praise he had shortly before added a new strophe in his "Canticle to the Sun." This was Saturday, Oct. 3, 1226, when he was in his forty-fifth year.

Saint Francis must surely be reckoned among those to whom the world of art and letters is deeply indebted. Prose could not satisfy the saint's ardent soul, so he made poetry. This was the first cry of a nascent poetry which found its highest expression in the "Divine Comedy," wherefore Francis has been called the Precursor of Dante. He taught the people the use of their native tongue in simple spontaneous hymns. In as far as Francis' representation of the stable at Bethlehem is the first Mystery play we hear of in Italy, he is said to have borne a part in the revival of the drama. If Francis' love of song called forth the beginnings of Italian verse, his life no less brought about the birth of Italian art. "His story," says Ruskin, "became a passionate tradition painted everywhere with delight, full of color, dramatic possibilities and human interest; the early Franciscan legends afforded the most popular material for painters since the life of Christ."

The Vision of Saint Anthony.

St. Anthony of Padua*

Anthony of Padua, for whom San Antonio, Texas, and for whom the Alamo was originally named, was a noted follower and contemporary of Francis of Assisi. This young nobleman was descended on his mother's side from a king of Asturias, and on his father's from the immortal Godfey of Bouillon. Being at Coimbra when a number of Franciscan martyrs were brought home from a foreign land, for burial, he meditated on their zeal for God's work and his heart became aflame with a fervent desire to follow their example and earn

*Compiled chiefly from *Catholic Encyclopedia*.

their glorious fate. He asked to be sent on a foreign mission, and was sent to Africa. He was there attacked by a malignant fever and sent back home.

Being extremely humble, he preferred to be the least rather than expose his own talents. His remarkable gifts were therefore discovered quite by accident. A number of persons were sent to Forli for ordination and when the time for ordination arrived it was found that no one had been appointed to preach. Different visitors were asked to address a few words, but every one declined, saying that he was not prepared. In the emergency the Superior commanded Anthony, who was thought only able to read, "to speak whatever the spirit of God put into his mouth." Anthony, compelled by obedience, began to speak, at first timidly and slowly, but soon was enkindled with fervor, explaining the Holy Scripture with such profound erudition that all were struck with astonishment. Thus was begun his public career. Francis, informed of his learning, directed him by the following letter to teach theology to the brethren: "To Brother Anthony; Brother Francis sends his greetings: It is my pleasure that thou teach theology to the brethren, provided, however, that as the Rule prescribes, the spirit of prayer and devotion may not be extinguished. Farewell! (A.D. 1224.)

It was as an orator, however, that Anthony reaped his richest harvest. He possessed in an eminent degree all the good qualities of an eloquent preacher: a loud, clear voice, a winning countenance, wonderful memory, profound learning, to which were added, from on high, the spirit of prophecy and an extraordinary gift of miracles. With the zeal of an apostle, he undertook to reform the immorality of his time by combatting the vices of luxury, avarice and tyranny. He spoke to the rich and poor, to those high in authority, and to the lowly, and his biographers tell us that when he preached whole cities and towns came out to hear him: and churches being too small, he sought the open fields in which to preach. Thirty thousand persons were often in his audience. His sermons were chiefly directed against hatred and enmity. So numerous and wonderful were the miracles attending his labors that he was called the "Wonder Worker."

The name of Anthony became celebrated throughout the world, and with it the name of Padua. The force of his miracles has never diminished, and even at the present day he is acknowledged as the greatest Thaumaturgist of the times. He was loved and honored by his brethren, and small wonder it is that the name of Francis and Anthony were perpetuated throughout the world by his Franciscan brethren.

Among the many miracles and legends which cluster around the name of St. Anthony may be mentioned the following:

At one time Anthony preached in Rome at the command of the Pope to some assembled pilgrims of different nations and languages, when behold! a "miracle of tongues," for each listener heard the sermon in his own native language and all went away amazed and edified.

In the neighborhood of Limoges lived Lord Chateauneauf, who always extended hospitality to Anthony, having a small house set apart for his special use. During one of his sojourns here, the VISION took place which has furnished the subject so generally adopted by artists in portraying St. Anthony. It was here that the Infant Jesus came to Anthony and permitted himself to be fondly caressed and embraced. Lord Chateauneauf who also saw the vision, was made to promise never to reveal it before the death of the saint, which promise was kept.

On one occasion St. Anthony came to the city of Rimini where were many heretics and unbelievers. He preached to them repentance and a new life, but they stopped their ears and refused to listen to him. He then repaired to the seashore, and stretching forth his hand he said: "Hear me, ye fishes! for these unbelievers refuse to listen! And truly it was a marvelous thing to see how an infinite number of fishes, great and little, lifted their heads above the water and listened to the sermon of the saint. This resulted in the conversion of many who had, from curiosity, incredulously followed him to see the result."

When St. Anthony died, the brotherhood desired to keep his death a secret, that they might bury him in their church, but the secret could not be kept, for the little children of the city, divinely inspired there to, ran through the streets crying, "Il Santo é, morto! Il Santo é, morto!" (the Saint is dead.) On his canonization a year later the church bells of Rome rang out their joyful peals, without visible human ringers.

The citizens of Padua decided to build a church to his memory at public expense. Thirty-two years after his death his remains were removed to the church built in his honor. Upon this occasion, the tomb being opened, the tongue of the saint was found intact, fresh and of a lively red color. An on-looker exclaimed: "It is clear that the tongue which always praised the Lord and made others bless Him hath merit before God."

His feast is June the 13th.

Such were the manner of men who came to America to teach and convert the Indians, spreading through the New World the Franciscan spirit and inspiration, and who founded the Mission schools and colleges and taught the heathen in the wilds of Texas.

Rear view od San Fernando Cathedral, showing old part.

The Church of San Fernando

The Church of San Fernando, although not a Mission Church, but merely a Parish Church, is older than the Church of the Alamo, its cornerstone having been laid May 11, 1738, while that of the Alamo Church was not laid until May 8, 1744. The Church was blessed November 1749. At the rear of the present Cathedral may still be seen a large part of the original Church, its dome, massive walls, and octagonal design showing the Moresque style of architecture.

The cornerstone of the new part was laid September 27, 1868. It was enlarged to meet the needs of the growing city of San Antonio, and in order that there should be no interruption in the services, the new Church was built around and over the old one. When the new one was sufficiently completed, the old roof and front were taken off, the old tile floor was removed and a wooden floor substituted, and pews put in. Later, a grand organ was installed and stained-glass windows purchased. The new Church was opened October 6, 1873, and was then designated as a Cathedral, since in the near future,

San Fernando Church when enlarged and named as a Cathedral.

the new diocese of San Antonio was to be erected. Mr. Francis Giraud, who was Mayor of San Antonio at this date, was the one who drew the plans for the enlargement of the Church. On September 3, 1874, the diocese was created, and the Very Rev. A. D. Pellicer, D. D. was appointed the first Bishop and was installed in his new See on Christmas Eve 1874. Right Rev. J. C. Neraz was the second Bishop of San Antonio, Right Rev. J. A. Forest the third Bishop, and the fourth is the present incumbent, the Right Rev. John W. Shaw, who still claims the ancient Church as his Cathedral and center of his diocese.

Bishop Odin, in 1840, in his diary, notes as follows: "The San Fernando Parochial Church was very much injured by fire in 1828, and partly repaired in the following years. In May 1841, we began to repair it entirely." It seems that there was a later fire in the old Church which destroyed a great part of the records and archives.

The Church of San Fernando has been the scene of many quaint, joyful, interesting, momentous and tragic events. From its tower the Texas sentinels first sighted the enemy in February 1836. Later from the same tower, Santa Anna's blood-red flag of "No Quarter" carried to the breeze its merciless message to the Texans in the Alamo.

The following translations of old Spanish documents relating to the founding of the Church may be of interest:

Royal Presidio of San Antonio de Bexar,
February 17, 1738.

Considering that the room appropriated at the time of the erection of this Presidio for the celebration of the Holy Sacrifice of the Mass, and now used as a parish church, has no tabernacle, font or other ornaments requisite for decorum of the Ministrations of the Sacraments; therefore, in view of the representation to the effect laid before me by Padre Don Juan Recio de León, Curate, Vicar and Ecclesiastical Justice of the town of San Fernando (outside this Presidio), I have resolved, jointly with the Justice and Town Council, for the better service of God, our Lord, the promotion of divine worship and public convenience, that a Parish Church shall be erected under the invocation of the Virgin of the Candalaria and our Lady of Guadalupe, for whom this population profess a particular devotion.

To this effect, and with the assistance of said Curate and Ecclesiastic Justice, and the Justice and Council of this town, I proceeded to select the most eligible site for the erection of said church, which site was marked out in a location convenient for both the residents in the town and in the garrison. There being no other resources for the construction of this edifice but the donations that may be offered by pious souls of both localities, I hereby ordain that the Justice and Town Council of San Fernando shall appoint to collect the donations, and with the proceeds thereof begin and superintend the work of construction; two trustees uniting in their persons both requisites of zeal for the service of God and skill, who shall faithfully appropriate the revenue they may obtain to the completion of our holy undertaking, and give a correct account in due form to the Justice and Town Council.

Thus, I, Prudencio Orobio de Basterra, Governor and Captain General of the province of Texas and New Philippines, have decreed and signed, to which I testify.

Prudencio de Orobio Basterra.
Signed before me, Francisco Joseph de Arocha.

Town of San Fernando, Government of Texas and New Philippines, the 18th day of February, 1738.

We, the Justice and Town Council of which we are members, Manuel de Nis and Ignacio Lorenzo de Armas, both ordinary Alcaldes, and the Ayidores, Juan Leal Goraz, Juan Curbelo, Antonio de Los Santos, Juan Leal Álbarez, Vicente Álbarez Travieso and Antonio Rodríguez in pursuance of the above decree, do hereby appoint the Chief Alguazil of this town, Vicente Álbarez Travieso and Francisco José de Arocha, trustees for the construction of a Parish Church under the invocation of the Virgin de la Candalaria and our Lady of Guadalupe, which construction is to be completed by means of the donations offered by the residents of this town and the Presidio of San Antonio de Bexar, on a site already appointed. Said Church shall be thirty varas in length and six in breadth, including vestry and baptismal chapel, its principal door opening to the east and fronting on the Plaza of this town, and its rear door to the West and fronting on the Plaza of the Presidio. With full confidence in the zeal and skill of the two aforesaid Trustees, we expect that they will use their utmost exertions for the workmanlike construction of said Parish Church, and give due and correct account of their receipts and disbursements.

In consequence whereof, we hereby notify them of their appointment, in order that without loss of time, they may take such measures as may be conducive to the completion of our Holy undertaking. And for due authenticity of these presents, we have jointly signed, the day, month and year, as above said; those who were unable to write making a mark instead of their signature ——, Ignacio Lorenzo, ——, Juan Leal Gorad, Antonio de Los Santos Juan Leal, Vicente Álbarez Travieso, ——, Antonio Rodríguez Mederos, Francisco José de Arocha.

Before adjourning, we the Justice and Town Council, notified the Trustees therein mentioned, of the above act who have accepted as they do, hereby accept the appointment of Trustees made in their persons and promised that, without loss of time, they will appropriate for the construction of said Parish Church such donations as they may receive for that purpose, and give due and faithful accounts of their receipts and disbursements to such judges or justices who may take cognizance thereof. Given and signed by the Justice and Town Council, ——, Ignacio Lorenzo de Armas, Juan Leal Goraz, Antonio Santos, Juan Leal, Vicente Álbarez Travieso, Antonio Rodriguez Mederos, Francisco José de Arocha.

Town of San Fernando, Government of Texas and New Philippines, the 25th day of February, 1738. The following amounts were received by the aforesaid Trustees, already mentioned, residents of said town and the Presidio of San Antonio, to be appropriated to the erection of a Parish Church to-wit: (Here follows the names and amount subscribed.)

Don Prudencia Orobio Basterra, Governor and Captain General of this Province, $200; Don Juan Rezio de León, Curate, Vicar and Ecclesiastic Justice, $25; Don José de Urrutia, Captain of the Company of said Presidio, $100; Don Manuel de Nis, Ordinary Alcalde of first vote, offered ten cart loads of stones; Don Ignacio Lorenzo de Armas Ordinary Alcalde of second vote, $10; Don Juan Leal Goraz, Senior Regidor, offered one yearling bull, worth $4; Don Antonio de Los Santos Regidor, $10; Don Juan Curbelo, Regidor, $10; Don Juan Leal Álbarez, Regidor, offered 10 fanegas of corn at $2 each $20; Don Vicente Álbarez Travieso, first Alguazil,

$20; Don Francisco José de Arocha, $10; Don Antonio Rodríguez Mederos, Collector of the town revenues, offered 20 cart loads of stones; JoséLeal offered 2 fanegas of corn and a yearling bull worth $8; Patricio Rodríguez, $10; Francisco Delgado, $10; Juan Delgado, $10; José Antonio Rodríguez, $20; Martín Lorenzo de Armas, offered one yearling bull, $4; Antonio Ximenes offered one yearling bull, $4; Bernardo Joseph offered one yearling bull, $6; Francisco Decal y Músquiz, $6.

Members of Presidial Garrison: Don Matheo Lezrez, Lieutenant in said Company, offered two yearling bulls, $8; Don Juan Galban, Ensign in said Company, $6; Ascensio del Raso, Sergeant in said Company, $10; Manuel de Caravaxal, $2; Juan Flores, $1; Antonio Martín Saucedo, $1; Francisco Flores, $4; Lorenzo de Castro, $2; Nicolás de Caravaxal, $4; Thoribio de Urutia, $1; Matías de la Cerda, 50 cents; Luis Maldonaldo, $2; Pedro Contrillo, $1; Cayetano Pérez, $4; José Padrón, $10; Sebastián Rincón, 50 cents; Joseph Ximines 50 cents; José Antonio Flores, $1; Andrés Hernandes, $2; Xavier Pérez, $4; Ignacio Urrutia, $10; Pedro de Urrutia, $5; Joachin de Urrutia $2; Miguel Núñez Murillo, $30; Don Gabriel Costales, Captain Commanding the Presidio de la Bahía del Espíritu Santo, $25. To which must be added the amount of alms collected on the 11th of May, the day of the laying of the cornerstone, $17.75. Total, $642.25.

We, the Justice and members of the Council of this town, assembled in ordinary session, for conferring on matters relative to our common welfare, in view of the decree therein above extended, of the Governor and Captain General of this Province, Don Prudencio Orobio de Basterra, in view also of the annexed instruments, and of the small amount of donations offered toward the erection of a church, have resolved that the donations shall be transmitted to Don Juan Recio de León, Curate, Vicar and Ecclesiastic Justice of this town and corresponding jurisdiction, in order that he be pleased to declared said church a Parish Church, under the above mentioned invocation and patronage, said decision and declaration to be transmitted to the Trustees appointed by us, who will state herein below, whatever further donations they may receive toward our pious undertaking.

Resolved and signed by the Justice and members of the Council of said town, the second day of May, 1738, to which I, the Secretary, do certify: Ignacio Lorenzo de Armas, Juan Leal Goraz, ——, Antonio Santos, Juan Leal, Vicente Álbarez Travieso.

I, Don Juan Recio de León, Curate, Vicar and Ecclesiastic Justice of this town of San Fernando, and the Royal Presidio of San Antonio de Bexar, in view of the decree of the Governor of this Province, February 17, 1738, and of other acts before mentioned, including the act of transferring to me the donations by the Council of this town, in date of the end of May instant.

I hereby declare that having waited on the Governor, Don Prudencio Orobio de Basterra, in his mansion and there exposed to His Excellency the indecent condition of the place appropriated for the celebration of the Holy Sacrifice of the Mass, the same being a room in the quarters of the soldiers of the garrison, having no safe place wherein to deposit the ornaments, without a Tabernacle and Font, with clods of earth for substitutes for an altar, the whole being eminently adverse to, and abusive of the decorum which should attend the ministrations of the Holy Sacraments; His Excellency's christian heart felt deeply all these inconveniences and in consequence, issued the before mentioned decree herein, and pursuant to which the illustrious Council of this city requested me to declare the new building erecting now at cost of donations offered by this poor population a Parish Church under the invocation of our Lady de La Candalaria and Our Lady of Guadalupe.

I, therefore, by virtue of the Ecclesiastic powers with which I am vested in the exercise of my duties and privileges, do declare that said church shall be the Parish Church of this town and the Presidio of San Antonio, under the invocation of the Holy Virgin Mary, Mother of God, our Lady "de La Candelaria" and our Lady of Guadalupe, whom I humbly pray to accept and look down with merciful eyes on this new edifice, tend to hold it, under her special protection and favor, moreover, San Fernando and San Antonio *being the guardians of this town and Presidio,* I claim also their rights to this church.

I request to be supplied with an authenticated copy of the donations, in order that I may forward it to his Eminence the illustrious Bishop of Guadalajara, who in view thereof will ordain whatever he judges convenient for the service of both majesties—God and the King.

I hereby tender my most heartfelt thanks to his Excellency for the zeal and love for religion he evinced in promoting an undertaking so agreeable to both God and the King, nor will I omit to give this their decree of the illustrious town council, but in presence of the small amount and inefficiency of the donations collected, I most humbly request them not to relax in their zeal for the completion of the new edifice so important to the service of God.

Considering that the Marquis of Casa Fuerte, late Viceroy of New Spain (may he rest in peace) when issuing his decree for the foundation of the town of San Fernando, ordered that Mass should be attended in the Presidio of San Antonio, contiguous to said town, until provisions should be made for the erection of a church, which provisions are still to be made, I request his Excellency the Governor to refer to the Illustrious and Most Excellent Viceroy of New Spain and obtain his action on the subject.

Signed at San Fernando de Bexar, the 16th day of June, 1738, in presence of my Secretary, to which I certify Don Juan Recio de León, Signed in my presence, Alberto López.

A. Ancient Church of San Fernando. B. Carved Baptismal Font, originally belonging to the Church of Mission San José. C. Ancient Mission Holy
Water Font of hammered copper with curious lid and fastening. D. Old door.

Royal Presidio of San Antonio de Bexar, the 15th day of June, 1738. I, Don Prudencio Orobio de Basterra, Governor and Captain General of Texas, certify that I have received the above documents: Prudencio Orobio de Basterra.

The Justice and Town Council of San Fernando to the Governor and Captain General of Texas.

The Justice and Town Council, in the names of their fellow residents of this town appear before your Excellency in due legal form, and as best suits the welfare and prosperity of our town and say that in the year 1731, when coming from the Canary Islands, we arrived at this destination, the King (May God preserve Him), having plentifully furnished at his own expense our transportation by and over land, we began building our houses agreeably to the orders of the late Viceroy Marquis de Casafuerte on the 28th of November, 1730, laying out a square for the erection of a church and other royal and public edifices. We are, however, still suffering the inconvenience to attend Mass and fulfill our other religious duties in one of the rooms appropriated to that effect, when the Presidio of San Antonio de Bexar was built; that place is so unfit for its holy destination, and moreover in such a ruinous condition that a strong Christian feeling only, may induce us to expose our lives under its roof. Your Excellency, feeling our sad situation and perhaps, prompted by a higher impulse, urged the residents of the town and soldiers of the garrison, to make their exertions for the construction of a church as becoming as the feeble resources of the country would allow, proceeded in company with the Town Council, to select a location to that effect and were pleased to contribute two hundred dollars of your own private purse toward the expenses of our holy undertaking, which generosity we cannot refrain from acknowledging here, at the risk of wounding your Excellency's modesty. At your Excellency and our virtuous Curate's example, the whole population and garrison cheerfully brought their offerings in proportion to their reduced means, however, and although the proportion and architecture of the new edifice are as modest as consistent with its destination, the amounts collected will hardly cover one-fourth of the contemplated expenses of construction and we have just reasons to apprehend a discontinuance of the work.

In this emergency, we deem it our duty to expose to your Excellency, that if we are not deceived by our limited intelligence, the expense of construction of a church ought to be supported by the Royal Treasury. We found our assertion on the very orders already alluded to of His Excellency the Marquis de Casafuerte, and which contains a provision that we shall attend Mass temporarily in the church of the Presidio of San Antonio until arrangements are made to build a church, which disposition may be construed in such manner that the King, our only benefactor and who has already shown us repeated evidences of his favor, had the intention to assume the expense of that important requisite for a *Catholic* town.

We might be reproached had we not applied to the viceroy; the reproach could, however, not be well founded, since we have repeatedly charged our Procuraters and Deputies to the Court of Mexico to present our request to that effect to His Excellency, with other representations touching the welfare of our community. Moreover, several persons who went to Mexico for their private business, and were received at the Court of Mexico, assured us, that, when they took leave of the viceroy, His Lordship was pleased to say: "Go my sons, I have already made provisions for the construction of your church." Our late Curate, Don José de la Garza, pretends to know to certainty, that the viceroy had appropriated for that purpose five thousand dollars of the Royal Treasury, still we never received advice of any such favor, and continue worshipping God in an indecent barracks room, our limited means precluding further pecuniary sacrifices.

Your Excellency, who may with just title be considered as the first promoter of our pious undertaking, is the only person to whom we recur for earthly relief in our sad situation.

We therefore beg that you be pleased in view of the impossibilities with which we are surrounded, to make your exertions, consider that the Viceroy may be informed as promptly as possible of the disadvantages under which we are laboring, and extend to us a slight pecuniary assistance, by doing so, he will serve both God and the King.

We beg your Excellency to receive kindly this supplication and to do as we request, by which you will confer on us justice and favor. We further swear to all the requisites, etc —— Ignacio Lorenzo de Armas, Juan Leal Goras — Antonio de los Santos, Juan Leal, Vicente Álbarez Travieso, Antonio Rodríguez Mederos, Juan Delgado.

Received the above document, a copy of which shall be extended in construction of the proceeding on the subject. The whole to be transmitted to the illustrious archbishop and viceroy, for his further action.

Thus I, Prudencio Orobio de Basterra, Governor and Captain General, have resolved and signed in presence of my assisting witness, for want of a notary public: Prudencio Orobio de Basterra, Manuel Ramírez de la Pusina, Matheo Antonio de Harbo.

Royal Presidio of San Antonio de Bexar July 3, 1738, I, Don Prudencio Orobio de Basterra: Governor and Captain General, ordain that Don Vicente Álbarez Travieso, Trustee for the construction of the Church of San Fernando, shall appear before me, to render an account of the donations received by him, toward said construction and declare if independently of the 642 dollars and 2 reals herein above mentioned, any other amounts have been offered and received.

Thus, I have ordained and signed in presence of my assisting witnesses for want of a Notary Public, Prudencio de Orobio Basterra, Manuel Ramírez la Pusina, Matheo Antonio de Harbo.

Agreeably to the above decree, appeared before me Don Vincente Álbarez Travieso, who declared that the herein above included statement of moneys received by him is true and correct, and further said that the following amounts received are to be added to said statement: From Francisco Hernández, $10; from Martín Flores, $4; from Juan Cortinas, $4; from José Móntez, $1; from José Pérez, $3; from José Martínez, $2.

The amount previously received as above stated, 642,¼.

Forming a total of six hundred and sixty-six dollars and two reals ($666.25.) in full of the donations received by the residents of the town and soldiers of the garrison, those who have not contributed thus far, being unable to do so, from extreme poverty.

San Fernando Cathedral as it is today.

In testimony whereof, I, the said Governor, and Don Vicente Álbarez Travieso, have both signed in presence of assisting witnesses, to which I certify. Prudencio de Basterra, Vicente Albarez Travieso, Manuel Ramírez de Puzina, Matheo Antonio de Harbo.

The 20th day of June 1738, I, Don Prudencio Orobio de Basterra, Governor and Captain General of this the Province of Texas, ordained that the present copy should be transcribed from the original documents which remain in my hands, the same having been compared and corrected in presence of Captain José de Urrutia, and Lieutenant Matheo Pérez, acting with assisting witnesses in absence of a Notary

Public. Prudencio Orobio de Basterra, Manuel Ramírez de Pusina, Matheo Antonio Harbo.

The original of the above was transmitted to the viceroy, signed Basterra. The viceroy later contributed five thousand dollars out of the royal treasury.

————

Legend of el Señor de los Milagros

THE LORD OF MIRACLES

————

In the dawn of the history of San Antonio, it seems there was no large crucifix available in the church of the village—the original having been, in some way, destroyed. Some piously inclined person, whether Indian or Mexican is not known, decided to fashion one. The cross was made under difficulties, and search as he might he could find no material for the figure of the Christ. To make it lifelike he required the lining of a membrane of a kid or lamb, also a certain fluid to preserve it. He finally decided to make the rounds of the village and ask for a lamb. He could find none. He went again and again and finally found a tethered kid west of the village. Finding the owner after a search, he begged her to sell it that he might kill it, saying that he would take only the membrane. The owner indignantly refused. He passed on, starting back to the village, for he was out near the Alazan. A very short time had elapsed when he heard a shot, and in a few minutes someone was running after him, frantically calling upon him to return. He hurriedly retraced his steps and found the little kid he had offered to buy lying dead. "Take it, take it!" said the owner excitedly. On inquiring what had happened, she said that he had hardly disappeared when a gun standing against the tree was in some strange fashion fired, and the kid was found shot dead. The only explanation was that she should have given him the kid for his pious purpose. "Now, there it is, take it," said the woman. The old man dressed the kid, removed the lining of the membrane and departed, deciding that the good angels must have tangled up the kid with the gun and had it fired just right. (That was miracle number one.)

When he got back home and fashioned his Christo to his satisfaction, he was still without the preserving fluid. Though he had sought the village over, none was to be found. Again he made a search in one of the store rooms of the church, where he had often looked before, and there was a bottle half full—all that he required. Where did it come from? (Miracle number two.)

His intentions were good; he hoped with this rude emblem of the suffering Christ to call to the minds of all beholders the cause of His sufferings—sin—and a greater sorrow for sin and a sincere and firm purpose of amendment. The crucifix completed, he placed it in a little shrine. Many stopped before it and reflected on the good God who had died to save each of them.

The story goes that when an artistic statue of the crucified Christ arrived from Spain this was discarded, but rescued by one to whom it had grown dear from association and who has passed it on to succeeding generations.

The legend says it was called El Señor de los Milagros because of the strange or miraculous manner of its making—but the uninformed think that it is because miracles are wrought in answer to prayers—some of the prayers being said before the said ancient crucifix. Some think it is called so for both reasons.

The pious believe that heartfelt and fervent prayers are answered anywhere, everywhere, in ways best for the petitioner—and so, while the crude ancient, unprepossessing statue is not a wonder worker, the one it is intended to represent is indeed El Señor de los Milagros and no doubt the sorrowing one who gazes at it realizes this fully.

General Lawrence De Zavala

**One of the Makers of Texas, Honored in London, Paris,
Madrid, and America, for Whom
De Zavala Chapter was Named**

(This sketch was read at De Zavala School, San Antonio, Texas, November,
1915, in connection with the ceremonies incident to the presentation of the portrait of De Zavala, a gift of Mrs. W. W. McAllister. The program was in charge of
the Parent-Teachers' Club, Mrs. H. A. Moos, President.)

Abou Ben Adhem (may his tribe increase)
Awoke one night from a deep dream of peace,
And saw, within the moonlight in his room,
Making it rich, and like a lily in bloom,
An angel writing in a book of gold.
Exceeding peace had made Ben Adhem bold,
And to the presence in the room he said,
"What writest thou?" The vision raised its head,
And, with a look made of all sweet accord,
Answered, "The names of those who love the Lord."
"And is mine one?" said Abou. "Nay, not so,"
Replied the angel. Abou spoke more low
But cheerily still, and said, "I pray thee then,
Write me as one that loves his fellow men."
The angel wrote and vanished. The next night
He came again, with a great awakening light
And showed the names whom love of God had blessed,
And, lo! Ben Adhem's name led all the rest!

The keynote of the life of Lawrence (Lorenzo) De Zavala was love of
his fellow men. He was ardently patriotic and possessed an insatiable
desire for increased knowledge. Duty was his watchword. These three
heart's desires ruled his life and he stands forth in the history of
Texas as the philanthropist and the scholar. Mirabeau B. Lamar in
his inaugural address, "all unconscious that the great patriot was
even then nearing the valley of the shadow of death," refers to his
friend, De Zavala, in these graceful and comprehensive words:

General Lawrence (Lorenzo) De Zavala, First Vice-President of the Republic of Texas; Signer of the Declaration of Texas Independence.

"Gentlemen, I should be doing injustice to my own feelings were I to resume my seat without paying to my predecessor in office that tribute of respect to which he is justly entitled by his public as well as private virtues. Through the period of a long life the ex-vice-president, Governor De Zavala, has been the unwavering and consistent friend of liberal principles and of free government. Among the first movers of the revolution, he has never departed from the pure and sacred principles upon which it was originally founded. This steady and unyielding devotion to the holy cause of liberty has been amply rewarded by the confidence of the virtuous portion of two republics. The gentleman, the scholar and the patriot, he goes into retirement with the undivided affection of his fellow citizens: and I know, gentlemen, that I only express your own feelings when I say that it is the wish of every member of this assembly that the evening of his days may be as tranquil and happy as the meridian of his life has been useful and honorable."

A gentleman, a patriot, a scholar and one who loves his fellowmen. What a fine ideal for the youth of any land; and for the youth of Texas; and for the pupils of this particular school which bears his name. You have a right to be proud of your school for the excellent work it has done and is doing and of the name it bears. No name emblazoned on history's pages is superior. You need yield to none in rank of namesake. Each great Texan achieved in his own line, and De Zavala's field of achievement was the alleviation of suffering, the uplift and awakening of his fellow men, in educating them and otherwise serving and ministering to them. He started and put in successful operation the first system of free primary schools, if not in the United States and America, at least the first in America this side of the Alleghenies. He founded and edited the first political newspaper in the same territory.

In personal attainment he had no equal in Texas. He read, wrote and spoke fluently English, French, German, Italian, Spanish, Portuguese, Greek, and Latin and other languages. His research work attracted worldwide attention, and among many honors accorded him he was made a member of the Geographical and Scientific Society of France, an honor of distinction even of the present day comparable with that of election to the French Academy. At the Court of St. James, England, and the Court of St. Cloud, France,* he was sought after and honored highly as well as at the Court of Madrid, and elsewhere in Europe. He was the author of the Constitution of 1824, and his name is the one signed first to that instrument as the president of the Congress adopting it. He openly advocated the separation of Texas from Mexico before many would dare to even think of it, and in a speech made at Harrisburg gave his views in so logical a manner that the legal phases were made clear to all. This speech was printed and sent broadcast over the State and did much to present the question of independence properly and calmly before the people of Texas. He was elected as a delegate to the Consultation which he had suggested and urged should be held and for which he set the date when it should be held. He was also a member of the Convention and was placed on every important committee whose work helped to form the Republic of Texas.

He was one of the framers of the Constitution and one of the signers of the Declaration of Independence. He was one of a committee of five appointed to design a flag for the Republic of Texas, and it was his design that was the one accepted as the flag of the Republic, which may be seen by reference to the journals of the convention in 1836. He was elected the first Vice President of the new Republic and later undertook, by

*The gold lace marked D., shown in a cut herewith, which adorned a suit worn by General De Zavala when he was ambassador to the Court of Louis Philippe, was ripped from his trousers by Mrs. Jane Harris, at Harrisburg, Texas, in 1836. When the Civil War broke out, inspired by the sacredness of the cause of the South, Mrs. Mary Jane Briscoe, daughter of Mrs. Harris, trimmed the cap of a young Captain with part of the gold lace which she treasured as a precious relic. In 1901, she gave each of his granddaughters, the Misses Adina and Mary De Zavala, a piece of the lace.

special request, the translation of the new laws and declarations into the Spanish language for the benefit of the great body of the people living in Texas. Before this date all legal matters were transacted in Spanish, the majority reading that language alone. De Zavala was a friend of Lafayette, Louis Philippe, Adams, Jackson and other prominent people of the time. He was a descendant of an ancient and noble line. His father and all his ancestors were patriots and he grew up with this love of liberty and righteousness deep in his soul. When quite a young man he exhorted his schoolmates on "Patriotic Conduct," "Liberty" and other kindred subjects. He later formed his friends and schoolmates into a society where they studied the serious political questions of the day and debated upon them. He edited a paper while still a young man at school, the better to disseminate his ideas and ideals. He also delivered lectures to his followers, members of his society and other bodies. These lectures and writings were always given with a view of instructing, elevating and encouraging the people at large and his friends and neighbors in particular. Young, ardent, enthusiastic, full of noble aspirations and honorable sympathies, he evinced a strong interest in the cause of the whole people and bodily declared himself their friend. Even as a boy the gravity and nobility and patriotism of his character and his mental and physical vigor commended him to those about him, and responsibility and command were entrusted to his hands at an age when most young men were still in college.

De Zavala's following became so great and his popularity was such that the Mexican authorities began to fear for their leadership. At this time he left for Europe, where he enjoyed the advantages of a regular collegiate education. Thus he spent much of his early life amidst scientific associations eminently calculated to impart polish and refinement to his manners and give expansion and vigor to his understanding. Before returning to America he traveled over Europe, and studied customs and conditions. The efforts that he made at Madrid, Paris, London and elsewhere for the recognition of the independence of Mexico gained for him fame as an eminent statesman. He was one of the most zealous friends of that whole train of measures, the adoption of which led ultimately to the severance of the Spanish colonies in America from the mother country. By the boldness and freedom of his declaration on this subject, while a delegate to the Spanish Cortez in 1820, and during the subsequent year he was one of the greatest factors in obtaining the freedom so ardently longed for. Returning from Europe, he was everywhere hailed as a hero. He arrived at New Orleans on the 20th of December, 1827, and spent several months there.

De Zavala was chosen a deputy to the first Congress, and the National Tribune those days reverberated with his eloquence. He took up the debate as a champion of popular rights, maintaining the thesis that fees were taxes, and that taxes should not be levied upon the people except by the consent of their representatives. In 1833, De Zavala was elected for the sixth time as National Representative. His triumphs at this period of his parliamentary labors are found published in the newspapers of that time. Now a man of mature and of large and profound experience, he spoke without hate and bitterness. He pitied the frenzy of his party friends, he despised the attacks of enemies, and showed that superiority and grandeur of soul which years alone, with a consciousness of good deeds and talents cultivated in the school of the world, could give. The envious appeared miserable pygmies by his side, weakly opposing what irritated them. He desired progress, light, and all the social improvements to which a nation had a right to aspire, and to this all his plans and inclinations tended. The "Old Alcalde," Governor Oran M. Roberts, often referred to him as the most farsighted and greatest constructive statesmen of his age, and as the one figure in Texas history over whom a halo is cast, in that it can not be even suspected that one thought of self entered into his lifelong work for the uplift of his fellowmen.

A. Silver Document Case with Chased Gold Lids or Tops, belonging to General De Zavala. B. Lake in the Crater of the Sierra Toluca de Nevada. C. De Zavala Home, opposite the battlefield of San Jacinto, Buffalo Bayou. D. Gold lace from pantaloons of Lawrence De Zavala, worn by him when ambassador to the Court of France when Louis Philippe was King.

Among the many incidents of his life, showing self-forgetfulness is one which does him much honor. He was in Mexico when a frightful epidemic of cholera occurred (the very thought of which caused all to shudder). De Zavala, among his other accomplishments, had studied medicine, taken his degree and practiced for several years. He immediately devoted himself personally to assist the suffering, aiding the poor and weak with his purse and knowledge of medicine. He gave his help to all who called for him, whether high or low, without price, giving his special service in the lazaretto, which he ordered established for those attacked by the plague. In those days of fear and consternation De Zavala forgot self and the Civil War and thought only of succoring the afflicted. In memory of this a monument and street bear his name. On another occasion, when Governor, in Mexico, a deputation of Indians appealed to him for succor and justice. They had appealed to their immediate authorities time and again without success. When they called upon De Zavala he received them kindly and heard their complaint. Upon investigation he found they had cause for grievance. Their village was situated at the foot of the Mountain of Toluca, where for ages the inhabitants of the village had received their supply of fresh water from a lake on the top of this mountain. Some wealthy owner or syndicate had diverted the course of the stream and deprived the Indians of water. De Zavala, taking a number of workmen with axes and other implements, accompanied by his escort, climbed the mountain, winding round and round its steep sides, until the summit was reached. Here in this beautiful and picturesque spot, he found where the water had been diverted by sluices. These he ordered cut, and the pure sparkling water went bounding down its old way to the Indian village at the foot of the Sierra de Toluca. Mrs. De Zavala, who was on her first visit to Mexico, accompanied him part of the way on this ride. As they came down they were very much surprised to find a large number of the inhabitants of the Indian village in the valley, intercepting their path, bearing garlands and baskets of flowers which they strewed in the pathway before Governor and Mrs. De Zavala, twining their horses with the garlands and decorating the trees along the path they were to follow. The thanks and appreciation of these poor villagers was touching, and it was indeed a beautiful and poetic sight.*

Of De Zavala as an author, Henry Stuart Foote, the historian, says: "From his connection with public affairs he became conspicuous as a friend to science and scientific men; this was but natural, since his own mind was the repository of a vast fund of valuable learning, which he was continually pouring forth for the benefit of his fellowmen. His scholastic attainments will not fail of commanding the respect of all who have read his two spirited and elegant historic volumes entitled "The Revolution of New Spain," in which he has given to the world a graphic and accurate narrative of all the revolutionary transactions in Mexico from the year 1808 to the year 1830, and in a temperate, dignified and philosophic manner has explained all the conflicting influences which marked twenty-two years of almost continuous intestine convulsions. But his chief glory certainly consists in having projected and put in successful operation a grand system of primary schools."

On another trip to Europe, about 1830, he again visited all the countries of Europe, spending much time in each, England, Scotland, Holland, Belgium, Germany, Switzerland and Italy, making his headquarters at Paris. His "Journey Through Switzerland," written at this time, is highly spoken of. Of his "Travels in the United States," a well-known critic and historian says: "This is one of the few books of travel in the United States worth reading, and is a fine picture of American manners, customs and institutions, with some notice of Austin's colonization in Texas. De Zavala aided Austin in effecting his release from imprisonment, lightened his confine-

*Mrs. De Zavala was written up in the Court Journals, in France, as being the most beautiful woman in the court circles.

Mrs. De Zavala, wife of the first Vice-President of Texas, who gave up her home to the sick and wounded soldiers after the battle of San Jacinto, and in order to be near at hand to minister to them, she camped in the field with her three small children.

ment, and materially assisted Texas in preparing for the inevitable conflict with Mexico." De Zavala resigned his place as minister to France because as a true patriot and an uncompromising friend of liberty he would not serve a corrupt government. His description of the ruins of Ushmal is the earliest extant, and was written in French and read before the noted Geographical and Scientific Society of Paris, of which he was a member. Among his other works were important state papers and political writings. "He was in every case the impartial critic, the wise and judicious public man, the historian, the philosopher, the economist and the man of state."

The historian, Foote, says: "The history of Vice-President De Zavala was marked with such a number of extraordinary adventures, both in Europe and America as well, to justify an elaborate biography at the hands of someone qualified for the task; and it is to be hoped that his intimate personal friend and former political associate, General Mirabeau B. Lamar, who has been for some time looked to on this subject, will yet find leisure to do full justice to the brilliant merits of one who lent much dignity to the Texan struggle for independence and liberty." But it must be acknowledged that his course had been such as to supply a new provocative to Santa Anna's ferocity, for on the 7th of August preceding the demand of his person, he had published an address to the citizens of Texas in which he very ably exposed the whole villainy of Santa Anna's course, and encouraged his brother Texans to heroic resistance. The reader will peruse, I doubt not, the concluding portion of this address, as it certainly had much effect at the time in imparting method as well as efficiency to the operations of the Texans.

It concludes: "The fundamental compact having been dissolved, and all the guarantees of the civil and political rights of citizens having been destroyed, it is incontestable that all the States of the Confederation are left at liberty to act for themselves, and to provide for their security and preservation as circumstances may require. Coahuila and Texas formed a State of the Republic, and, as one part of it is occupied by an invading force, the free part of it should proceed to organize a power which would restore harmony and establish order and uniformity in all the branches of the public administration, which should be a rallying point for the citizens whose hearts now tremble for liberty. But as this power can be organized only by means of a convention, which should represent the free will of the citizens of Texas, it is my opinion that this step should be taken, and I suggest the 15th day of October as a time sufficient to allow all the departments to send their representatives."

His colleagues in the first Congress of the Republic of Texas, over whom he presided as the vice president of Texas, were constantly addressing him by one title or another to which he was properly entitled, but as a Democrat he opposed all distinctions and titles and it was distinctly distasteful to him to be addressed by a title. It is of record in the proceedings of the first Congress that he addressed them on the subject and asked them to address him as plain Mr., saying that he did not wish anyone to feel that he was above or beyond them for an accident of birth or a title—that to be an honest man and a citizen of a free republic, able and willing to serve his family, friends and fellowmen, ought to be privilege enough for any man. That titles were man-given, but that an honest man was the noblest work of God.

He was also an empresario, bringing out and colonizing at his own expense a number of families in De Zavala's Colony—extending from the Sabine River on the east to the Trinity on the west and the Gulf of Mexico on the south and a line through Nacogdoches on the north.

His present resources were always subject to the call of unfortunate friends, and there are many descendants of those friends whom he has tided over rough places still living in

San Antonio. He was too noble to be suspicious, too brave to be envious, too magnanimous to be jealous. His name is indelibly stamped on the pages of Texas history as the gentleman and the patriot, but pre-eminently the philanthropist and the scholar. It is perpetuated in the name of one of the counties of Texas, in the name of streets, schools, companies— a town in East Texas within the borders of his empresario grant, is named for him. His name is inscribed on the $50,000 monument at Galveston, given by Henry Rosenberg; a battleship was named for him by the Republic of Texas. An oil painting by a celebrated artist was purchased by the State of Texas and ordered hung in the Senate chamber, at the right of the speaker's desk, where it may be seen. Mexico and Yucatan has honored him for his philanthropic work and work done as a Statesman in the National Congress. The name of Yucatan was changed to Yucatan De Zavala, and streets have been named and monuments erected in his honor. London, Madrid and Paris honored him.

One writer thus sums up his life, "A man of talents, of rare virtues, scholarly and gentlemanly accomplishments, forbearing, patient and constant, prudent in private life and to crown all that he was in every sense of the word an honest man whose word was as good as his bond. Of all the signers of the Declaration he risked most. He was the wealthiest man in the colonies at the beginning of the revolution. He knew no day of rest from the moment, when in his youth he consecrated his efforts to humanity, to the close of the eventful year of 1836, when in the midst of unremitting labor for the new republic he had helped to found, his great soul passed to the eternal life. Having passed through the dark and stormy times of the revolution, in which he took an active part and which he was largely instrumental in bringing to a successful issue, he was now fast approaching his end. His long imprisonment in the damp dungeon of San Juan de Ulloa; his harassing duties in aiding to organize the government and framing the laws of a new nation, and other duties resting upon him, gave him no time to attend to his health or even think of it. The immediate cause of his death was the overturning of a canoe in which he was crossing Buffalo Bayou with his small son, Augustine De Zavala. He rescued the boy, placing him upon the overturned canoe, and swam with him to the shore. He contracted a severe cold, which developed into pneumonia, from which he died November 15, 1836. On learning of his death Congress passed suitable resolutions of regret and adjourned on motion of Mr. Ellis as a further manifestation of the respect that body had for their late vice president. They further named a committee of three to consider and report to the Senate the most suitable manner for Congress to manifest its respect for his memory. The Telegraph and Texas Register of November 26, 1836, contains this obituary: "Died on the 5th inst. at his residence on the San Jacinto, our distinguished and talented fellow citizen, Lorenzo De Zavala. In the death of this enlightened and patriotic statesman, Texas has lost one of her most valuable citizens, the cause of liberal principles one of its most untiring advocates and society one of its brightest ornaments. His travels have procured him an extensive acquaintance with mankind; his writings have justly elevated him to a high rank as an author; and the part he has played in the revolution of his country and his uncompromising exertions in favor of Republican institutions have erected to his memory a monument more durable than brass. His death will be lamented by the admirable and interesting family which he has left and the large number of friends which he has acquired through a life devoted to the cause of liberty and the service of mankind."

All Texas mourned his loss, and in particular San Antonio. To friends in the Alamo and the town of Bexar he had set a special courier to warn them of the coming of Santa Anna.

Brown concludes the story of De Zavala in these words: "He presents one of the most spotless and exalted characters of modern times, and his memory should be cherished by the children of Texas as one of the purest patriots of this or any other age."

"How far away is the Temple of Good?"
   Said a youth at the dawn of day;
And he strove in a spirit of brotherhood,
To help and succor, as best he could.
The poor and unfortunate multitude
   On their hard and dreary way.

He likewise strove with adversity,
   To climb to the heights above;
But his dream was ever of men made free,
   Of better days in the time to be,
And self was buried in sympathy,
   He followed the path of love.

He was careless alike of praise or blame;
   But after his work was done,
An angel of glory, from heaven came,
   And wrote on high his immortal name,
Proclaiming this truth, that the Temple of Fame
   And the Temple of good are one.

For this is the lesson that History
   Has taught since the world began;
The great, whose memories never die,
   That shine like stars in our human sky
And brighter glow as the years roll by,
   Are those who have lived for Man.

—J. A. Edgerton, in Rocky Mountain News.

"The De Zavala Daughters"

Descendants of the Heroes, Pioneers, Founders and
Statesmen of Texas,

and

THE DE ZAVALA CHAPTER

About 1889, a band of patriotic women in San Antonio, Texas, associated themselves and met occasionally to keep green the memory of the heroes, founders and pioneers of Texas; to formulate methods of arousing the dormant patriotism of the majority of their fellow-citizens; to devise ways of inculcating and disseminating a wider knowledge of the history of Texas; and of instilling a love and proper pride in town, city, county and State; acting on the belief that patriotism, like charity, begins at home, and that if one does not love his home he will not love his country, and that like every virtue, patriotism should be fostered.

This band was called into existence on the invitation of Miss Adina De Zavala. They wrote historic articles, gathered historical data, and in various ways endeavored to arouse public sentiment for the care and restoration of the Missions of Texas, and all historic places, and everything pertaining to Texas; and for a more general display of the Texas flag.

On November 6, 1891, in Houston, Texas, at the residence of Mrs. Andrew Briscoe, a society was organized composed of the wives, daughters, and lineal female descendants of the men who served the Republic of Texas. The Association was suggested by Mr. Guy M. Bryan, and urged by his niece, Miss Betty Ballinger, his daughter, Miss Hally Bryan, and by Mrs. Mary Jane Briscoe. Among the ladies assisting in the organization were Mesdames M. Looscan, M. G. Howe, J. M.

O. Menard, W. E. Kendall, C. H. Hume, W. R. Robertson, and Ernest Vasmer.

Believing that more good in general historical and patriotic work could be accomplished by the united efforts of the descendants of the pioneers over the State, the San Antonio ladies, descendants of the heroes of Texas, joined hands with the women who had organized for purposes similar to the San Antonio band, and De Zavala Chapter was founded, Miss Adina De Zavala being elected President.

The historic locality of San Antonio afforded a rich field of effort for De Zavala Chapter, and labor as they might there was always urgent work ahead and more funds needed for its prosecution. However, they were determined and patriotic, and year by year they grew in numbers, in record of work accomplished, and in the affections of the people.

This Society started the campaign to save the Missions of Texas, and succeeded in awakening considerable interest, and Mission San José was repaired, and fenced, and a custodian employed by the Society at a cost of several hundred dollars.

Ben Milam's grave was rescued from oblivion, and a neat monument was erected which now marks his last resting place, near the center of Milam Park.

The work of placing tablets on all historic buildings, battlefields, sites, roads and trees was inaugurated; and of marking with name tablets, the schools named in honor of the heroes of Texas.

A tablet was placed upon the Veramendi House—the residence of the Vice-Governor Veramendi—the house where Bowie wooed and won his bride, Ursula Veramendi; and where brave Ben Milam was killed—the house connected with so much old-time history of San Antonio and Texas.

A marble tablet was placed upon the main building of the Alamo Fortress to emphasize its importance as the scene of the sublimest sacrifice recorded in modern history.

Historical paintings, manuscripts, writings, data, old and rare books, relics, and other articles of virtue pertaining to Texas were collected; and all such entrusted to their care are sacredly kept.

A picture of one of the relics, the old bell "San Antonio," a most cherished gift of Mr. Moses Oppenheimer, will be found in this volume.

Many of the old and historic buildings, street names, etc., were long saved to the people by the efforts of this society. A resolution was secured from the School Board of the City of San Antonio, naming the public schools in honor of the Texas heroes; the School Board using the names and assignments as suggested by De Zavala Chapter.

This society welcomed all artists to the City of San Antonio and planned a free School of Art. On application to the City authorities, the old Market House on Market Street was leased to them for a number of years, the building overhauled and cleaned up, and the material obtained and placed on the ground for the repair and proper fitting up of the building for a School of Art—Art in every line—painting, sculpture, architecture, etc., was to be fostered. Mr. Pompeo Coppini and others agreed to give their services to the school for certain hours each week. In fact, all arrangements were complete—when the School Board and the City became involved in a lawsuit, the Market House was claimed by the former, and sold, and the School of Art was without a home. The De Zavala Daughters next planned to use part of the Fortress of the Alamo for this purpose. Selfish "interests" prevented this, but the society continued to do all in their power for the advancement of art in every phase.

They contributed largely for the purpose of presenting pictures of historic persons to the school houses of Texas; and for a handsome silk Texas flag given to the University of Texas, and also contributed to the purchase of the silk Texas flag placed in the Texas room at Mount Vernon.

Numberless other things were done by this society, working always toward the highest ideals and the uplift of present and future generations of the citizens of Texas.

The largest amount of money ever obtained by an organization from the State of Texas was secured by the De Zavala Daughters for the payment of the balance due on their notes given to Charles Hugo (of Hugo, Schmeltzer Co.) through the Chairman of their Alamo Mission Fund Committee, for the purchase of the Alamo Fort—Sixty-five Thousand Dollars ($65,000.00) being the amount appropriated by the State of Texas—De Zavala Chapter having already expended about Twenty Thousand Dollars ($20,000.00) towards its purchase.

The main building of the *Alamo Fortress*, of which they had just secured the purchase, and the CHURCH of THE ALAMO were delivered to the custody of the De Zavala Daughters, and immediately, a set of selfish and ambitious persons—caring nothing for the good of the people of Texas, or children of Texas, or of the proper keeping of the Alamo—began to plan to secure control of that sacred shrine. A syndicate which had options on adjoining property decided that the Alamo Fortress stood in the way of the enhancement of the value of lots owned or controlled by them and they applied to the De Zavala Daughters to tear down the old ALAMO FORTRESS. These ladies replied that even the wish to do such a thing was sacrilegious, and with great care explained the history of the Alamo—but, it was personal gain versus patriotism—and the said interests refused to yield to patriotism and announced a determination, "by fair or foul measures," because it stood in front of their property (i. e. in which they were interested)—to bring about the destruction of the main building of the Alamo Fortress just purchased by the De Zavala Daughters and the State of Texas.

About this time, the property east of Alamo on the corner of Houston and Nacogdoches Streets was sold, and an attempt was made by the St. Louis purchasers to bring about the destruction of the main building of the Alamo Fortress, which is 191 feet in length running from Houston Street, south, along the east side of Alamo Plaza. The Hotel Company was not satisfied with the two side street frontages, but desired to face the hotel on Alamo Plaza. As the property they had acquired was back of the Alamo and ran along the east side of the Alamo ditch or acequia which was then plainly visible, they could do this only by tearing away the Alamo Fort—the main building of the Alamo where the heroes died—and they endeavored to interest a number of San Antonio businessmen with the hope that the latter would use their influence to bring about the destruction of the Alamo Fort proper which stood in the way of an Alamo Plaza frontage for their hotel. The following letters may be of interest:

St. Louis, Mo., August 30, 1906.

Miss Adina De Zavala, President De Zavala Daughters,
    San Antonio, Texas.
Dear Madam:

About ten days ago as the representative of St. Louis parties I bought the north half of the Gallagher property adjoining the Alamo in San Antonio. It is the earnest desire of my clients to improve this property in a manner creditable to ourselves and to the city, and if proper encouragement is given by the Daughters of Texas, and the citizens of San Antonio, a splendid structure costing approximately $500,000 will be erected. Will you kindly present this letter to your society at the earliest possible moment and advise me of whatever action may be taken?

If my clients decide to erect a hotel on the site, it will be perhaps the handsomest building of the kind in the southwest. Before they can determine upon their course of action, however, they must have some positive assurances that the owners of the Hugo-Schmeltzer property (meaning the owners of the

*Bracketed words are by writer.

—212—

main building of the Alamo Fort*) intend to tear down the building (the main building of the Alamo Fort) now occupied by that firm, and that the ground on which it stands will be converted into a park. This, I was informed while in your city, the State of Texas or the De Zavala Daughters have agreed to do. If this information is correct, we are not only prepared to go ahead with our plans, but to materially assist your society in carrying out the work.

In order to assist your organization, I beg to advise that we will be willing to assume the entire expense of tearing down these buildings (the main building of the Alamo) and removing the dèbris, and also to contribute toward the expense of the landscape work necessary to convert the premises into a park. I have written the Business Men's Club on this subject and enclose herewith the letter addressed to the president of the club. I have also taken the liberty of enclosing to the president of that club a copy of this letter to you, in order that all parties interested may have full and complete understanding of our plans and purposes so far as they have been matured up to this time....

Very sincerely yours,

CHAS. M. R_____

To Mr. _____,
    Pres. Business Men's Club,

San Antonio, Texas.

Gentlemen: As representative of the St. Louis parties who recently bought the Gallagher property, at the corner of Houston and Nacogdoches Streets, I lay before you a proposition in which we have interest in common. The parties I represent have made a large investment in your beautiful city, and it is our intention to improve the property in a manner that will be highly creditable to the city as well as to ourselves. The need of a first class fire-proof hotel in your city to accommodate the ever increasing tourist and health seeker's travel is so apparent that he who runs may read.....I can frankly say that we would prefer to erect a hotel on the site if certain improvements can be brought about, and it is in this matter that we seek your co-operation and assistance.

I was advised that the Hugo & Schmeltzer building (main building of Alamo Fort) was bought by the State of Texas and confided to the Daughters of Texas with the understanding that they would wreck the building (the main building of the Alamo Fort) and convert the property into a beautiful park. This unsightly building has long been an eyesore.... Is the Business Men's Club in position to bring about the early wrecking of the building in question? If so we can materially aid in that work. We would be willing to pay the expense of tearing down the buildings and removing the dèbris, and also to contribute toward the expense of the landscape work necessary to convert it into a park.......

It will not only clear Alamo Plaza of a highly objectionable structure, but will open the vista of the post office and add another beautiful building....With this accomplished, property values in that section will be greatly enhanced. I would thank you to lay this before the businessmen of San Antonio for a full and free discussion. If they think well of it, we would be pleased to discuss it in detail with such of them as may care to join in the undertaking and take a certain amount of the stock of the hotel company which responsible parties here are willing to guarantee a 6 per cent per annum net income upon......

Yours very truly,

CHAS. M. R_____

St. Louis, Mo., Aug. 30, 1906.

The President of the De Zavala Daughters replied to the above letter and explained that the building sought to be destroyed was the main building of the Alamo Fort, and the building in which the majority of the heroes died, believing that the explanation would end the matter; but the time to acquire a frontage on the Alamo Plaza for their property must have seemed opportune, for the stockholders and promoters would not abandon the idea. In the attempt to acquire the frontage, no stone was left unturned to bring about the destruction of the Alamo Fortress proper, and the most disgraceful methods were resorted to. For years the battle waged between the De Zavala Daughters and various companies or syndicates, joined by a few self-seeking and envious individuals. When the Hotel Company gave up the struggle, an Amusement Palace Company took it up, and different interests entered the contest from time to time. During one of these harassing struggles, about 1913, the upper story of the Alamo Fortress proper was battered down, and, by the cooperation of a San Antonio local official or officials. So strong were the ancient walls that the sacrilegious destruction was effected with the greatest difficulty and only after the most strenuous exertions. One of the most historic parts of the Alamo thus fell a sacrifice to private greed and unsatiable ambition.

Engaged in the conflict to save the Alamo were the most prominent women of Texas, socially, intellectually, morally, and patriotically, and all that loving interest and private purse could do was done, and most of them are still engaged in patriotic and unselfish labors. The majority of those chiefly responsible for the Alamo trouble have passed from the scene, and they did not accomplish their purpose.